AUSTON MATTHEWS

A LIFE IN HOCKEY

KEVIN McGRAN

Published by Simon & Schuster

NEW YORK AMSTERDAM/ANTWERP LONDON
TORONTO SYDNEY/MELBOURNE NEW DELHI

A Division of Simon & Schuster, LLC
166 King Street East, Suite 300
Toronto, Ontario M5A 1J3

This Simon & Schuster Canada edition September 2025

SIMON & SCHUSTER CANADA and colophon are trademarks of
Simon & Schuster, LLC

Manufactured in the United States of America

1 3 5 7 9 10 8 6 4 2
Online Computer Library Center number: 1492497950

ISBN 978-1-6680-6309-5
ISBN 978-1-6680-6311-8 (ebook)

This book is dedicated to Paddy and Eveleen. The best parents you could hope for if you're a kid who loves hockey and words equally.

Go raibh maith agat

Contents

CONTENTS

Prologue

When Auston Matthews was twelve and playing spring hockey, he showed up late to his baseball game. His two sporting passions overlapped.

He showed up in the fifth inning, hit a grand slam in his first at bat, then hit the game-winning home run in the seventh inning. The dugout was ecstatic because there was a second game on tap and their best hitter had arrived. But the coach and team were soon disappointed, the coach shaking his head in disbelief. The kid everyone called Papi wasn't going to play in the second game of the doubleheader. He had to get back to the rink.

This was in the unlikely hockey breeding ground of Scottsdale, Arizona, in the heart of the Southwestern American desert. Somehow this American son of a Mexican immigrant fell in love with Canada's game. He loved the action. He loved the pace.

At five, he skated on fake ice. At eight, he was better than ten-year-olds. At ten, he was better than twelve-year-olds. By fifteen, he was already projected to go number one in the 2016 NHL Draft. At seventeen, he signed a pro contract in Europe. At eighteen, he was taken first overall by the Toronto Maple Leafs and scored four times in his first NHL game, an unmatched feat.

And after his first game, the most unusual, nontraditional journey to become the best player in the history of hockey's most storied franchise was under way.

Matthews, the twenty-sixth captain of the Maple Leafs, is on his way to being the greatest player in the team's history. Its greatest goal scorer. Its most decorated player in terms of regular-season awards.

Some of the moments are of his own doing. He's the one who fell in love with the game. He's the one who brings the passion. He's the one who puts in the work. He's the one who developed that shot. He's the one who brings the moves. He's the one scoring the goals.

But some of the moments really do come down to chance. How did a woman from Mexico fall in love with a sports fan from California when the two didn't even speak the same language? How did one of hockey's greatest players get his start in a region without natural ice rinks? How did an NHL team end up in Phoenix and stay there against all odds just so Auston Matthews could watch the likes of Daniel Brière and Shane Doan and fall in love with the sport? How did a kid from the trailer parks of Eastern Ontario end up running a small rink that featured the synthetic ice Matthews got his start on? How did a Ukrainian hockey player end up coaching in Mexico and get coaxed into coaching Matthews in Scottsdale, Arizona? How did a kid from the no-name hockey state of Arizona get discovered by the prestigious US National Team Development Program? How did the greatest American hockey player of his generation end up playing in Zurich? How did hockey's self-anointed most fabled franchise fall from grace so quickly that it drafted first overall in 2016? And how has all of that changed the game since?

This is Auston Matthews's unusual and unique story.

AUSTON MATTHEWS

CHAPTER ONE

A Four-Goal Debut

Auston Matthews carried the puck down the right wing into the Ottawa zone, leading to a mad scramble in front of the Senators net. Matthews chopped at it. William Nylander took a shot that ricocheted to Zach Hyman, who carried the puck behind the net and fed Matthews on the right side of the crease. And in the blink of an eye Matthews shovelled a one-timer past the Ottawa goalie Craig Anderson.

Auston Matthews, the can't-miss rookie, didn't miss. He had his first NHL goal. It came on his first shot, at 8:21 of the first period of his first NHL game, the first goal by anyone of the 2016–17 season.

There may be no greater feeling in hockey than scoring. For goal scorers—players who make their living as the go-to guys for their teams—it's the adrenaline rush that drives them. For the fans who watch, seeing their team score, or their favourite player score, is another form of elation, validating all the time spent loving their team and reading about the player in the off-season. For the media covering the game, it's the story they want to tell: the kid making good, getting that first goal.

It had all fallen into place in the first period of the first NHL game Auston Matthews played. There would be no waiting. An easy, feel-good story to tell for Leaf fans all too accustomed to bad things happening to their favourite team. For the twelfth time in league history, the first overall pick from the previous draft scored in his first game.

And then Matthews scored again.

The second goal came with 5:42 left in the first period, on his second shot of the game. He won a puck battle with Mark Stone at the blue line, lost it briefly but got it back from two-time Norris Trophy winner Erik Karlsson, then lifted the puck over Marc Methot and beat Craig Anderson with an odd-angled forehand.

"What a goal, Matthews, magnificent," play-by-play caller Paul Romanuk told his *Hockey Night in Canada* audience. "You see that second goal he scored? Not many guys do that," Coach Mike Babcock said after the game. For just the second time in NHL history, the first overall pick scored twice in his first game. Matthews joined Alex Ovechkin with the honour.

But Matthews wasn't done rewriting the *NHL Official Guide and Record Book*.

Another goal, his hat-trick goal, came on a one-timer from inside the right circle on a feed from Morgan Rielly 1:25 into the second period. The game was in Ottawa, but Leaf fans travel well, and the ice at the Canadian Tire Centre was showered with hats. He had scored three goals on three shots.

"Oh my goodness, what a debut," Romanuk told viewers.

He was already acting like a veteran. The first two goals got big-time "cellys," or celebrations. The third was more muted, pointing at Rielly to thank him for the pass. In the stands, Matthews's mother, Ema, was jumping up and down, giving out high fives.

Matthews had become the first number-one overall pick to score three times in his debut. Four other players had done it as far back as 1943, what the NHL calls the onset of its modern era.

The Montreal Canadiens forward Alex Smart scored January 14, 1943, against Chicago.

Quebec Nordiques forward Réal Cloutier did it October 10, 1979, versus Atlanta. He'd already played five years in the WHA.

Dallas Stars forward Fabian Brunnström accomplished the feat October 15, 2008, against Nashville. He was twenty-three and undrafted but had been a pro in Sweden.

Impressively, New York Rangers forward Derek Stepan did it October 9, 2010, against Buffalo. He was twenty, two years removed from being a second-round pick in 2008, after spending two seasons at the University of Wisconsin. Matthews was the youngest to have done it, having turned nineteen on September 17.

Sportsnet's cameras turned to Auston's parents, Brian and Ema. Ema was wiping tears from her eyes. At the second intermission, rinkside reporter Christine Simpson caught up with the parents.

"Those were tears of joy," Ema Matthews told Sportsnet's viewing audience. "I feel very excited. This is what Auston has been dreaming since he was six, to be playing right here in the NHL."

"I hope that nobody's going to wake me up here anytime soon," Brian Matthews said. "This is unbelievable."

Christine Simpson—perhaps only half jokingly—wondered to the parents if Auston had a fourth goal in him.

He did. The fourth goal followed a give-and-go with William Nylander. Matthews lifted the puck past Anderson after blowing by a defender in the slot. "You are looking at the first player ever to score four goals in an NHL debut," gushed Romanuk.

"I think everybody was like, 'What's going on here?'" Matthews told reporters that night. "Like I said, you don't really draw it up like that."

Zach Hyman, his left winger that night and for most of their time together on the Maple Leafs, recalled the evening in wonder.

"It was a surreal experience. I think it was surreal for him. I remember being in the locker room with him. After the second period, he had three by then. I think he was a little bit in shock himself. Like, how can you not be? Pretty special. You got four goals, or they're all scored a different way, right. Just a great debut."

Karlsson—just about as gifted a player as there was in the NHL at the time—was equally impressed.

"He got four scoring chances, and he scored four goals," said Karlsson that night. "Two of them, most people probably can't do. Good for him, and good for Toronto having a player like that."

Most rookies get one souvenir puck for their first NHL goal. Matthews got four. "I'll probably give them to my mom. She usually does something nice with them."

It's not like the Senators didn't know what Matthews could do. They, more than any team, should have been prepared. Their assistant coach was Marc Crawford, who had coached Matthews the season prior in Switzerland. "He said, 'This guy is good. He can do this, and he can do that,'" said Anderson. "It's not like we didn't believe him. But there wasn't an extra emphasis on him.

"Him able to do the things we talked about—pickpocketing, stealing the puck, quick release—that night, everything went right for him. Every time the puck was on his stick, he made something magical happen. He lived up to the hype."

Earlier in the day, Matthews's teammates had been talking about his maturity level, given he was just nineteen and the youngest player on the team.

"He's not like a kid," said veteran forward Leo Komarov. "He's more like a guy who's played in this league already."

"He's not afraid of anything," said veteran defenceman Roman Polák.

"He's a man," Coach Mike Babcock told the media gathered in

Ottawa for the game. "He's nineteen years old, but he acts like he's twenty-seven. He has great maturity. If you meet his mom and dad, you're thoroughly impressed with the kind of people they are, and the respect he has for his mom and sisters, the kind of guy he is. Don't get me wrong, we would have drafted him anyway, but that makes him more special."

After the game, Matthews joked the last time he scored four times was probably "in mites." But he showed his colours with his next comment.

"It's really something you can't write up," Matthews said. "And it was pretty special having my parents here for them to share the moment with me."

Family, for Matthews, is everything. His father, Brian, was a technology officer who played college baseball and encouraged his kids to play sports. His mother, Ema, was a former flight attendant who left Mexico to pursue her dreams and encouraged her kids to do the same. She worked two jobs, including as a barista, to help make ends meet. Older sister Alexandria was trying her hand at being a social media influencer with lifestyle, beauty, and fitness videos, and younger sister Breyana would pursue golf. They're a tight-knit group.

"They've been a huge part of my career, it was only right for them to be there for the first one," said Matthews.

In fact, Brian Matthews—ever the dad, the coach, and one-time college athlete—would usually talk to Auston after a game, just to check in.

"When the moment's right, he does a pretty good job separating hockey from life in general," Auston said to the *Toronto Sun*. "It's not always hockey, hockey, hockey. That helped when I was younger, to let go a little bit. I can only imagine how emotional my mom was getting up there. I saw a couple of videos of them."

As the goals piled up, the reaction from fans was understandably excited. But it was the reaction from current and past NHLers that really stood out. Twitter, as X was called then, was abuzz.

"What a way to start a career," posted Maple Leafs great Doug Gilmour.

"Feels like I'm watching mite hockey where there's that one kid who's just way better than everyone else," posted Martin St. Louis.

"Welcome to our beer league," tweeted Penguins defenceman Kris Letang.

"Since the start of this game, I didn't even get a chance to drink four beers, and he's got four goals," said LA Kings sniper Marián Gáborík.

"Most guys would be thrilled to score four in a month," posted ex-Leaf Viktor Stålberg.

"I feel like I'm watching one of the 99 overall created players I used to make in *NHL 2002*," wrote Marlies goalie Garrett Sparks.

Ryan Callahan tweeted to his ex-Rangers teammate Derek Stepan that his three-goal debut against Buffalo "is not looking so impressive anymore."

Paul Bissonnette: "Would pay money to see Auston Matthews's DMs right now."

And Aaron Ward: "That moment Auston Matthews gets four in first career game, causing you to reflect on your NHL career and wondering if you even got four in practice."

But the best deadpan probably belonged to the best deadpanning goalie in the league in that era: Panthers goalie Roberto Luongo. He declared, "I've just decided that Reims [James Reimer] will play *all* of the games versus the Leafs this year."

"What's the big deal? I scored four goals . . . in my career. #matthews #bust," said Frazer McLaren. In fact, he scored two of his four career goals (over 102 career games) with the Maple Leafs.

Canadian actor Stephen Amell, star of the TV show *Arrow*, which was going head-to-head with the Leafs game on TV that night, also chimed in. "After Auston Matthews's fourth goal, I'm just going to accept that the only person in Toronto watching *Arrow* is my mom."

Even Craig Anderson got into it. The next time the two teams faced each other, the Ottawa netminder asked Auston to autograph his goalie stick. "Thanks 'four' making my first game memorable," Matthews penned.

Matthews had the world's attention. The NHL tried to put it all into context with North America's other major league sports. Citing the Elias Sports Bureau, the league said: "No player has ever hit three home runs in his MLB debut; the last to hit two was Trevor Story on April 4, 2016. The last player to record three touchdowns in his NFL debut was Marshall Faulk on September 4, 1994. The most points recorded by a player making his NBA debut is 43, achieved by Wilt Chamberlain on October 24, 1959."

What might have mattered to Matthews more was happening back in Arizona. The people who were close to him, his former coaches and teammates, were gushing with pride. His minor hockey Arizona Bobcats tweeted they'd seen it before, posting the score sheet of a four-goal game by Matthews when he was fourteen.

There was Sean Whyte, a journeyman pro hockey player from the Ottawa Valley, who settled in Scottsdale and ran Ozzie Ice, which featured the synthetic surface where Matthews took skating lessons.

"I was in my office at the hockey rink, and I had the TV on. I was putting my skates on, and he ended up scoring, and I was just like, 'Oh my God, that is so amazing. First game, he scores a goal. How unbelievable is that?' So I'm beaming. And I go on the ice, coaching my team in practice, and then someone came running out, someone said he just scored another one. And I was like, 'Oh my God, how cool is that?' A little while later, they tell me he just scored a hat trick, and I turned to my team and said, 'You know what, guys? Free time. Do what you want. I'm going in.' And I went in and started walking in my office and got to see the fourth goal. I was like, 'This is history right now.' Some of my players came up as well and started watching, too, so it was a pretty cool moment."

Boris Dorozhenko, a Ukrainian Russian hockey player who was coaching in Mexico when the Matthews family approached him to teach their son his skating techniques, said, "For me, it was normal. When he was a youth, he did it many times, scoring four or five goals a game. So nothing changed for him."

Justin Rogers, one of Matthews's first teammates in minor hockey, said, "We knew from the start he was going to be special. And it was so exciting. We all got goose bumps. Part of you thinks maybe we are frauds down in the desert playing hockey, but then you see him produce the way he does and to have the love of the game. You don't have to be born in Minnesota or Toronto. You can be born anywhere."

Pat Mahan, a Minnesotan transplant who coached Matthews on the Bobcats along with his own son and put Auston up in hotel rooms to help the Matthews family defray the costs of a travelling team, said, "On one hand, obviously, it was surprising. On the other hand, it wasn't surprising at all. For anybody to do that in any game, much less your first game, it's unreal. But after the fact, what I thought was, 'The world is now going to realize who they're really dealing with.'"

"I was watching, and I was incredibly happy for Mom and Dad," said Stanley Cup champion Claude Lemieux, who ran a hockey academy in Scottsdale when Auston was a youngster. "I couldn't believe it. And I knew it was the start of something special."

There was Laurence Gilman, who would become assistant GM of the Leafs in 2018, but had heard of Matthews when he was a youngster and Gilman was assistant GM of the Coyotes. "When he scored when he went down the left side and then drove the net, I thought, 'My God, this kid is for real,'" said Gilman. "He displayed some spectacular, not just skill, but speed, strength, and courage to drive the net as hard as he did. And that's been a hallmark of his game since day one."

On the Ottawa bench was Marc Crawford, Matthews's coach the season prior in Switzerland, now an associate coach with the Senators. "It was amazing, such a great happening," said Crawford. "Such a debut for Auston."

His former billeting teammate in USA Hockey's National Team Development Program, goalie Luke Opilka, was with the Kitchener Rangers. "I thought it was amazing. I was so happy for him. I was super excited. Like, that's the way to make a splash."

Ryan Shannon, the former NHLer who became close to the entire Matthews family in having Auston as a neighbour and teammate in Zurich, was more taken in by the reactions of Brian and Ema. "It still gives me goose bumps," said Shannon. "It started with fist pumps and hugs, and they were crying. And then the second one went in, and it was kind of like, 'Yes.' And then they kind of got used to it after the third. And then it was like arms up in the air and shock and astonishment after the fourth."

The Swiss like their coffee and cake, and at the next day's practice in Zurich, Auston's four goals were the talk of the breakfast table.

"It was so fun to just be around the Swiss guys and the imports that had played with him," said Shannon. "There were jokes, like, 'He never scored four goals here. The NHL's a joke.' Like, 'This league is better.' But no one was surprised. Obviously you got to be shocked at four goals in a debut. That doesn't happen, right? But you can see it. He is special and works really hard at it."

Mike DeAngelis, a much-travelled defenceman from Kamloops, BC, who had become the director of the Jr. Coyotes at the Ice Den where Matthews got his start, added, "For me, it was the defining moment, that whatever path he took was the right path."

Four goals in an NHL debut. It simply hadn't been done in the NHL's modern era. Not by Connor McDavid, the Newmarket phenom who'd been chosen first overall the year before Matthews. Not Wayne Gretzky, who held the NHL's all-time leading scoring record for thirty-one years with 894 career goals. He'd famously learned the game under the tutelage of his father in a backyard rink in Brantford, Ontario. Not Alex Ovechkin, the Russian son of two Soviet Union–era athletes who surpassed Gretzky's seemingly unbreakable record in 2025.

No one.

The first to do it was a nineteen-year-old American raised in the desert community of Scottsdale, Arizona, the son of a Mexican mother and an American father, a boy who only became a hockey fan of Canada's sport because a team in Winnipeg relocated to Arizona and the NHL adamantly ensured it stayed there—at least for a while.

To be fair to history—and for those who would like to split a few hairs—Reg Noble of the Toronto team (they played without a nickname) scored four goals in his first game in the newly formed National Hockey League in its first season of 1917–18. Harry Hyland of the Montreal Wanderers scored five against Noble's team in that same first NHL game, a 10–9 win by the Wanderers over the Toronto team. And Joe Malone scored five for the Montreal Canadiens that same night, December 19, 1917, when the Canadiens beat the Ottawa Senators 7–4 in the new four-team circuit.

The NHL had formed the season after the National Hockey Association had folded, playing under the same constitution and same rules, and mostly the same players. So pretty much everybody had plenty of professional experience. Noble had been with the Toronto Blueshirts. Malone had already won the Stanley Cup a couple of times (with the Quebec Bulldogs) and had been the leading scorer in the NHA three times. Hyland had started his career in 1908 with the Montreal Shamrocks and spent eight seasons in the NHA with the Wanderers. His "first" season in the NHL was his last in professional hockey.

In other words, none would be considered rookies in the professional sense back then. In fact, the Calder Trophy for the rookie of the year wasn't even created until 1936.

So technically speaking, Matthews had done something that hadn't been done since the absolute dawn of the league, a span of 36,092 calendar days.

Split hairs if you must.

And yes, the Leafs lost the game 5–4 in overtime to Ottawa. Matthews—showing a maturity beyond his years—took the blame for the loss, on a goal by Kyle Turris thirty-seven seconds into the extra period.

"That last play was 100 percent my fault," Matthews told reporters after the game. "We came here to win, and we didn't get that done. It's a learning point for me and my team. It would have been nice to get the win."

Still, Matthews didn't just live up to the hype that preceded the Maple Leafs taking him first overall that June. He exceeded it. In his first game in the NHL, which propelled him forwards to an awards-filled, multimillion-dollar career. He was on his way to becoming one of the greatest goal scorers of all time and the greatest Maple Leaf ever.

Think about it: If you were going to create the greatest Maple Leaf of all time, perhaps you'd try to duplicate the upbringing of Dave Keon, who, in 2016, was named the greatest Maple Leaf of the franchise's first hundred years. The Maple Leafs took over sponsorship of a team to buy the rights to the kid from Noranda, Quebec, in the days before the draft, developing him in their own feeder system starting with the St. Michael's Majors.

If you were going to create the greatest American hockey player of all time, perhaps you'd try to duplicate the path of Mike Modano, the first overall pick of the Minnesota North Stars in 1988 who went on to a 1,499-game career. Modano was born in Livonia, Michigan, a fan of the Red Wings, and wore number 9 in part because of Gordie Howe. His family had to move to Westland, Michigan, just so he could play in one of the best minor hockey programs in the United States with AAA Little Caesars.

If you were going to create the greatest goal scorer of all time, you'd try to copy the path Alex Ovechkin took. His mother, Tatyana Ovechkina, is a two-time Olympic gold medallist (1976, 1980) and world champion (1975) in basketball. His father, Mikhail, was a soccer player.

If you were going to create the greatest player of all time, then it's Wayne Gretzky's path you'd want: backyard rinks in the cold winters of Brantford, Ontario, and a father who coached not just games but skills. Drills included skating around bleach bottles and tin cans, and flipping pucks over scattered hockey sticks in order to be able to pick up the puck again in full flight. Walter Gretzky gave the advice to "skate where the puck's going, not where it's been."

All those greats have a few things in common: growing up in a northern, snowy climate. Rinks at the ready. Hockey on television. Playing in highly competitive leagues filled with other great players. Growing up in a community that lives and breathes the game.

One thing you might not want to do if you're creating the greatest Maple Leaf of all time, or greatest American hockey player, or greatest goal scorer, is to start things off the way things started for Auston Matthews.

That is, in Mexico.

CHAPTER TWO

Mexico

Auston Matthews's story starts with his mother, Ema. She grew up one of eight siblings—six girls, two boys—on the family ranch near Hermosillo, Mexico. Her father, Rafael, raised cattle and horses. Her mother, Alicia, took care of the family, went to the market, and did the cooking.

"Growing up in Mexico, it was very simple," Ema told ESPN in 2021. "Being on the ranch, in that world, it's amazing. It's seeing natural animals, quiet, no traffic, just you and the beautiful green in the desert. It's another world. You grew up very humble because you see how privileged people are."

As Ema told Kaplan, there was no electricity. They lugged water from a well. Still, all the kids went to school. The family was supportive, encouraging each of their children to follow their dreams. Ema wanted to become a pilot, but pilot training was expensive. "As a woman back then, it was different." She became a flight attendant instead.

At nineteen, Ema left home to work for a now-defunct airline called Aero California that had regular flights to Los Angeles.

One day in 1990, there was a problem with the plane. A technician named Brian Matthews came aboard to see what needed to be done. He was a student at Loyola Marymount University, was a pretty good baseball player, and a sports fan. This was a part-time job to get him through college. He didn't really want to take the call to the plane, but he did.

He had one look at Ema and it was love at first sight.

"She spoke no English," Brian Matthews told *The Globe and Mail*. "I spoke no Spanish. I got fluent in about six months."

Brian lived in Culver City, California, a mere ten-minute drive to Loyola Marymount University, a twenty-minute drive to LAX, and about fifteen minutes to the Great Western Forum, then the home of the Los Angeles Kings.

Just two years before the couple met, Canada's cultural identity was shaken to its foundations when the unthinkable happened: On August 9, 1988, the Edmonton Oilers traded Wayne Gretzky—the Great One himself—to the Los Angeles Kings, turning the place known colloquially as the Fabulous Forum into the Western capital of the hockey universe.

American kids who might never have been exposed to hockey now were taking up the sport or were playing the roller version of the sport. Hockey suddenly mattered to those to whom the sport had never mattered before. California would later start producing high-end players. Up until Gretzky's arrival, only six players born in California ever made it to the NHL, the best being Oakland-born Lee Norwood. Since the Gretzky deal, the number is closer to fifty.

The San Jose Sharks followed. Then the Anaheim Ducks. Almost an entire American Hockey League division is based in California. All because Oilers owner Peter Pocklington needed cash, and the fastest way of getting some was to trade hockey's greatest player.

Thankfully, the Kings were good.

Brian and Ema would watch Kings games together. He did his

best to explain this weird ice sport to Ema—as Ema and Brian would later have to explain so that Auston's Mexican relatives could see what he was up to.

"There was a vibe," Brian Matthews told *USA Today* in 2017. "The Kings had Gretzky, and [Marty] McSorley, and then Jari Kurri. They were fun to watch. They scored goals. They put up points. They were winning."

Eventually, Brian's work in the tech industry took them to San Ramon, California, where Alexandria was born. Then, on September 17, 1997, Auston Matthews was born.

Before Christmas that year, they moved to Scottsdale, Arizona, where Brian Matthews had roots. It was just a couple of years after the Winnipeg Jets had moved to the desert. Nearly five years after Auston's birth—and on the day of his first skating lesson—his younger sister, Breyana, was born.

Ema's cooking was decidedly Mexican. Talk around the dinner table was only partly in Spanish, but mostly in English because older sister Alexandria had been teased at age five for speaking Spanish in class. Auston is a little hesitant to speak Spanish outside the friendly environs of his family, but he can.

Among Brian's family in Scottsdale was his brother Billy. Auston was two when Uncle Billy—a Coyotes season-ticket holder—took him to his first NHL game. Was it the action? Was it the colours? Was it the atmosphere? Was it the Zambonis? Brian believed it was the Zamboni, which Auston called "El Trucke." Whatever the reason, it was love at first sight between a kid and a sport.

"If the Coyotes hadn't come, then Auston most likely would be in baseball or some other sport," Brian Matthews told *USA Today* in 2017.

The Matthews family has athletic blood. Not only did Auston's dad, Brian, make it as a college ball pitcher, but his Uncle Wes played wide receiver for four games with the Miami Dolphins. And Auston's great-grandfather was a high school football coach at Muskogee Central High School in Oklahoma.

The family decided the kids should each play two sports. Auston chose baseball and hockey. The eldest daughter, Alexandria, played soccer, while the younger, Breyana, would find her own athletic niche on the Arizona State University women's golf team. Both can beat him at tennis, a sport he takes particularly seriously as an adult.

Auston turned out to be very good at baseball. Now he sometimes shows off his hand-eye co-ordination and baseball prowess when he takes batting practice with the Toronto Blue Jays. He hits home runs. He's that good.

His dad, Brian, was a right-handed pitcher who challenged left-handed Auston in the batter's box. Fastballs. Sinkers. Stuff most dads couldn't throw at their kids. "I was throwing everything at him, mixing it up," Brian told *The Hockey News* in 2016. "He never knew what was coming. But his hand-eye co-ordination was uncanny."

Auston played catcher. Coaches told him there was more money to be made on the diamond than the ice rink.

Brian related the story to Don Granato, Auston's coach at the US National Team Development Program, of Auston playing in a spring hockey league at the same time as he was playing baseball. Sometimes the two schedules would overlap. Auston played his hockey game and joined baseball mid-game. "He showed up in the fifth inning, hit a grand slam in his first at bat, then hit the game-winning home run in the seventh inning," Granato told Sportsnet.

Smiles in the dugout turned to frowns when Brian Matthews told the baseball coach that Auston was heading back to the rink and wouldn't be able to play the next game. "The coach went crazy,"

Granato said. "He said, 'Your kid just hit two home runs in three innings and you're not bringing him back?'"

When time constraints forced him to choose between sports at thirteen, baseball lost. "Auston was a better baseball player than he was a hockey player, but the game wasn't fast enough for him," his mom, Ema, told *The Hockey News*. "He needed motion."

Ema and Brian knew little about hockey when Auston first started playing. But that didn't stop him.

"My parents spent my whole childhood doing everything for us, and they were never really doing anything for themselves," Matthews told ESPN.

CHAPTER THREE

Ozzie Ice

The day of Auston Matthews's first skating lesson is etched in family lore, for good reason: It was the day his younger sister, Breyana, was born, April 21, 2002.

Ema was supposed to be induced that day, but it conflicted with Auston's first lesson. She gamely delayed Breyana's birth an hour or so to allow for what turned out to be a fairly meaningful first step—or first skate—for one of hockey's superstars.

"She understood," Brian told ESPN in 2016, recounting his wife's reaction. "What was another hour?"

There were only a handful of rinks to choose from. AZ Ice Arcadia is where Auston started, taught by the late Jim Rogers. Rogers was a Coyotes season-ticket holder who worked his way up from janitor at Arcadia, eventually buying the rink, all with the goal of making sure ice hockey, of all sports, could flourish in the desert. Auston Matthews would become his most famous student.

"My dad was always talking about Auston's work ethic," said Justin Rogers, Jim's son and Auston's frequent teammate on the Valley of the Sun Hockey Association (VOSHA) Mustangs. "He was the first one to say that 'I didn't make Auston Matthews the way he was. I was blessed to coach Auston.' He talked about Auston in that way from when he was probably six years old. He really thought Auston was very special.

"He was the six-year-old kid who could raise the puck. He was phenomenal."

The VOSHA Mustangs, run by Rogers, was an organization that had a *Bad News Bears* feel about it. Kids would show up with football gear. Or with plastic roller hockey sticks. Or with equipment carried in garbage bags. "It was the wild Wild West, that stereotypical what you'd imagine minor hockey in Phoenix back then would look like," said Justin Rogers. "My dad was the coach who was willing to take on any kid in the Valley, whether they had played before or whether they were a super-duper elite athlete—or first time ever walking into a rink.

"We were kind of that outcast, weren't good enough for the other guys. And Matthews showed up, and we were stoked. It was like, 'Holy smokes, this kid is pretty good.' He could actually skate forwards and backwards. That's not something we're used to in our program."

With Matthews, the VOSHA Mustangs Under-8 team, deemed to be one of the weakest in the Valley, actually won tournaments.

Young Auston would have been at the rink every day if he could have been. He signed up for club hockey with the Jr. Coyotes. In 2004, at seven, he was playing with eight- and nine-year-olds with Jr. Coyotes Mites. In 2005, he was playing Squirt with ten-year-olds. Playing with older kids was a theme, partly because of the dearth of hockey players in the region, partly because he was such a good player.

All the while, though, it was the Ozzie Ice training facility in Scottsdale, less than a mile from where the Matthews family lived, that became his home away from home.

It was unlike any rink any Canadian hockey player would have played in. The facility had two small rinks, each sixty feet by eighty-five feet. They both had regulation nets and boards, but one surface was real ice, the other synthetic.

The owner was Dwayne Osadchuk, who'd wanted to showcase the synthetic ice that he had patented. Osadchuk was born in Edmonton and grew up playing shinny on frozen ponds, forming rolled-up newspapers into shin pads. He didn't like what he saw in Phoenix as far as the big rinks were concerned. He thought they charged too much and never had any openings for kids.

"I got mad at the bigger rinks," said Osadchuk. "They were charging way too much. Their attitude was 'no kid from Arizona will make it to the NHL.'" That wasn't how Osadchuk saw the world.

"Kids can make it if you give them a chance, you know. That's what we did. So that's why we built it."

When the Ozzie Ice surfaces weren't rented or booked, the idea was to replicate pond hockey. All kids, all ages could come and play. "We built this for the kids to train and learn and have fun. And it goes back to the old pond-hockey days. And the little kids, the big kids, high school kids, they all skated and played hockey together, like we did on the ponds. There was no checking or pushing or stuff like that. It was more stickhandling and skills and so forth. And it taught the big kids to share with the little kids."

Matthews was the very definition of a rink rat, taking lessons at Ozzie Ice from a former NHL player in Sean Whyte, and later "Uncle" Boris Dorozhenko, a product of the Soviet hockey system who would become an important figure in his life and a close family friend. Whyte was a trailer park kid who beat the odds by both making the NHL and getting a business degree. Whyte was born in Sudbury, Ontario, but grew up in a trailer park in the Ottawa Valley and started playing hockey in Petawawa, which, as in the same way as in Phoenix, was small enough that if you go to tryouts, you make the team.

The family wasn't wealthy, and hockey can be an expensive sport. So when Whyte's father bought the gear, Whyte was thrown when he found out that it was so expensive. He knew if his father was spending that kind of money, he'd better be good. He'd shoot five hundred pucks a day. When his dad came into the bedroom to wake him at 5:00 a.m. for practice, Whyte would flip the sheets and reveal he was already in his gear. That was his mentality. He played four years of junior and was drafted by the Los Angeles Kings in 1989, a year after they traded for Wayne Gretzky.

He signed at twenty and went to camp. The league was showcasing a game between Gretzky's Los Angeles Kings and Mario Lemieux's Pittsburgh Penguins in the 1990 preseason at the Suncoast Dome in St. Petersburg, Florida. More than 25,000 fans showed up—at that point a record crowd for the NHL—and it was only a preseason game. And hockey would soon be on its way to Florida.

Whyte played in that exhibition game. Gretzky scored. Lemieux had a sore back and missed it. The Penguins won 5–3. After the game, Whyte was told he did well but was going to be cut. They told him he was going to Phoenix. He was happy. The other farm team was in New Haven, Connecticut.

"I got off the plane and it was like a thousand blow dryers hitting me," said Whyte. "I got my hockey bag on one shoulder, my clothing bag on the other shoulder. I walk outside and there's palm trees and blue skies and a guy goes by on a Harley without a helmet on. And I'm like, 'I'm home.'"

His NHL career amounted to twenty-one games over two seasons as well as minor league trips to Tulsa, Cornwall, Worcester, Fort Worth, and El Paso. But Phoenix was home. He spent two and a half seasons with the IHL Phoenix Roadrunners and his final four with the Phoenix Mustangs of the WCHL. But four surgeries over his last two seasons put an end to his playing days in 2001.

The hard-nosed right winger was looking for what was next, preferably in Phoenix. He was lost but found his way, getting a business degree, a major in project management, and graduating summa cum laude. While he was back at school, he worked at Ozzie Ice. He offered skating lessons. Whyte worked eight-to-ten-hour days, his feet aching from wearing skates all day.

During all that, along came a six-year-old named Auston Matthews who wanted some lessons. He had taken a learn-to-play lesson at Arcadia, the rink in Phoenix. Now Matthews wanted to get serious about skating. After one lesson, the family went home. Brian came back and signed Auston up for a full season. Matthews was so impressed with skating that gift ideas for Christmas and birthdays were gift cards for skating or hockey lessons.

"I don't know what to do, Sean," Brian said to Whyte. "He doesn't think of anything else. He doesn't do anything else. Baseball and tennis, I know. I don't know anything about hockey. What do I do?"

Sean asked Brian if he wanted to learn. He said yes.

"I did a ton of lessons with him, too," Sean said.

Brian learned to skate, learned the game, played shinny, joined leagues just so he could share in Auston's world. He coached Auston as well.

It's something a Canadian family might take for granted. You skate with your mom or dad. They probably teach you. But Auston was leading the way here, the son demonstrating this strange ice sport to his American dad and Mexican mother.

It was fairly clear that Matthews was soaking up the lessons. He never complained that Whyte was asking too much. There was no eye-rolling that adults look for around children, a signal to take your foot off the pedal. No whining. No complaining.

Young Auston would be at the rink at six in the morning, then head to school, and come back after school.

At the rink—as elsewhere in life—Auston went by Papi. It was a term of endearment his mother gave him at birth.

One day at the rink, Auston's parents couldn't find him and began asking his friends and teammates if anyone had seen Auston. The kids looked at each other and shrugged. One asked, "Who's Auston?" Then they figured it out. They were looking for Papi.

Ozzie Ice was losing money. He came up with a plan, part of which was a revolutionary idea: a three-on-three hockey league—small area games, small area practices, small area drills, for kids. Brian Matthews, sensing more opportunity for his son, was an enthusiastic backer.

As Brian Matthews would find out, there was no template for youth hockey in a new market as there would be in Canada or northern states. There was no right or wrong way to train kids for hockey, only what was available.

So three-on-three hockey in a small rink with fake ice? Where do we sign up?

It is in fact the development model now but was unheard of then. Small pockets of kids around North America were practising and playing on small ice surfaces, sometimes reluctantly. Parents traditionally want their kids to play on a full two-hundred-foot ice surface.

But if you think about it, what good is it for an eight-year-old to skate two hundred feet? That's simply a speed game. But kids learn puck-handling skills on small surfaces—puck retrieval, puck protection. How to create a shot with no space. How to make a play with someone right on top of you. Short bursts of speed.

Does that sound like any hockey player you know who wears number 34 for the Toronto Maple Leafs?

"A lot of the skills I've developed today are from that," Matthews told author Mike Traikos for his 2019 book *The Next Ones*. "It was my own little backyard rink. I was there constantly. I had every team's jersey so I could fill in and play for them and have fun. I'd be there all the time."

From an early age, Matthews was already better than his age group—and obsessed with hockey. Matthews wanted to play all the time, and Whyte made him a deal. If any of the teams were ever so shorthanded that they couldn't ice a team, Matthews could play. So Matthews had a jersey of every colour represented in the league and would sit beside Whyte, who was the timekeeper and stats keeper and just about everything else, ready to go.

Whyte would watch the games, of course. But Matthews's eyes were focused behind the action, toward the dressing rooms. He'd count players going into the room for the next game. It was supposed to be nine to a team. If it got down to five, Matthews would get the tap. It was a routine song and dance, but Whyte did his best to get Matthews more playing time on shorthanded teams.

One day, Matthews tapped Whyte on the shoulder.

"Hey, Coach, that team has only five players," Matthews said.

"I don't know, Auston, they're much older," said Whyte.

Matthews playing against older players—by a year or two—was not a problem. That was the reality of Phoenix-area hockey; the best kids—regardless of age—would cluster together.

But this was a big age gap. And size gap. They were bantams, thirteen- and fourteen-year-olds. Auston was no more than eight, as Whyte recalled.

A deal was a deal, though, and Whyte figured Matthews was talented enough to play. And if he wasn't, what harm would it do?

Whyte went into the room with the bigger kids and introduced young Auston.

Whyte left. A few minutes later two of the boys came out to complain. They didn't want to play with a little kid. They'd get by with five players.

Whyte stood firm. The kids relented. Matthews could play.

Then Whyte sat at his post and smiled every time Matthews scored for the team that initially didn't want him.

"They won 14–6, and Auston scored seven or eight goals. Those two kids came up to me after the game and go, 'Hey, Coach, next week if we're short, we want that kid.'

"Meanwhile, he's, like, half their age."

When young Auston first put on skates, the area's hockey infrastructure was so sparse that new and different training ideas were easily implemented. The hockey community in Phoenix was small but diverse; its hockey history was long but thin.

There were the Apaches, who lasted one season (1958–59) in the California Hockey League.

The Roadrunners nickname was particularly popular, with teams sporting the moniker in the Western Hockey League (1967–74), the World Hockey Association (1974–77), the Central Hockey League (1977–78), the Pacific Hockey League (1977–79), the International Hockey League (1989–97), and the ECHL (2005–09). Then there were the Mustangs (1997–2001) in the West Coast Hockey League, and the Polar Bears (2001–2011) of the Western States Hockey League. There was a roller hockey team called the Cobras in the mid-1990s.

Many players, like Whyte, stuck around in their retirement, drawn by the good weather.

Hockey's popularity gained more traction with the arrival of the Winnipeg Jets, transforming into first the Phoenix Coyotes and then the Arizona Coyotes. While the locals went to games, it was the new arrivals in Phoenix who were giving life to minor hockey, a melting pot of locals curious about the game, folks from the Midwest and the East Coast, and even Canadians who'd moved to the city. The weather was pleasant all year round.

Housing was cheap. And Arizona's economic opportunities were blossoming.

The Phoenix area rapidly went from 650,000 in the mid-1960s to five million today—one of the key reasons the NHL wanted Arizona as a market.

Helping put it all together was Mike DeAngelis, a native of Kamloops, BC, and a product of the Penticton Knights and the University of Minnesota Duluth. But the defenceman became more famous because of his Italian heritage, playing internationally for Italy at three Olympic Games and nine World Championships. He finished his playing days with the WCHL's Phoenix Mustangs in 2001, settled in the area, and helped pioneer youth hockey in the region. "This was the last stop at the end of my career," said DeAngelis.

The Matthewses also got to know the Mahans. Pat Mahan was a Minnesota transplant and a beer-league aficionado who took to coaching in Phoenix because his son, Mike, took to the game. "I grew up in Minnesota and we had outdoor rinks at every block," said Mahan. "Travelling was from Burnsville to Bloomington. Just across the bridge."

Not so in Arizona. Travel meant going to other states: Colorado, Texas, Utah, California, Nevada.

It wasn't long before Mahan hooked up with some more famous names: Claude Lemieux and Ron Filion.

Lemieux played some of the final years of his NHL career with the Coyotes and took a liking to the place. By 2004, it felt like Lemieux's career was over (though he came back for one season with San Jose in 2008–09). NHL Commissioner Gary Bettman imposed a season-long lockout on the players in pursuit of a salary cap, so Lemieux got into the business side of things.

The Coyotes left Phoenix for the West Valley suburb of Glendale in 2003, and Lemieux was convinced an ECHL team would work in Phoenix. He became president of the Roadrunners in the rebirth of an old minor league team. He chose as his coach his good friend Ron Filion. They'd played youth hockey with the Riverains du Collège Charles-Lemoyne in Sainte-Catherine, Quebec, in the 1981–82 season. The Lemieux–Filion relationship continued with the Trois-Rivières Draveurs of the QMJHL in 1982–83, the Verdun Juniors in 1983–84, and on through life.

Claude Lemieux won the Stanley Cup four times and the Conn Smythe Trophy once, while his pal Ron Filion played pro in France.

Phoenix-area minor hockey was about to get all the richer for their reunion.

Lemieux and Filion both became deeply involved in the youth hockey scene. Claude's son, Brendan, was a very good hockey player and would one day follow in his father's footsteps to the NHL.

Filion lasted only two years as coach of the Roadrunners, but Lemieux hired him again to run the Lemieux Academy. "We didn't have a whole lot of talent in Arizona, or at least I didn't think we did," said Lemieux. "There weren't many to select from."

So the region might not have had a high volume of kids wanting to play hockey, but for the ones who did, high-level skills training and coaching were readily available.

"We have to fabricate players," said Filion. "We don't get the top athletes. They go to baseball or football. We get kids like Auston once in a while, passionate about hockey because he saw a game. Very rarely do we get the top athletes, so we really have to put on our working boots and try to work with kids."

Matthews, though, was different. He could have been a great athlete at any sport. He chose hockey.

"He was probably much better at baseball than hockey, [but] that's not where his passion was," shared Brian Matthews in *The*

Arizona Republic. "He got so addicted to the fast pace of hockey, constantly moving and doing stuff, and attacking and hitting."

Young Auston had been in and out of teams. The Coyotes, the Roadrunners. Sometimes he only played tournament hockey, the family eschewing fall-winter league play.

For a couple of years up to age twelve or so, he concentrated mostly on skating and skills training with Boris Dorozhenko, who at times was allied with the Valley of the Sun Hockey Association, the Lemieux Academy, and on his own with Next Generation Hockey. That meant a lot of spring and summer hockey tournaments, but little by way of club or league play in hockey's traditional fall-winter season.

DeAngelis couldn't imagine a Canadian family making that decision.

"They would probably feel like their child is falling behind. And that's not the best thing. And 'We've got to keep up with the development of the rest of the kids of that age group,'" said DeAngelis. "Whatever the circumstances were, Auston just didn't play a lot of fall-winter hockey. It didn't seem to bother the family. For whatever reason, they just weren't concerned about it. And he was probably just doing it because it was fun and he liked it and it just came natural to him. And the dad thought it was fine, but I think a more established hockey family from Canada would have been panicking if their kid was not playing in the fall-winter."

In 2007, Claude Lemieux, Ron Filion, and Pat Mahan joined forces to form the Arizona Bobcats, a team that would travel to places like Colorado, Utah, California, and Texas to represent Arizona hockey.

To that point, the Arizona kids were out of their league. The other teams had bigger pools of players to draw from, and longer-established programs. If the Arizona kids were going to compete when they travelled, they'd need to form a Triple A team, drawing the best of the best from their local leagues, and even drawing kids from out of state if need be.

Billets were found for kids from as far away as Utah and Idaho. Then they decided they'd go farther afield and head to hockey country, places like Minnesota and Michigan.

"We needed to take them where the competition was harder, show them what it's like to play against better kids so that we could develop them," said Mahan.

"At that time, Auston was playing locally, and he was playing with kids two years older than him. And still he was still dominant," said Mahan. "At one point, Brian saw what we were doing, so I asked him to come join us. And it was expensive. Brian was a working man. They were a working family. They have three kids, and they treat them all the same. Everybody's equal. I told him, 'Trust me. We'll get Auston where he should go, and this is what we're doing.' And he trusted us."

Finally, in 2010 when he was thirteen, Matthews joined the Arizona Bobcats with Filion as his head coach. "He was above the group," said Filion. "You could see there was something special about him. The biggest thing that speaks to me was his love for the game, the fact that he always wanted to be on the ice."

It didn't matter which age group Filion was working with, Matthews wanted on the ice.

"He had that passion."

Even at home, in the family garage, Matthews obsessed about getting better at hockey. Brian drilled holes in broken sticks, then attached pucks as sticklanding training aids. Matthews stickhandled in the family garage while Brian poke-checked or tried to scoop the puck. The idea was to challenge Matthews to make quick decisions against a stronger opponent.

"The garage has been repaired numerous times," Brian said to *The Arizona Republic.*

It was expensive because hockey is an expensive sport. But for Arizona families, there were greater distances to travel. How expensive? "I could have put my kid through Harvard twice, rather than play travel hockey all those years," joked Mahan.

He estimated $30,000 US a year for flights, hotels, and meals, with registration fees for winter, summer, and spring hockey for an elite team. The Matthewses weren't rolling in money as Brian worked his way up the corporate ladder and Ema held jobs like barista.

"So I would take Auston with me and Michael. He would stay with us in the hotel. So I could help him out that way because Brian couldn't leave both his daughters," said Mahan.

Some families who recognize they have a hockey-playing prodigy on their hands might have moved to more of a hockey market. Claude Lemieux ultimately did, moving to Toronto and getting his son into the GTHL Red Wings program. Heaven knows some families do whatever they can to get an address within the limits of the Greater Toronto Hockey League. Any league would have welcomed Matthews. But that was never on the table for the Matthews family.

"It had a huge impact on the family today and who he is, because he could have played anywhere in the country," said Mahan.

While it may be surprising on the surface, it wasn't if you knew the Matthews family. "Brian's a very smart and competent man," said Mahan. "Obviously, nobody knows if you're going to make the NHL. But Brian believed in him and taught him if you want something, you've got to work for it. It doesn't matter where you live. That's just how he is. He didn't ask my advice but trusted me. When he put him with us, he could have put him anywhere.

"I don't think they ever seriously considered moving him

anywhere because they're a family. They are very tight-knit. Principled. Great family.

"Brian was like, 'If we're going to get there, we're going to get there. Let's go to work,'" said Mahan. "And Auston always did. And he probably missed out on some stuff as a kid. But he was always having fun. He was always happy."

And he was better than everyone else. But how had Auston gotten so much better? He'd put in the work, with help from the unlikeliest of sources in the unlikeliest of places: a former Ukrainian hockey player living in Mexico.

CHAPTER FOUR

Uncle Boris

In 2004, Auston Matthews was six years old and madly in love with hockey. Boris Dorozhenko, the Ukrainian-born, Russian-trained hockey player and mathematician living in Mexico City, was about to make a trip that would change both of their lives.

He called an old friend, Robert Lopez, who'd made a career promoting hockey among Latino kids. Lopez had been coaching the University of Washington Huskies when his friend and mentor, the late Pat Quinn, suggested he take a job coaching kids in Mexico. That's where Lopez and Dorozhenko met.

His contract over, Lopez had set up shop in Scottsdale, Arizona. Dorozhenko asked if he could bring his Mexican team to Arizona for exhibition games and a training camp. They called it "Euro Hockey Camp" for marketing purposes, leaning on Dorozhenko's Ukrainian background. Brian Matthews signed up Auston.

"If I had known somebody from Texas, I probably would have taken my kids to Texas," said Dorozhenko.

Dorozhenko's Mexican peewees made mincemeat out of teams in Peoria, Chandler, and Gilbert, Arizona. The best player was a ten-year-old named Hector Majul, who would play pro in Italy.

"Brian definitely couldn't believe that a kid from Mexico was a better skater than everyone on the ice that he could see," said Majul.

Brian Matthews and Dorozhenko hit it off, Boris quickly becoming "Uncle Boris" to Auston. Auston ate up Boris's unusual skating lessons and training techniques.

"I've got to believe in that first camp, Brian Matthews saw the progress that Auston made in one week, that was tremendous, and saw how I was skating," said Hector.

That convinced Brian that Dorozhenko should coach Auston. Now Brian had to convince Dorozhenko to move to Scottsdale. It wasn't an easy decision, but Dorozhenko had made difficult decisions before, taking on even bigger challenges.

More than a decade earlier, he was in Ukraine, playing hockey in the Soviet Championship League, and he wasn't always getting paid. The Soviet Union had collapsed in 1991, and while there were then hopes for democratic reform and an end to the Cold War with the West, there wasn't a lot of extra money to pay players to play hockey.

The lucrative Kontinental Hockey League wouldn't be formed until 2008–09. Dorozhenko's playing days were almost over anyway. There wasn't much of a future in Ukraine. There had to be a future elsewhere.

It just happened to be in the hockey hotbed of Mexico.

The Mexico Ice Hockey Federation—and really, who knew they even had one in 1994—was looking for an executive director to grow the game.

"The Soviet Union was collapsing when I made the decision to move to Mexico City," said Dorozhenko. "Life in Soviet Union at that time, there was not much by way of opportunity. It was decision by economic reason. The Soviet League was a good league, but at some point, there was no way to keep playing without getting paid. So I got this opportunity to move to Mexico. I definitely didn't speak any Spanish or any English. It was my big adventure. And the people advised me the ice hockey in Mexico was represented by maybe thirty or forty players in the whole country. But the idea was to move there and build something. They offered me a decent salary, reasonable money for this. Maybe ten times more than I was earning."

And Mexico, which had joined the International Ice Hockey Federation in 1985, was on its way to becoming an ice hockey nation, with Dorozhenko spreading the word, convincing kids to take up the sport, and even getting some surprisingly nice results in Canada, of all places.

"I made this really revolutionary decision," said Dorozhenko. "My dad told me, 'Okay, son, you can go. We will always be here for you. If something goes wrong, you have your home here.' And I said, 'Okay, I'm going there for maybe a couple of years and try to do my best.' And I did it. But then two years make a transformation to fifteen years. I actually did something there. I started national teams and youth teams. First peewee Quebec participation by Mexican team." One of his teams even won a game at the Silver Stick Tournament in Sarnia. Things were going well for Dorozhenko in Mexico.

"I was pretty established there," said Dorozhenko. "We grew the organization from fewer than a hundred people to something like fifteen hundred. It was a big transformation. On the basis of this group, I started to build the national teams. At a certain moment, I decided to bring our teams to the United States. One of our visits was to Arizona. That team was really spectacular. We won a few games. And many people in the United States were shocked that Mexicans could skate so well. One of these visits, I got asked, 'Why not come here and show us. Do a camp, or a master class, show us what you're doing with your boys.'"

Dorozhenko is not a traditional coach. At least, his coaching techniques are very different from what Canadian kids experience from house league to Triple A as they get sliced off to their level.

"When you develop hockey players in non-hockey communities, you need to be very attentive to each individual," said Dorozhenko. "When you work with a big, huge number of people in a hockey community, you can have as many kids as you want. You can select the best kids, and definitely there's a chance a kid from this group will become a professional hockey player. But when you work with a reduced group of people, you need to develop different philosophies. You need to be very attentive. You need to develop individual skill so they can be at least competitive against kids."

When Canadian kids go to tryouts, there are so many different levels from house league to Triple A that they know they'll get picked for a team at their level. But back when Dorozhenko was working in Mexico and Arizona, there was only one team, and each player had divergent skills.

"You just have this group to work with, and you need to make them competitive," said Dorozhenko. "This pushes you to use your own resources, natural resources, to accelerate the process and make this more productive and make the kids really learn and prove it during the games. So I developed a system, a skating system, which is very different than well-known, old hockey systems. Stretching and on-ice work. A lot of edge work. A huge part of it is the edge work. Definitely work without sticks. It's different.

"I don't know how I became so popular because my camps, they're not fun," he continued. "I admit it, it is not fun for many people. The kids want to shoot the puck, and I make them skate without the puck for a long time. And make them do the same thing for the thousandth time before I give them the puck. But people are still coming."

Players go through a series of exercises that make them mostly vulnerable—bouncing on their skates from a seated position, 360-degree jumps at the red and blue lines, and holding the stick horizontally in front of them while skating backwards. Getting comfortable on the edges of the skate blade is at the heart of Dorozhenko's philosophy, as he focuses on using the entire blade to become stable.

"It's all about your edges," said Matthews's Maple Leafs teammate Matthew Knies. "There's a lot of power-skating techniques you don't see anywhere else. Jumping on the ice. Manoeuvring in awkward areas to control your balance. A lot of focus on mobility and movement. As a kid, to be able to practise that stuff at a young age, to get to be a more powerful skater, it's huge."

Knies is another in what's becoming a long line of NHL players to come out of Dorozhenko's skating schools in Scottsdale.

"He made me an overall better skater. When you [finally] add the puck in there, with your body control, your upper body control, it's pretty dangerous stuff what he can put together there and what he can do for you and make younger players do."

Dorozhenko's prized pupil back in Mexico City in 2004, Hector Majul, had played soccer but tried out for hockey at six after seeing the sport while waiting for his sister to get changed after figure skating practice. Dorozhenko brought ten-year-old Hector with him to Arizona because he was familiar with the complicated drills and could demonstrate them to others.

"That's where I met Papi," said Majul. "It was kind of hard for kids to pick up the exercises the first few days. But I do remember Papi, he was the one guy that picked it up very quickly."

What Dorozhenko taught Matthews was the basis of what any athlete needs to learn to be great. "It was a system of how to work. Establish a plan and understand that everything counts. Nutrition, proper practice, smart practising. You don't just go pull the weights. Because sometimes people are so strong, they look like Arnold Schwarzenegger, but they can't move."

Dorozhenko has built a reputation on not just what he did for Matthews, but what Matthews became. And he's thankful for it.

"Definitely, my system is a lot of skating, is a lot of drills, which are very different. You can't find these drills in any drill book. But when they are watching that, they're like, 'What for? Like wow, we don't understand.'"

At Ozzie Ice, watching as Dorozhenko put his kids through drills, Sean Whyte understood. And he sees it pay off now.

"You watch Auston now and you watch him shoot a puck, whether he has both feet planted, whether he's in stride, whether he's falling off the back, or if he's off the outside edge of his off foot, he's still getting good quality shots off," said Whyte. "And I truly attribute that to all of his training with Boris. The level to which he pushed these kids out of their comfort zone is only going to benefit you in those crunch moments when you aren't truly set or prepared to make a pass, take a shot, receive a pass, you know, or for that matter, just get hit and stay standing."

Claude Lemieux became a fan as well, helping Dorozhenko get a visa and eventually bringing him into the Lemieux Academy as a skills coach.

"His gift was more the teaching part of it. He had great skill as an instructor," said Lemieux. "What he was able to teach was to separate the upper body from the lower body. I bought into it because that's something I couldn't teach. I could teach them how to shoot. But it wasn't so much about stickhandling. It was just about being able to have your feet going in one direction and your upper body going in another direction. You watch Auston, that's why he's so shifty.

"Auston was an incredibly dedicated student," Lemieux continued. "He didn't say much. He was the hardest worker. He did all the drills. He didn't complain about it, versus some of my other boys, including my own son. They wanted to shoot the puck."

The results, Dorozhenko said, speak for themselves.

"Auston, definitely he is the top, top guy," said Dorozhenko. "He's like family. I have a really good relationship with many top players, but just very few of them do I have the same type of relationship as I have with Auston. This is probably a very, very familiar and unique relationship."

But it almost didn't happen. After that initial camp, Dorozhenko simply took his team and went back to Mexico. Brian Matthews urged Dorozhenko to return.

"I remember when I got back to Mexico, Brian gave me a call and said, 'Hey, have you decided?' I said, 'Decided what?' They said, 'We talked with you about moving to Arizona.'"

The move wasn't on. But another camp was. That's when the full-court press happened.

"So I came one other time, and I was here probably two or three weeks. And then I get back to Mexico, and Brian after that visit told me like, 'Boris, how much time do you need to make a decision?' And I said, 'Well, I need a month, at least two months. Leave me alone for a month, and I will put my stuff together, and I will think about this.'"

About ten days later, Brian called again.

"He told me one thing I remember. It was 'Boris, did you make your decision?' I said, 'You gave me a month.' He said, 'Yes, but the kids need you.' Then something clicked in me."

That something was Auston Matthews.

"Seeing how much Auston loved hockey helped me to make this decision. We had a conversation. He was a young kid, and Brian always told me like, 'Boris, believe me, my kid has a big, big, big heart for hockey. Huge heart. He just needs help.' And I said, 'Well, then let's talk with Auston.' I said, 'What do you want to do?' He said, 'I want to be a National Hockey League player.' I said, 'Seriously?' He said, 'Yeah.' And I said, 'Okay.'

"So I packed my stuff. Within a week, I was here in the US. The hockey organization helped me get my work visa, and I started officially working here with the group." A lifelong bond was formed.

Dorozhenko spoke almost no English but bonded immediately with Brian, who was fluent in Spanish thanks to his wife, Ema. Since he was relocating quickly and had nowhere to stay, Dorozhenko moved in with Auston's grandparents, Bobby and Beverly Matthews. He ended up staying with them for two years, establishing a special bond with Auston that helped develop one of hockey's best, and least likely, phenoms.

Other people were taking notice, not so much of young Auston Matthews, but of Dorozhenko's unique skating drills. If any hockey family knows the importance of skating, it's Russ and Geoff Courtnall.

Playing sports was a big thing in the Courtnall household when Geoff and Russ were growing up on Vancouver Island. Hockey, of course, was what the Courtnalls became famous for. Geoff won the Stanley Cup in 1988 as a member of the Edmonton Oilers, part of a 1,048-game NHL career. Russ played 1,029 NHL games, though the Cup eluded him.

Their success is testament in some ways to their father, Archie, who found an ingenious way to get his sons more ice time when they were younger. The best rink back then where they were growing up was at the Victoria Racquet Club, which ran a minor hockey association. It was a private club. You had to be a member to play there, and the Courtnalls couldn't afford that, so Archie coached so he could get his sons in.

"The best part about it was the ice time," said Geoff Courtnall.

They not only could practise and play with their club team, but they could get into the two-hour morning shinny session before school, 5:00 a.m. to 7:00 a.m.

Archie also ran a summer hockey program with power skating as a key component.

"He had a guy named Phil Blake, who was a figure skater and hockey player who taught us power skating," said Geoff.

The emphasis on a special coach for skating stuck with both boys as they became NHLers and later fathers with sons who wanted to play hockey, too.

It was the summer of 2007 when former NHLer Russ Courtnall brought his eleven-year-old son, Lawton, to Park City, Utah, at the request of another former NHLer, Claude Lemieux. They'd been teammates on the Montreal Canadiens in the 1980s, Lemieux drafted by the storied franchise in the second round of the 1983 draft. Russ—as every Leaf fan of a certain age remembers and regrets—was traded to Montreal in an ill-advised transaction in the fall of 1988 for enforcer John Kordic.

Lemieux ran a youth hockey camp June 30–July 25, 2007, at the Park City Ice Arena, with the help of his good friend Ron Filion and his son's skating coach, Boris Dorozhenko. Each of them had their own links to Auston Matthews, then just nine years old and at the camp.

The camp was divided into four one-week segments. The first two weeks were exclusively for players who were currently playing at USA Hockey's AAA level and who had 1995, 1996, and 1997 birthdates, while the second two weeks were open to players of all levels and age groups.

Matthews was in all four weeks.

Russ was blown away, not by the youngster Matthews (at least not yet) but by Dorozhenko and his unique coaching methods.

"Boris is a mathematician, played hockey, blew out his knee, and created this theory on skating," said Russ. "He watched so much video of the best skaters and then started coming up with these ideas. And now everybody's talking about edge work. But as far as I know, as far as I'm concerned, Boris was the first guy to do it. And now everybody's doing it, but nobody does it like him, I can tell you that much."

One unique feature to a Dorozhenko skating lesson: no pucks, at least to start. Another: competition among the players to do the drills the best.

He might have twenty-five kids, separated into five lines. The lines weren't separated by age or region. They were divided by skill. The kid at the front of each line was one who Dorozhenko knew could do the drill the best.

"Sometimes you'd have a nine-year-old kid in the front of the line and a sixteen-year-old kid in the back, and all these kids were thinking about was how to get to the front of the line," said Russ. "There was Auston, my son [Lawton], this kid named Speedy [Jose Suares], this kid named 81 [Eddy Wong], Hector from Mexico, all these kids who travelled with Boris, and they were in the front of the line, in each line. And all these other kids, they might have been better hockey players, they might have been older. But they had to work their way to try to get to the front. And they never wanted the puck. They never thought about a puck. They were just thinking about this drill."

The drills were so difficult, Russ gave them a try, to his lasting regret. "I was known for my skating skills. Yeah, and I couldn't do his drills. And Auston was there, maybe nine, and he did them."

At that point, Russ invited Dorozhenko to BC the following summer for a camp Russ was going to run.

"After the hockey season, we set up these camps because, selfishly, I wanted my son Lawton to skate with Boris and learn from Boris. So there was a group of kids that tagged along with Boris, and Auston was one of them."

If Dorozhenko was taking his coaching skills on the road to Canada, Matthews was part of the package deal.

"He came with me everywhere," said Dorozhenko.

Over the next years, there would be Russ–Dorozhenko (Next Gen) camps all over the North American Northwest: Victoria, Nanaimo, Vancouver, Whistler, and Coeur d'Alene, Idaho. Matthews and a few other of the best kids from Dorozhenko's Arizona hockey school were always part of the camps.

"They were from Mexico, they were from Arizona, they were from different parts of the United States and Canada. It was awesome, like the International Hockey School of British Columbia," said Russ.

Boris would rent a home for most of the kids and hire sitters.

"Boris was more than just teaching hockey," said Russ. "He was teaching life skills. So he had a mixed bag of kids. They had to make their beds. They rented houses and moved around to these camps. They went to training camp with him. They trained off ice. He was militant, almost. But they loved him. To this day, they still love him."

Whenever the camp was in Victoria, Matthews—who was a year or two younger than everybody else—stayed with Lawton in the home of Lawton's grandmother Cathy.

"[Auston] always looked up to the adults. And he listened to everything you said. He was a super well-behaved kid. My mom absolutely loved him," Russ said of Matthews. "I give Brian and

Ema, the parents, so much credit because they loved him so much. They allowed him the freedom at a very young age to go away and travel with Boris. Without Boris, he would have missed out on four to six weeks of training every summer. That's why I want people to remember to give the parents a lot of credit, even though they weren't there. They were both working, trying to provide for Auston."

And Auston took the travelling hockey camps seriously.

"Auston was a hard worker and a great student," said Russ. "We never had a problem with him. He had a big smile. He was a quiet kid, very well behaved. It was like he knew the opportunity he had was so precious. And his parents were allowing him to have that opportunity."

Spring hockey was also part of the camp experience. Russ ran a team called the BC Bruins, one that would feature a future real Boston Bruin, Jake DeBrusk, at a tournament in Whistler, BC.

Most of the players in the tournament were twelve, but Russ Courtnall wanted ten-year-old Auston on the team. He got some pushback from parents. Why, they wondered, would they let a kid two years younger on the team? And he's from Arizona, so he can't be that good.

To that point, Russ Courtnall had never seen Auston in a game, only camps and practices. He knew Auston was a good skater and stickhandler. He just didn't know how good. But he couldn't get the parents to shut up.

"So I said, 'This kid's the best hockey player in the United States,'" Russ recalled. "I was going around bragging about the kid. Had no idea, no clue. And sure enough, he turned out to be the best player. The first game in Whistler, he scored five points.

"It shut up all the parents."

The Matthews family learned to trust in Dorozhenko. "Brian at some point told me many years ago that I felt like a brother to him because some missing part of him was Billy."

Billy Matthews, the uncle who had brought Auston to his first games, had died. Dorozhenko had never met him, but he understood. And he'd never let the Matthews family down.

Dorozhenko had links all over the world, and he had a good relationship with a youth team from Ukraine, Druzhba-78 Kharkiv. The team was a regular participant at one of the most famous hockey tournaments in the world, the Quebec International Pee-Wee Hockey Tournament.

There was a standing invitation to join the Kharkiv team if Boris thought he had a player who could play at that level.

"I said, well, I have one kid, but the family doesn't have much money," Dorozhenko told the Ukrainians in time for the 2010 tournament.

Boris and Brian talked things over. It was a unique opportunity to play in that tournament. There were no other Arizona teams going. The list of all-time greats who'd played there was amazing. It really was a special tournament. All the Matthewses had to do was pay for a flight to New Jersey, where the Ukrainians were having a camp as part of another tournament.

The Ukrainian coach, understandably, wanted to see Matthews play first before he committed to having him join the team for the Quebec tournament.

The flight landed in Newark. The team had already played the first period. Matthews joined them for the second period.

"He jumped plane and scored three goals right away," said Dorozhenko. "The coach called me right away and said, 'Yeah, and definitely, we'll take him. No question.'"

Matthews got on Kharkiv's minibus to Quebec City's Colisée, once home to the Quebec Nordiques. For twelve-year-olds from

Wayne Gretzky to Mario Lemieux to Connor McDavid, it was the place to be, the most prestigious peewee hockey tournament in the world.

"It was a test for him," said Dorozhenko.

It wasn't just a hockey test. These were kids from Eastern Europe, an entirely different background. And they were in a French-speaking Canadian city.

"They speak Russian, but they all spoke English," Matthews told Sportsnet. "I remember my first couple times . . . playing with them: I had no friends, homesick and stuff. That was kind of my first time away from home."

He wore number 8, not his familiar 34, on the blue-and-yellow Kharkiv sweater. They lost 5–4 in a quarterfinal to Detroit Compuware in a game that saw his team surrender two goals in the final 2:09 of regulation.

"It was kind of a heartbreaking loss," Matthews told Sportsnet. "The late goal, I remember it pretty well. I think they lost one game all year. They were kind of the world's top team, and I think they ended up winning the tournament." Matthews had three goals and three assists in three games.

The Quebec media wanted an interview with the "Ukrainian" phenom. When he started talking, they were astonished.

"How come your English is so good?" he was asked.

Matthews didn't realize they thought he was Ukrainian and offered a simple answer.

"I learned it in school."

When it was over, the Ukrainian coach called to thank Boris.

"You don't even imagine how big a star you have created," the coach said. "He's not going to be a big star for just his teams. He's going to be a big star in the National Hockey League. Remember my words."

Years later, Geoff Courtnall remembered this hockey-playing kid everyone called Papi who used to stay at his mom's house whenever his brother Russ was running summer hockey camps in Victoria.

Russ's son, Lawton, was a pretty good hockey player. When Lawton was accepted to Western Michigan University to play hockey starting in 2016, Geoff wondered what happened to the other guy who stayed in his mom's house.

"I said to Russ, 'Whatever happened to that Papi kid? He was a good player, good skater.' And Russ goes, 'That's Auston Matthews. He's going first overall in the draft.' I was like, 'Oh my God, you've got to be kidding me.'"

It was a good news story that got better as far as Geoff was concerned.

"Auston was a very nice, appreciative kid," said Geoff. "My mom loved taking him and Lawton everywhere. My mom was obviously a big factor for us being successful. She drove us to all our sports. We played soccer, baseball, and hockey growing up. My mom drove us to all of our events and waited for us, watched our practices, gave us shit when we weren't working hard or whatever.

"She would do the same with Lawton and Auston. She treated them like they were her own."

CHAPTER FIVE

Winnipeg Jets to Phoenix

It was January 16, 2006, when three of the greatest NHL goal scorers of all time were in the same place at the same time: Wayne Gretzky, Alex Ovechkin, and Auston Matthews.

That night, Gretzky was coaching the Phoenix Coyotes. Alex Ovechkin was in his rookie year. And Auston Matthews was eight years old, watching in the stands, one of 14,110 fans lucky enough to be in Glendale Arena.

Alex Ovechkin was about to score "The Goal"—one of the most talked-about moments of the season, if not the decade.

The Great Eight fell down after skating at full speed, yet managed to maintain control of the puck while reaching back with his stick while sliding on his back. The puck behind him and flat on the ice, he managed a no-look hard shot from an awkward angle to beat goalie Brian Boucher, the final goal in a 6–1 Washington win.

"That was pretty sweet," Number 99 told reporters after the game. "He's a phenomenal player. Not only is he doing well, but he loves the game. And it's easy to see he loves to be on the ice. He is that good."

It was Ovechkin's second goal of the night, and the thirty-second goal in his career as he started his chase for Wayne Gretzky's all-time NHL goals record of 894.

"The best goal I ever scored," said Ovechkin. "I just went down and shot."

Future Number 34 was there because he was already madly in love with hockey. The Winnipeg Jets had moved to Arizona to begin a new life as the Phoenix Coyotes a year before Brian and Ema moved their family to the area. As mentioned, his Uncle Billy had season tickets and took Auston to his first game when he was two. Matthews was immediately transfixed by what he saw.

"He was more fascinated with the Zamboni and the remote-control balloons that flew around and dropped things from them," his father, Brian, told *The Arizona Republic*. "It was fun, but it obviously left an impression on him."

By five he wanted to play hockey so he could be like his favourite players, Shane Doan and Daniel Brière.

By the time Matthews was interviewed about Ovechkin's career-defining goal, much time had passed. Matthews was already in the NHL, ready to take on Ovechkin and the Capitals. Ask him once, ask him a thousand times, his answer is the same:

"Probably one of the best goals ever."

But none of it would have happened—and Matthews might have pursued another sport—if not for the economic conditions that forced the Winnipeg Jets to move to Phoenix in 1996, and for Commissioner Gary Bettman's insistence that the oft-troubled franchise stay there for as long as it did.

The mid-1990s were not kind to NHL franchise stability as the league had its eye on nontraditional hockey markets in the Sunbelt states.

Wayne Gretzky was a hit in Los Angeles. Even Matthews's father and mother watched Gretzky's Kings, who went to the Stanley Cup Final in 1993.

"We have gone from the last page to the front page of the sports sections, and from last to first on the sportscasts," Gretzky told the *South Florida Sun Sentinel* in 1993. "I never dreamed we'd be ahead of the Lakers or the Dodgers in popularity."

As much as Canadians hated the idea, putting teams in the fast-growing and big-TV-market cities, including the American Sunbelt, was inevitable.

In 1993, the Minnesota North Stars relocated to Dallas, where the franchise would win its first Stanley Cup in 1999. In 1995, the Quebec Nordiques left with their stable of stars for Colorado, winning the Cup for the first time in 1996. In 1997, the Hartford Whalers became the Carolina Hurricanes and would win the Cup for the first time in 2006.

In between, in 1996, the Winnipeg Jets became the Phoenix Coyotes, and until 2024 would be the league's problem child.

The Winnipeg Jets had been losing money. A charter franchise of the rebel World Hockey Association, the team gained notoriety when it paid Bobby Hull a whopping $1 million (over five years) to defect from the Chicago Blackhawks and the NHL. Signing Swedish stars like Anders Hedberg and Ulf Nilsson propelled the team to further national prominence, competing for the Avco Cup five times in the WHA's seven-year history, winning it twice.

The Jets were one of four WHA teams absorbed by the NHL in 1979. The rosters of the four teams were largely gutted, revenge exacted by NHL owners who complained about losing players to the rival league and inflated salaries. The Jets did okay, making the playoffs in eleven of their sixteen NHL seasons. But they only ever won two rounds, and typically ran into the Edmonton Oilers and simply couldn't get past Wayne Gretzky and Co.

By the mid-1990s, NHL salaries were rising, and the Canadian dollar was tanking. Canadian teams drew most of their revenue in Canadian dollars and had to pay players in American dollars. By the time the sale of the Jets to Arizona interests was confirmed, it cost $1.37 Canadian to buy $1 US.

It was well before the salary cap evened the playing field for big- and small-market teams, a time that was untenable for small-market Canadian teams, notably Quebec and Winnipeg.

Auston Matthews almost didn't see the Phoenix Coyotes play hockey because they almost didn't come to Arizona.

In April 1995, Jets owner Barry Shenkarow announced that a two-year effort to keep the team in Winnipeg had failed, and he intended to sell it to Richard Burke of Medina, Minnesota. There was a huge outcry in Winnipeg—no fan base may love its team more—and Shenkarow called off the sale to continue to look for a Manitoba saviour. By August, no buyer had emerged, and Burke bought the team along with Steven Gluckstern, intending to move it to Minnesota's Target Center, home of the NBA's Timberwolves.

It was an ideal situation, Minnesota being an ideal hockey market and having been recently abandoned by its North Stars.

By October 1995, that plan failed because ownership determined the Target Center wouldn't generate enough revenue to support the hockey team. Burke had sought an $8 million annual public subsidy from what was a city-owned facility. Burke looked briefly at St. Paul, Minnesota, where its Civic Center rink needed about $20 million in upgrades. He said no, and the Jets flew to the desert.

"I'm happy because now I know the team is moving for sure," star forward Alexei Zhamnov said when the move was made official in late 1995. "Last summer, it's crazy—every week team moves, next week team stays. But right now everybody knows the team moves to Phoenix. I mean, this is business. I don't care where I play. I just want to play hockey and enjoy hockey."

So it was off to Phoenix, one of the fastest growing metropolises in the United States.

The city of Phoenix was founded in 1870 by Euro-American and Mexican settlers who saw potential for agriculture with canals near the Salt River. The Second World War brought US Army air bases and factories to supply them. In 1940, about 65,000 called the Valley of the Sun their home. By 1960, the population rose to half a million, attracted by the warm weather, relatively low cost of living, and availability of jobs. Construction and housing had become the core of the local economy.

Big cities typically show off their size—that they've "arrived"—by bringing the big leagues to their communities. The NBA was first in, granting an expansion franchise—the Suns—in 1968. They were most famous in their early years as a franchise for losing a coin flip to the Milwaukee Bucks for the right to draft first in 1969. The player up for grabs: Lew Alcindor, better known as Kareem Abdul-Jabbar.

The Jets were the second big league team to land in Phoenix, which by 1996 was the sixth-largest city in America. They were renamed the Coyotes thanks to a name-the-team contest. Also considered: Mustangs, Outlaws, Wranglers, and Freeze.

Coincidentally, there was that minor league team with the nickname Roadrunners, who had a little Looney Tunes fun, reminding all that the Coyote could never catch the Roadrunner.

Regardless, the NHL was in the desert. Could it work? What did Arizonans know about hockey?

The Coyotes had eight picks in the 1996 draft. With their second choice, twenty-fourth overall, they took speedy, skilled centre Daniel Brière, who would become one of Matthews's favourite players, along with Shane Doan, who had been the Jets' first-round pick in 1995.

"Hockey was in its infancy stage when I got there," Brière said to me. "Our practice rink was fairly new in North Scottsdale, the Ice Den. Minor hockey was just starting, and there weren't a lot of players."

In a season preview, *The Arizona Republic* predicted the Maple Leafs would finish last that season in part because of the goaltending of "Denis" Potvin. Not a good start. Of course, they meant Felix Potvin, not the Hall of Fame Islander defenceman.

The mere idea of playing hockey in an area without natural ice rinks seemed absurd. But Gary Bettman, who became the NHL's first commissioner on February 1, 1993, was continuing the league's Sunbelt strategy borne of the huge success of Wayne Gretzky playing in Los Angeles for the Kings following a blockbuster trade on August 9, 1988.

The Kings were must-see television. The stars were coming to see them. Interest in hockey had never seemed higher in the United States. Hockey fans were already getting used to the term "non-traditional markets." San Jose joined in 1991. Tampa (and Ottawa) joined in 1992.

The December meeting of the NHL Board of Governors at The Breakers in Palm Beach, Florida, set the course for the NHL's future. The board elected Gary Bettman as the league's first commissioner, coming in from the wildly successful NBA, where he had been senior vice president and general counsel. The league was almost giddy with excitement concerning its Sunbelt strategy.

"This could be the NBA of the nineties," Ken Wilson, then president of sales and marketing for the Mighty Ducks of Anaheim, told the *South Florida Sun Sentinel*. "We're in a similar position as they were in the early eighties before the league took off and exploded."

The NHL in Phoenix would prove to be a challenge from the get-go, a harbinger of things to come over the next two decades. To start, the team was going to play in America West Arena, where the

NBA Suns played. While it offered 17,500 seats for hockey, only 15,000 had a clear view of the entire rink. That was fewer than in the 15,393-seat Winnipeg Arena the Jets were leaving. The floor could barely accommodate a two-hundred-foot rink, and that was only due to some hasty re-engineering. The configuration left a portion of one end of the upper deck hanging over the boards and ice, obscuring almost a third of the rink and one goal from several sections.

Ownership was almost immediately in flux. Jerry Colangelo, owner of the National Basketball Association's Phoenix Suns, and businessmen Steven Gluckstern and Richard Burke were the original purchasers. Burke bought out Gluckstern in 1998 but was unable to attract more investors to alleviate the team's financial woes. There were rumours the team would move. Paul Allen of Microsoft fame wanted to move the team to Portland, Oregon, where they could share a facility with the NBA Trail Blazers.

"The rumours happened mostly in the summertime," said Brière, a Coyote until 2003. "I was training there early in my career. I heard all the rumours, and a few of us players were wondering where we would be next. We were hoping that it wouldn't happen. Phoenix is a really amazing place to live, so we were hoping to stay put."

They did. Sort of.

In 2001, Burke sold the team to Phoenix-area developer Steve Ellman, with Wayne Gretzky as a part owner and head of hockey operations. The team was barely competitive, losing up to $40 million a year at one point. The deal at America West was not favourable.

The team made a deal with a suburban council in Glendale in the West Valley. Ellman committed to building a new arena. In December 2003, the team moved into Glendale Arena, which became known as Jobing.com Arena during the 2006–07 NHL season. Simultaneously, the team changed its logo and uniforms, moving from a multi-coloured kit to a more streamlined look. In 2005, Ellman sold the Coyotes, the National Lacrosse League's Arizona Sting, and the lease to Gila River Arena to trucking magnate Jerry Moyes, who was also a part owner of Major League Baseball's Arizona Diamondbacks.

There was just as much turmoil in the front office. Gretzky had taken over as coach to start the 2005–06 season, the year Matthews saw Ovechkin score "The Goal." But Gretzky's longtime agent, Mike Barnett, was let go as GM in 2007, as were Vice President of Hockey Operations Cliff Fletcher and Assistant GM Laurence Gilman. In came Don Maloney, and assistants Brad Treliving and Gretzky's brother Keith Gretzky.

All along, it was widely known that the Coyotes were leaking money, were suffering massive losses, and that the NHL was paying the team's bills. Things were always a mess in Phoenix. But they were about to get messier.

Commissioner Gary Bettman was working the back rooms and had found Jerry Reinsdorf, owner of the NBA Bulls and MLB White Sox, to buy the team from Moyes.

Moyes had another idea. In the spring of 2009, he put the team into bankruptcy with the idea he'd sell it to Canadian billionaire Jim Balsillie and let him move the team to Hamilton, Ontario. Balsillie wanted a seventh team in Canada and had previously tried to purchase the Predators and the Penguins but had been rebuffed. There ended up being a massive legal battle over the summer of 2009.

"We generally try to avoid relocating franchises unless you absolutely have to," said Bettman. "We think when a franchise is in trouble, you try and fix the problems. We don't run out on cities."

Prime Minister Stephen Harper and Ontario Premier Dalton McGuinty—from opposite ends of the political spectrum—were united among those lining up for another team in Ontario.

"This is a great market," said McGuinty. "You talk to folks living in this community here. How long does it take to get a hold of season tickets at the Air Canada Centre? We could easily fill up another arena somewhere in Southern Ontario with rabid hockey fans."

Harper said it was ultimately the NHL's business but added, "I'd love another team in Canada . . . Particularly Southern Ontario can support another team."

The NHL playoffs were on, but the Leafs were out, so the hockey conversation locally was all about a second team.

Balsillie had tendered a $212.5 million bid, and another $50 million to the City of Glendale to break the Coyotes' lease at Gila River Arena, and promised to pay a reasonable relocation fee to the NHL. Was it going to be in Hamilton's Copps Coliseum? Could the Leafs share the Air Canada Centre? Could Balsillie convince Kitchener-Waterloo to build an NHL rink?

Folks wondered if Captain Shane Doan could invoke his "no movement" clause in his contract to force the team to stay in Arizona, should the Canadian side prevail.

When word first spread that the Coyotes were in bankruptcy protection, looking for Balsillie to move them to Canada, Doan was in Bern, Switzerland, representing Canada at the World Championships, preparing to play Latvia. His phone lit up with calls and texts.

"It'd be Winnipeg to Phoenix and now back up to Canada," Doan told CanWest News Service. "You know what, I don't know. It's one of those things. There's a bunch of people saying it will never happen, too." *The Arizona Republic* caught up to Doan on July 1. He was spending his summer in Canada, following the coverage of the bankruptcy hearing.

"They're constantly saying how bad things are in Phoenix," Doan told the paper. "You hear, 'It's awful. It's terrible. It's the worst organization ever. The team shouldn't ever have gone there.' And I'm telling you, you hear this stuff every single day."

Despite his nationality, and despite starting his career as a Winnipeg Jet, Doan's loyalties were clear.

"We should be here [in Phoenix]. And don't tell me we shouldn't. Don't tell me everything I've given you over the past thirteen years wasn't worth it. And I'm sure the fans feel the same way."

The affair was messy. Wayne Gretzky was a minority owner, and it looked like he was going to lose millions. Jerry Moyes, the majority owner, was going to lose more if the NHL prevailed over Balsillie. The City of Glendale was on track to spend more than $2 million to lawyers and consultants to fight the move of the team.

Judge Redfield T. Baum ended up being the hometown folk hero the story needed. He had a bit of a southern drawl. When he spoke, it was with home-spun common sense. If an actor were to portray him in a movie, it would be Jimmy Stewart playing an American archetype: the small-town guy not taking any nonsense from the big-city lawyers brought in to fight their cases.

In the end, Baum didn't really rule at all. He simply denied both Balsillie's and the NHL's bids—although he left the NHL some wiggle room to revamp its "bid" for the team in bankruptcy protection if it dropped its stance that neither Moyes nor Gretzky were creditors.

The judge cited the NHL's right to preserve who it admits as members, to control where its members play their home hockey games, and to set a relocation fee—all issues that drew the attention of the NFL, NBA, and Major League Baseball to the point the other leagues were granted legal status in the proceedings.

This "is the end for the efforts of PSE (Phoenix Sports and Entertainment), Balsillie, Moyes, and the Coyotes to force a sale and relocation of the hockey team," the judge ruled. Balsillie, now denied an NHL team for the third time, was gracious in defeat.

"From the beginning, my attempt to relocate the Coyotes to Hamilton has been about Canadian hockey fans and Canadian hockey," said Balsillie. "It was a chance to realize a dream. All I wanted was a fair chance to bring a seventh NHL team to Canada, to serve the best unserved hockey fans in the world. I believe I got that chance."

The folks in Glendale, risking being left with a white elephant of an arena with no tenant, were elated. Spokesperson Jennifer Liewer said the city was looking forward to hockey "for years to come." They'd find out later that wouldn't be the case, but for now the team remained. The judge took issue with the league's insistence that it be able to pick and choose who gets paid. The league believed Moyes personally—not the team—owed Gretzky up to $9.3 million when the Great One deferred salary to help the team through its financial squeeze.

"There has been no determination that the Moyes and Gretzky claims are not 'legitimate creditors,'" the judge wrote. "It would be inherently unjust for this court to deprive them of their possible rightful share of any proceeds without first providing all involved a fair trial on their claims."

The judge gave the NHL a chance to revamp its bid, although he didn't set a deadline: "In hockey parlance, the court is passing the puck to the NHL, who can decide to take another shot at the sale net, or it can pass off the puck."

That the judge sided with the league about its "territorial restrictions" was viewed as a landmark victory for sports leagues, which had been heretofore powerless to stop renegade owners from switching cities.

"We are pleased that the bankruptcy court has confirmed the league's rights to select its owners and the location of its franchises," said Deputy NHL Commissioner Bill Daly.

The Coyotes got to stay. Their arena deal was a mess. They played far from their fan base. They weren't very good. But the area's biggest impetus for youth hockey was still viable.

Auston Matthews was about to turn twelve, an impressionable age for a sports-minded kid. He was still a year away from joining the Arizona Bobcats program that would propel him to the US National Team Development Program.

It's hard to imagine what might have happened if the Coyotes had left. Would he still have loved hockey without a team to root for? Other kids—potential teammates—might have lost interest. Or perhaps the parents coaching the kids might have lost interest. Whatever was fuelling that solid base of future hockey stars coming out of the Scottsdale area would have been less hot. The quality of hockey that pushed Matthews to be better would have declined. But the NHL held firm. The league had to remain in the Phoenix area. The Coyotes had to stay. The NHL prevailed in bankruptcy court. And Matthews could still watch the Coyotes.

Hockey players are coming out of all the Sunbelt areas these days. Jason and Nick Robertson, Trevor Moore, Brendan Brisson, and Jason Zucker are all California-born. Quinn and Jack Hughes, Shayne Gostisbehere, and Jakob Chycrun are Florida-born. Blake Coleman, Seth Jones, and Tyler Myers are from Texas.

But none might matter as much as what Matthews means to Arizona hockey, or in the even bigger picture, to American hockey.

"Is there a team in Florida and Dallas and Phoenix and Anaheim?" Brière wondered. "It's amazing what those players from those markets can do. I know Auston is in a big market here, but for Arizona minor hockey to have a spokesperson like that, I think it's fantastic. We're lucky. I think it's great for hockey."

And there's a fun little twist to Brière having been Matthews's favourite player. Brière has a hockey-playing nephew, Zaac. His favourite player? Auston Matthews.

CHAPTER SIX

Uncle Sam

When Auston Matthews's future teammates were looking at the roster of players invited to USA Hockey's National Team Development Program camp in May 2013, they saw a kid from Scottsdale, Arizona, on the list. They weren't that impressed.

Some figured it was either a mistake or one of those things that happen from time to time. A kid is born in one place but raised in a hockey market. Dylan Larkin saw "Arizona Bobcats" beside Auston Matthews's name and his only thought was "I've never heard of the Arizona Bobcats."

A few, like Noah Hanifin, knew who he was from playing in tournaments when Boris would loan Matthews to teams.

"Arizona is not a normal hockey background," said Hanifin.

Matthews was finally in a real hockey market: Michigan. Going up against kids from real hockey cities and established hockey programs. He was the unknown.

"I had a chip on my shoulder and wanted to prove something, because, you know, they come out with lists of who they think is going to be on the team, and I don't think I was on any of those lists," Matthews told Sportsnet.

"And that didn't really bother me because nobody had really seen me play. But that's definitely motivation."

On the ice, hometowns and youth teams don't matter. It was tryouts. Everyone was equal at the blow of the first whistle. And Matthews separated himself from the pack quickly.

The group was divided into three teams: Red, White, and Blue. Matthews was on the Blue team.

It came time for a penalty shot. He did the "Jason Blake," as players called it. It's a move now banned from NHL shoot-outs, because of the backwards motion of the puck, but one Blake—an ex–Maple Leaf—was known for. Come in with speed, get the goalie going one direction, and do the spinarama—a 360 turn—to deposit the puck to the empty side of the net.

"I was like, this kid's a little different," said Charlie McAvoy. "He scored. And you could see that he was just jumping off the page. He had a ton of skill."

Hockey lifer Don Granato was the coach. And he knew what was coming. In the spring of 2013, Matthews and his family had been invited to Ann Arbor, Michigan, to take in the program and learn what USA Hockey could do both developmentally and for his education.

Matthews had brought his equipment and joined the practice with kids two and three years older than him, like J.T. Compher. He fit right in. He stayed out after practice, too.

Granato looked at a colleague and said, "Please tell me we have this kid signed already."

They didn't.

Matthews had already been drafted, fifty-seventh overall, in the 2012 WHL Bantam Draft by the Everett Silvertips. And they needed scoring. The Canadian Hockey League is always the US program's main competition for top American-born sixteen-year-olds. The

CHL pays its players a paltry amount: about $50 a week for first-year players to $150 a week for players in their final year. It typically amounts to substantially less than minimum wage, given the travel and practice time.

Scholarships to a Canadian university await players who do not make it to the pros. But certain teams in the CHL are often accused of under-the-table deals with families, or agents, to secure the talents of stars.

The USNTDP didn't have to worry. The Matthewses were sold long before anyone would talk dollars and cents. The power of putting on a Team USA jersey and representing your country is simply too strong. While Matthews's goal from childhood was to play in the NHL one day, the steps along the way were always going to include two years in Ann Arbor, Michigan. The US program locked him up.

Watching Matthews play in his first week with the program, Granato was so happy he phoned his brother, Tony, a former NHLer who was at the time an assistant coach of the Pittsburgh Penguins.

"I remember talking to him, saying, 'Hey, there's a kid here that could be as good as any player you have.'"

Tony's response: "Are you out of your mind?"

Tony Granato, of course, was coaching none other than Sidney Crosby, so he can be forgiven his initial astonishment. But Don held firm: "He's got all the attributes."

It didn't start great for Matthews, beginning with some teenage hijinks. But he and McAvoy quickly became friends.

"Our billets were on the same street," said Matthews. "I don't know who came up with this genius idea. But we had a rope, and one guy had a car, and we just thought it would be fun."

What exactly would be fun? Using the rope to tie a bike to a car. Someone drives the car; someone else is on the bike. See how fast they can go.

"I went first, and it was all smooth. And then Charlie went, and he took a bit of a tumble, and we all got in trouble," said Matthews.

"We both ended up taking turns, but he was a lot more coordinated," said McAvoy. "So I'm the one who fell off and got the road rash all over my body.

"Donny [Granato] called me the next day. It was the first day of the program, and he was like, 'Man, is this what we're getting in here for the next two years?' I'm like, 'Never doing that again, never getting out of line again.' You live and you learn. You grow up fast."

They can laugh about it now.

"It was really stupid," said Matthews. "But looking back on it, we were just kids, and kids make stupid decisions and dumb choices sometimes, and that was definitely one of them. You learn from it."

More seriously, though, Matthews broke his left femur in the second game of the U17 Team's 2013–14 season, from a knee-on-knee hit. The big stage would have to wait. Surgeons inserted a pin into his leg. He was outfitted with a cast and given a wheelchair.

"It was a hard day when the team called and we got the news," Ema Matthews told Gare Joyce in his book *Young Leafs*. "It was the first time he'd had a serious injury. We hadn't been through anything like it."

Frustrating though that may have been, he got a call from one of his idols, Shane Doan. The same thing had happened to Doan back in junior hockey, and the Coyotes legend wanted Matthews to know it wasn't the end of the world.

On top of recuperating from such an injury, there was school and the rest of his life as he billeted with Brian and Heidi Daniels and their sons, Cole and Camden. Matthews had a bedroom on the second floor of a house in a suburban subdivision. When he broke his leg, they offered him a room on the main floor, but he declined.

"You could tell he was disappointed when the other kids would leave for the road trips, but he just stayed home and hung out with the family," Heidi told Joyce. "We would take him in, drag him to my older son's football games, and wrap up his leg with blankets."

Matthews was shy at first, but fit in quickly, and over his two years in the house he relished being the new "older brother" to Cole and Camden after having lived all his life with sisters. Over the course of two hockey seasons with the Danielses, there was plenty of sports to be played, baseball chief among them, as well as what turned into full-contact ministicks, or as the family called it: "knee hockey." There were also real sticks, two-on-two with a tennis ball banging the walls.

It was teammate Luke Opilka, also in the Daniels house, and Cole, the older "billet" brother, against Matthews and Camden.

"It was competitive, it was awesome," said Opilka. "Whether we were playing Ping-Pong, shinny hockey in the basement, or basketball, his competitive drive was second to none. I thought I was pretty competitive, but he outclasses me for sure. It was never cheap. It was always very fun."

Once, Matthews lost, and he hurled his stick and struck somebody in the ankle.

"I've never met a more competitive kid," Camden Daniels told NHL.com. "If he lost, you weren't going to hear the end of it for a couple days."

He helped with chores around the house and garden, shovelling in the winter, spreading mulch in planting season. He kept his room clean, brought down his own laundry, and made his own breakfast and lunch. While Ema's cooking gets rave reviews by any who try it, Heidi wouldn't put herself in the same category, though she did try to make one of Auston's favourite meals: a lettuce wrap with ground beef and spices.

When the dads found out he was a player at USA Hockey, they

would offer father-like coaching advice that Auston would politely accept.

It was only once in a while, and only after Auston had left with Cole and Camden, that the Danielses would tell the other parents just how good a hockey player he was, that he was expected to go first in the draft.

"The other parents would say that you'd never think that just talking to him," Daniels told Joyce.

But you wouldn't hear much about ice hockey.

"Whenever we went out to dinner or anything and some of my friends would be with him . . . everyone knew how good he was, and he would just play it off like it was nothing basically," Camden Daniels said. "You would have never thought he was doing what he was doing."

The bond remains, even though Matthews went off to Switzerland and Toronto. When he made his NHL debut October 12 against the Ottawa Senators, the Daniels family was busy but kept tabs. He scored once. He scored twice. He scored three times, and the family's phones started blowing up. They got home and put on the game.

"We said, 'Just wait. He's going to score a fourth one,'" Heidi Daniels said. "And sure enough, he did."

"I'm really proud of him," Heidi told NHL.com. "He worked really hard to get where he is, and it doesn't surprise me at all. I think he's taking it in good stride . . . He never let it get to his head, that's for sure."

Matthews was an eager patient through his rehabilitation and physiotherapy. Once he started skating again, he would do his moves. He would participate in shoot-outs. Whenever he'd score—which was often—he'd wink at the team trainer as if to say, "Get me back in there."

He was out till December, ready in time for the 2013–14 World Hockey Challenge in Nova Scotia. It featured the best players under the age of seventeen in Canada, the United States, Sweden, the Czech Republic, Russia, and Germany. Canada featured four teams: Ontario, Quebec, Pacific, and Atlantic.

Matthews got four goals and four assists—one point behind future teammate Mitch Marner, on the Ontario team—as Team USA won gold. Word was getting out.

Donny Granato did something else he doesn't usually do. He called a player's parents. Usually it's the other way around. But Don had been around hockey long enough to know what happens when NHL scouts "discover" prodigies like Matthews. He felt "compelled" to warn Brian and Ema of what was coming.

"I said, 'Brian, you probably have to get your family ready for complete chaos.' He said, 'What do you mean?' And I said, 'Do you have any idea how good your son is?' 'No.' 'Well, I guess in a year from now, he's probably going to be the top pick in the draft. Your life is going to change pretty dramatically.'"

Matthews wasn't finished winning gold medals internationally and making a name for himself.

The World Under-18 Championships don't really resonate in Canada, because they happen in late April and early May. They compete for eyeballs against the Stanley Cup playoffs. And Canada is somewhat hamstrung, rarely able to send its best teams since the pool of available players largely comes from CHL teams that fail to make the playoffs.

But for the rest of the hockey world, the U18s matter a great deal. It is, after all, a World Championship and a harbinger of the future of hockey.

The 2014 tournament was in Finland that year, and the US team was stacked: Jack Eichel, Dylan Larkin, Alex Tuch, Noah Hanifin, and, of course, Auston Matthews. He was the youngest player on Team USA, recovered from the broken leg. He won gold at the U17 World Challenge and moved his way up to the U18 Team by the end of the season. He was sixteen. Most of the players at the event—including future teammate William Nylander of Sweden—were seventeen.

With two goals in a 5–2 gold medal showdown with the Czech Republic, Matthews led Team USA to gold at the World Under-18s.

Nylander would turn eighteen four days after the tournament ended and get drafted seven weeks later, eighth overall, by the Toronto Maple Leafs. Matthews still had two years to go until he would be drafted. But the secret was out. The scouting reports started to ooze with praise.

"If there's a better player than Auston Matthews, would you introduce him to me," said TSN scouting guru Craig Button in the *Edmonton Journal. SB Nation College* hockey gushed, "He's the top available player in 2016 right now, and I'm sticking with my assertion that he's a little bit ahead of where Jack Eichel was last year. Max Jones was great at the World U17 Challenge, but Matthews is the top overall prospect for 2016 right now."

When he was back home in Arizona that summer, skating with the pros, Sarah McLellan, then of *The Arizona Republic,* caught up with Matthews. She noted how he fit in with the pros, the way he carried the puck with authority, his speed, the fact that he—at sixteen—was already six feet tall, and the way his shot found its way under the crossbar, one of the signature moves he'd unveil later to great success as a Maple Leaf.

"Some day I want to be that role model for kids from Arizona that you can play hockey and do it well," Matthews told her.

He was preparing to head back to Ann Arbor, Michigan, for his final year with the US National Team Development Program. All his life, he had played above his age group. Even as a sixteen-year-old he'd played with the seventeen-year-olds at the USNTDP.

This upcoming season—2014–15—he'd be playing, really for the first time, with his age group.

Everything was routine. The players arrived in late August, their billets awaiting them. The first day was for orientation, which included on-ice practice, weight training, off-ice conditioning, life skills, study table, and team meetings. The nutritionists handed the billet families meal expectations.

For the most part, they went to school each day, Pioneer High School, getting out an hour earlier than the rest of the kids. Their time on the ice counted for the gym credit they were missing.

They were at the rink around 2:00 p.m. for sessions on the ice, in the gym, and in front of the whiteboard and video screens. Then it was home for dinner at around 5:30 p.m. And do it all again tomorrow.

"That program is strenuous," said McAvoy. "You're practising for an hour and a half a day. You're working out an hour and a half a day, like you're doing all those things that you've got to do: Come home and do homework and try and have your leisure time and then get up and do it all over again.

"I think it was a 6:30 alarm every day. Leave the house at 7:00, 7:40 was first period. We lived about twenty minutes away from the school."

Though the USNTDP touts the number of NHL players it has helped produce, the message to parents is mostly about education. Every student athlete is expected to earn a GPA standard to maintain eligibility for competition. In addition, each player must work to achieve their NCAA eligibility as they plan to participate in Division I college hockey upon graduating from high school, in programs such as Boston College, Boston University, Harvard

University, Miami University, Ohio State University, the University of Michigan, the University of Minnesota, the University of Notre Dame, and the University of Wisconsin.

The USNTDP has two teams: the Under-17 Team and the Under-18 Team. Both take part in the United States Hockey League, the top junior program in the United States, one that is probably a step below the major junior leagues of the CHL and a step above Junior A.

The key for the USHL, like Junior A, is that its players are eligible for the American college system. Players in the CHL in those days were considered "professional" by the tall foreheads of the NCAA and ineligible to play with "amateurs" in the US college system.

The two teams also play a season's worth of exhibition games against university programs. The competition for the U18s and U17s is invaluable. Again, though Matthews's teammates were his age, his opponents were older, as old as twenty for USHL teams, even older for university teams.

"That's humbling and good development," said Joseph Woll, a goalie in the program a year behind Matthews and now his teammate with the Leafs. "We held our own. It goes year to year depending on how good the teams are. Like Auston's team might have been the best team that program has ever seen. The whole team is in the NHL. They did a good job against the colleges." Matthews still managed twenty goals in twenty-four games against USHL opponents, part of what would be a record-setting year of offence for the Arizona product at the USNTDP.

The next big international tournament for Matthews would be the 2015 World Junior Championship. Matthews, just seventeen, made Team USA's World Junior Championship roster for the 2015 tournament co-hosted by Montreal and Toronto, a place he would soon call home. He was one of the youngest players in the tournament meant for nineteen-year-olds. It's rare for eighteen-year-olds to be in the tournament, much less seventeen-year-olds.

By age nineteen, most players are already drafted by NHL teams, or they've been passed over. So the World Junior tournament isn't a big sell for amateur scouts. But this tournament was different.

The big storyline in that tournament was Connor McDavid leading Team Canada against Jack Eichel, leading Team USA. The two were the prohibitive favourites to be drafted first and second overall in the 2015 draft. At eighteen, they were also younger than most of the players in the tournament, but they dominated the headlines and gave scouts a reason to watch.

But so did the presence of Matthews, who wasn't eligible to be drafted until 2016. He was still growing. He scored the USA's first goal of the tournament, a game-winner it turns out, in a 6–0 win over Germany at the Bell Centre in Montreal.

"He's a special player," USA GM Jim Johansson told *The Boston Globe* when Matthews made the team. "The interesting part is he missed the first three months of the season before. I think a lot of people don't know that or forgot about it. To do what he's done over the course of fifteen months of hockey has been really impressive and very consistent."

The Russians, though, ousted the Americans in the quarter-final in Montreal. Matthews did what he could. Russia was up 3–1 when Matthews's line went to work. Matthews applied pressure. Matthews and Nick Schmaltz passed back and forth behind the net. There was plenty of movement. Pivoting. Trying to find an opening. Schmaltz took a shot and Igor Shesterkin stopped it. Matthews gobbled up the rebound and fed it to Zach Werenski, who got the Americans to within one. But that was as close as they got. Matthews and the Americans never made it to Toronto for the medal round. The Canadians, led by Connor McDavid, defeated the

Russians for gold. McDavid's fate was sealed. He'd go number one, Eichel number two, and Matthews would have to wait.

"He would have been right at the top of that mix. We would have had a healthy discussion and debate as to who they would want as number one," Director of NHL Central Scouting Dan Marr told *Yahoo!* "Just talent wise, Connor has the cleverness, creativeness, and finesse to his game where I would say Auston has more the power forward game where he's really driven on the play, but his puck skills are just as good."

As high profile as the World Junior (Under-20) Championship (held in the Christmas season) is in Canada, the target for the USNTDP is the World Under-18s in May. Matthews already had one gold medal from the 2014 event.

Matthews's life was about to change at the 2015 IIHF U18s. Maybe that's too dramatic. Maybe it's more that another path for Matthews was about to emerge, one that he would eventually follow, though he didn't know it in April 2015 with the World U18s in Zug, Switzerland.

Matthews led the tournament with eight goals and seven assists in seven games as the US won gold for the second year in a row with Matthews on the team. Two of those goals came in the semifinal, a 7–2 win by the Americans over Canada. Matthews assisted on the game-tying goal in the USA's 2–1 win over Patrik Laine and Team Finland in the final. He was named the tournament's most valuable player.

"That was a really big deal," Matthews later told me. "All the time and effort you put in is geared towards that tournament. I have a lot of really great memories."

But a funny thing happened. His parents, Brian and Ema, joined him at the tournament. And they had a look around Switzerland. And they liked it.

Matthews was still seventeen. He wouldn't be eligible for the NHL Draft until 2016. And his two years with the US National Team Development Program were over with a remarkable résumé. He scored fifty-five times for the U18 team that season and obliterated Patrick Kane's record of 102 points. He had one U17 gold medal, two U18 gold medals, and one IIHF U18 MVP title. And he had nowhere to play the next season. He basically had a gap year.

The Everett Silvertips were hoping he'd join them. They had taken him years before in the Bantam Draft. The Matthewses had visited Everett, Washington, and told GM Garry Davidson they'd wait until after the U18s to make their decision.

"I think he would be what we call a 'seven' in our business: a franchise player," Davidson told *The Everett Herald* in April 2015 as the tournament was under way. "He and his people and his family told us they wouldn't make a decision until after the U-18 . . . We'll just patiently wait until that's over, then reach out to them and see exactly where they're at."

The clock was ticking. The phone was ringing. It was Switzerland on the line.

CHAPTER SEVEN

The Shanaplan

When he was general manager of the Maple Leafs, Brian Burke faced a great deal of criticism from fans and media for the way he went about trying to build a winner in Toronto. He traded two first-round picks and a second for Phil Kessel, an enigmatic but talented scorer. His critics looked longingly at the Pittsburgh Penguins and wondered why Burke couldn't build a winner in Toronto the way it was done in Pittsburgh, through the draft.

Burke would scoff: "They won a goddamn lottery."

He wasn't wrong. The Penguins indeed won a controversial lottery in 2005, giving them the ability to pick a generational talent in Sidney Crosby, and the result was three more Stanley Cups.

Burke was undeniably bitter. He was GM of the Anaheim Ducks in 2005. They picked second after Crosby was off the board, selecting Bobby Ryan. And as good as Ryan was as a hockey player, he was no Sidney Crosby.

But Burke wasn't completely right, either, because the Penguins also had drafted wisely, taking the likes of Evgeni Malkin, Marc-André Fleury, and Kris Letang, and not making big trades until they were ready to contend.

Building a winner is a tricky business. It requires a certain skill on behalf of managers and scouts, and a fair bit of luck when it comes to the draft lottery. And patience.

This much Brendan Shanahan knew when he took over the hot seat at the Air Canada Centre, installed as the president of the Toronto Maple Leafs in the spring of 2014.

The hiring seemed inspired. First off, he was a Toronto kid, having grown up in the rough-and-tumble west-end community of Mimico, where nothing was given, everything earned. He was born into a sports-loving, hockey- and lacrosse-playing family who worshipped the Maple Leafs even through the bad old days of the Harold Ballard years.

And he was good at hockey, too, exceptionally so. He was a power forward left winger drafted second overall in 1987 by the New Jersey Devils. He won the Stanley Cup three times. Throw in a World Championship as well as an Olympic gold, and he is a member of the elite Triple Gold Club. There was a Canada Cup gold medal, too, all part of a Hall of Fame career.

He cared about the game, too. He was an integral voice that got the league out of its hooking, holding, and neutral-zone trap era and into a more wide-open version that gave the skilled, speedy players a place to shine. That was at the end of the lockout that cost the league its entire 2004–05 season, emerging with Shanahan-inspired new rules in the 2005–06 season.

His vision and voice set him up for a post-playing career in the league's head office, joining hockey operations in 2009. By 2011, he succeeded Colin Campbell as senior vice president, taking on the duties of sheriff. He would dole out suspensions and fines to players who had crossed lines with headshots and cross-checks, and other overly aggressive players. It became known as the "Shanaban." It was generally deemed to be the most thankless job in hockey. On April 11, 2014, he left that for a job that might even be more thankless—trying to turn the Maple Leafs into a winner.

Maple Leaf Sports & Entertainment was in the midst of a corporate-wide rebirth. In 2012, Rogers and Bell, both major telecommunications companies, bought the company. They each owned 37.5 percent, with Larry Tanenbaum owning the rest.

At the behest of George Cope, who then ran Bell, Burke was fired before the lockout-shortened 2012–13 season. Dave Nonis, senior vice president and director of hockey operations, took over. The Leafs had a memorable seven-game playoff series against the Boston Bruins—for all the wrong reasons—that included an epic Game 7 meltdown. Cries of "It was 4–1" still resonate with a fragile fan base that remembers a Bruins late-third-period rally and a 5–4 loss in overtime. Still, the playoff appearance had given the Maple Leafs team a sense—false, it turns out—of hope.

American sports executive Tim Leiweke had taken over from Richard Peddie as chief executive of MLSE on April 26, 2013, two weeks after that meltdown. He made a bold prediction that summer, telling Bloomberg that he was planning a Stanley Cup parade. "I have it planned out, and it's going to be fantastic," Leiweke said in an interview with Bloomberg's Hugo Miller and Eric Lam. "If you can all dream about that and get that in your mind, we'll have something we're all driven toward."

Then he watched as the 2013–14 Maple Leafs team sat comfortably in third place in the Eastern Conference standings with only fourteen games to go, a second playoff appearance in a row about as certain as rain on a holiday in Ireland. The Leafs, however, would go 2–12–0 down the stretch, dropping all the way to eighth from the bottom in another sensational meltdown. Change had to come. Leiweke got to work.

Over a very short span, he redirected each of the organization's franchises. He promoted Masai Ujiri to run the basketball Raptors within two months of taking over the reins of MLSE. The Raptors would go on to win the NBA championship in 2019.

He reset the course for Toronto FC of Major League Soccer, bringing in star players Michael Bradley, Jermain Defoe, and Sebastian Giovinco as FC became a force, winning a domestic "treble" in 2017 in taking the MLS Cup, Supporters' Shield, and Canadian Championship.

And for the Maple Leafs, Leiweke took his time. He likened FC to a boat and the Raptors to a yacht, both easy to turn around. The Leafs, however, "are a massive cruiser, and it takes a lot to turn them around, and it takes a lot to shift strategy," he told Bruce Arthur, then with Postmedia. "This is not a task you take lightly. I needed some time to understand what was right and wrong here."

Brendan Shanahan was hired. The path he would lay out would become the "Shanaplan." The hiring offered hope.

"Hiring a person of his calibre, with his résumé, was pretty exciting for us as players, and I think for everyone, for fans as well," said nine-year Maple Leaf Tyler Bozak. "How he sees the game and knows the game so well from being inside of it for so long, that definitely gave us a lot of hope that the team was going in the right direction."

Now Shanahan was going from neutral observer as a league official to number-one cheerleader for the team he grew up loving. He came in just days after what looked like a promising season turned into a debacle. Dropping from a comfortable playoff spot, though embarrassing, did have a bright side. Their reward was William Nylander, taken eighth overall that year. Given his production and game-breaking ability, Nylander would go much higher if that draft were to be redone. The Leafs got themselves a gem.

What Shanahan knew was that in 2015, there was an even bigger reward for a bad team that won the draft lottery: Connor McDavid. Not just him, but there was some fairly high-end talent available in both 2015 and 2016. Bad teams would be rewarded.

The "Shanaplan" was something akin to a five-year plan to give hope, a direction that maybe had to do with skill rather than enforcers. But there wasn't a great deal of change to the team to start the 2014–15 season, with Shanahan essentially sitting back and watching.

The changes that first season, such as they were, were mostly in the front office.

Shanahan had brought in some new recruits, minds that would be central to the early part of the team's revival.

Kyle Dubas was hired July 22, 2014, scooped up from the OHL Soo Greyhounds. He was hired as assistant general manager in part because he was young—just twenty-eight—and saw the game with new eyes, through the lens of analytics. He had risen up from stick boy on the Greyhounds to management, looking for angles that others didn't see. There was a war being waged among hockey watchers: between those who trusted their eyes and those who trusted their spreadsheet.

"He's not tied to any old ideas," Shanahan told the gathered media. The status quo hadn't gotten the franchise anywhere, reasoned Shanahan. Better to try something new, something different.

Mark Hunter came in October 21, 2014, as director of player personnel. His London Knights (he was co-owner and GM) favoured highly skilled players with high hockey IQs. Then fifty-one, he was a bit old school but just starting out in the analytics world—it was truly in its infancy—measuring scoring chances per sixty minutes and zone starts. But Shanahan truly liked that Hunter was generally deemed to be the game's greatest scout of teenage talent. A lot of draft picks were on the horizon. Hunter and Dubas would prove invaluable.

In between, on August 19, 2014, Shanahan had his coup de grâce, hiring Brandon Pridham. Shanahan knew Pridham, then forty, from when the two worked at the NHL together. Pridham started in the NHL's Central Scouting department and worked his way up from there, basically writing the NHL's collective bargaining agreement and the rules to the restrictive salary cap system. If there was a loophole, Pridham would be the first to find it. The Leafs would need his skills in burying contracts for nonproductive players in the minors and maximizing the use of Long-Term Injured Reserve to get the most cap relief possible, right down to the last dollar.

For the 2014–15 season—at the end of which Connor McDavid would be available—Dave Nonis was still GM. Randy Carlyle was still coach. Dion Phaneuf was still captain. Phil Kessel was still eating hot dogs. Allegedly, anyway, though he would embrace the mythology later with the Pittsburgh Penguins.

The season hadn't even started and there was already controversy, which was a daily occurrence in the Leafs of that era. Assistant Coach Steve Spott had some ideas for the power play that he told some of his colleagues he couldn't put in place because Phil Kessel didn't like them. That didn't help the public perception that this group was a coddled bunch, which would be okay if they won, but they just couldn't find that gear.

"I feel like those years, we had lots of hope," said Tyler Bozak, the Maple Leafs' top centre from 2009 until 2018. "We had pretty good players, and we'd always start the year off quite well. And then just a slow decline throughout the year."

Shanahan seemed to know this, letting it play out for a while, and the 2014–15 Leafs tanked down the stretch just like the 2013–14 team. Only this time, it was more or less on purpose.

Carlyle was fired just days into 2015, the team holding down a playoff spot, replaced by interim coach Peter Horachek. The team became sellers at the trade deadline, sending Daniel Winnik, Cody Franson, and Korbinian Holzer to greener pastures, while flipping Olli Jokinen and getting draft picks in both trades.

Under Horachek, the team went 9–28–5 in what felt like a tragicomedy.

"He was such a good man," said Bozak. "He deserved better."

They went a stretch of ten games without winning, and eighteen on the road without a win, and the team's PR department debated with the beat media about whether overtime losses should count as losses when talking about a losing streak.

A young Morgan Rielly learned a lesson in media when he said the team had to stop acting like "girls" in part of a long, and otherwise thoughtful, interview amid all the losing. And then there's a game in New Jersey after which goalie James Reimer called out his team for their poor play, and then so did Coach Peter Horachek, telling his players to check their "give-a-shit meter."

Twitter branded Phil Kessel a coach killer. He stopped talking to the media for a bit, then one day in Florida gathered all the media around him at a practice for a spirited defence of his captain, Dion Phaneuf, after a false and vulgar tweet regarding Phaneuf's wife, Elisha Cuthbert, and teammate Joffrey Lupul made it to TSN's trade deadline show as uncurated tweets from viewers scrolled through the bottom of the screen during its broadcast.

Later that same night, the road losing streak only ended because both Panthers goalies were hurt. Roberto Luongo bravely stood in the Florida net unable to move.

Their brightest prospect, Nazem Kadri, was suspended by the team for missing a meeting before practice.

"It's tough in a market like Toronto, when little things start going wrong. It kind of magnifies them more than they should be magnified," said Bozak. "That can take your confidence away a lot more than it should. In a market like that, when things aren't going well, it's tough to be confident. I personally think confidence is such a huge part of, you know, playing well and doing the right things out there. I think when you're playing confident, you obviously are playing a lot better and everyone's playing a lot better. So it was not a fun end of the year. But you know how it is with Toronto. There's always hope going into the next season. There's always hope from the media, from fans, from us as players. As bad as we did finish that year, you still believe that next year is what's going to be better."

The 2014–15 season mercifully came to an end. The Leafs had missed the playoffs by a whopping thirty-one points. Remember, they were in a playoff spot in January with a 21–16–3 record. Under Horachek—handcuffed by trades—they went 9–28–5. They finished fourth from the bottom.

Shanahan had seen enough.

Sunday, April 12, 2015, was to become known as Bloody Sunday. Shanahan cleaned house: Out were Nonis, Horachek, assistant coaches Steve Spott, Chris Dennis, and Rick St. Croix, director of player development Jim Hughes, and director of pro scouting Steve Kasper—as well as Rob Cowie, eighteen other scouts, and strength and conditioning coach Anthony Belza.

A new regime was in charge: Shanahan, aided by Dubas, Hunter, and Pridham.

Shanahan had said all the right things about drafting and developing talent, about being patient.

Shanahan was saying a rebuild could take three or four years, unless . . . Shanahan's eyes were fixated on one player: Connor McDavid. The prize of the 2015 draft. The Leafs had a 9.5 percent chance to get him. "It would certainly speed things up," he said.

The draft had changed since the last time the Leafs had drafted first overall and selected Wendel Clark. In those days the last-place team drafted first. It was simple: Finish last, draft first.

Through the years, it became apparent that some very special eighteen-year-olds were going to be available in the draft, and the NHL had endured some embarrassment when teams like the Penguins and Devils both tanked for a chance at Mario Lemieux in 1984, as had the Quebec Nordiques, who had set their sights on Eric Lindros in 1991.

The league had tried all sorts of machinations to give more than one team a shot at a franchise-altering talent. It settled on a lottery system. And even that changed over the years when one team—the Edmonton Oilers—kept winning it.

The NHL Draft lottery was created in 1995. Only non-playoff teams were involved. The winner of the lottery, which was heavily weighted to the worst teams, would move up four spots, so only the worst five teams had a chance at the number-one pick.

Five times between 1995 and 2009, the last-place team won the lottery and kept its selection. Twice, teams from further down moved up, but not to first overall. Six times teams moved up to take first overall.

Tampa Bay traded for the top pick in 1998, selecting Vincent Lecavalier. The Penguins won a different kind of lottery in 2005—the draft after the year-long lockout—to win Sidney Crosby.

In 2010, the last-place Oilers won the lottery and retained the first overall pick, taking Taylor Hall. In 2011, the last-place Oilers retained the first overall pick (Ryan Nugent-Hopkins) when eighth-place New Jersey won the lottery and moved to fourth overall. In

2012, the twenty-ninth-place Oilers won the lottery and moved from the second overall pick to number one. Again. That became Nail Yakupov, who didn't work out. Three years in a row, the same team had the first overall pick, despite the presence of the lottery.

There was another movement to change the system because teams knew some special young teenagers were on the way.

In 2013, the league changed the draft lottery rules, making it a bit simpler: It was still a weighted system that favoured the worst teams. The team that won the lottery picked first. The Avalanche moved from second to first to take Nathan MacKinnon in 2013. The Panthers moved from second to first to take Aaron Ekblad in 2014.

In 2015, Connor McDavid was the top prize for a bad team, someone worth tanking for. The league tweaked the lottery yet again by changing the odds. The worst teams saw their chances slimmed, and the better teams from the non-playoff group were given more of a chance.

The Buffalo Sabres were the worst team, awarded 20 percent of the possible number combinations created by numbers on Ping-Pong balls. (That was down from 25 percent the season prior.) The Boston Bruins had a 1 percent chance as the team with the best record among the non-playoff teams.

The Leafs, as mentioned, sat at 9.5 percent.

The league tried its hand at must-watch TV that season. It brought McDavid, Dylan Strome, and Noah Hanifin—deemed to be among the top prospects—to CBC headquarters, where the draft lottery would be broadcast live. Jack Eichel, who would go number two overall, was listening in on a conference call.

McDavid showed up in a blue suit, with a blue-and-white checkered shirt. McDavid was from Newmarket, Ontario, had grown up a Leaf fan, and was the best prospect to be available in the draft since Sidney Crosby in 2005. The teams also sent representatives to the

CBC studios. For the Maple Leafs, it was Brendan Shanahan. He wore a shamrock for luck. But it was Edmonton's lucky night. For the fourth time in six seasons, the Oilers would draft first overall.

"They've got some luck," Shanahan said that night, a bit relieved the Leafs were able to retain the fourth overall pick. "You [worry] about sliding down to five. Happy we're at four. There are some good players there." That pick would turn into Mitch Marner, Auston Matthews's favourite right winger, and a sensational game-changing talent himself. But the Leafs were ever so close—frustratingly so—to getting McDavid.

The winning numbers were 1–5–6–14 for Edmonton. But it was the order they came out where the Leaf angst lay. Ping-Pong balls numbered 1 to 14 were in a black briefcase, to be loaded into a mini bingo cage in a room unavailable to the public. League officials and representatives of teams involved in the NHL Draft lottery were inside, as was a single journalist acting as a pool reporter, Lance Hornby of the *Toronto Sun*, the Toronto chapter chairperson of the Professional Hockey Writers Association.

For the teams not going to the Stanley Cup playoffs, this would be their biggest moment of the season. A red button to vacuum up the balls was pressed at ten-second intervals. Neither the time-keeper nor the button presser looked at the machine. The first Ping-Pong ball drawn was number 5. That left the Leafs with twenty-five chances to win McDavid. The Oilers had thirty-nine chances. Arizona had thirty chances, already dropping behind Edmonton. Buffalo had fifty-two, still in the lead.

The second ball out was 14, dropping the Leafs, Oilers, and Coyotes down to seven chances. The Sabres had twelve possibilities at the top spot remaining.

When number 6 was pulled next, the Leafs were in the driver's seat. They had four chances to win with the 5–14–6 combination.

If 2, 7, 8, or 13 popped up, the Leafs would win. Buffalo had three chances (3, 11, 12); Edmonton had two (1, 10); Arizona was eliminated. There were two dark horses: Carolina needed 4; Columbus needed 9.

If you look closely at the video of the bouncing balls, number 2—a Leaf number—was on the cusp of being drawn last. But it bounced to the opening a fraction of a second too soon. By the time the button was pressed to vacuum up the final ball, number 1 had pushed number 2 out of the way.

The Oilers had won again. They'd pick first overall for the fourth time in six seasons. Ryan Nugent-Hopkins. Taylor Hall. Nail Yakupov. Now McDavid. The lottery gods have been good to them.

If there was a lesson to be learned, it's that fourth from the bottom—and its corresponding 9.5 percent chance—wasn't good enough.

Shanahan took his eyes off McDavid. There was another generational player on the horizon: Auston Matthews. He'd obliterated the USNTDP record book. He had two U18 gold medals and one tournament MVP title.

All he needed was a place to play. His already unusual path to the NHL was about to take another European turn.

CHAPTER EIGHT

Swiss Mister

It was late in the afternoon on August 7, 2015, in Zurich, Switzerland, and the temperature sat at 34°C. Clouds had turned to sun. This was hardly hockey weather, but it was time for hockey news. Big hockey news. The rumours were true.

Auston Matthews was about to stun the hockey world with an unprecedented decision.

A teenage hockey player's path to the NHL Draft is generally straightforward: For an American or a Canadian and even a whole bunch of Europeans, the choices are the Canadian Hockey League, the USHL, or the NCAA. And hockey players themselves are generally conservative. They do what the guy before them did. If it worked for him, it'll work for me. That sort of thing. New ideas? Heresy. They take a long time to gain traction in hockey circles. For Canadian teens, for example, that means playing major junior hockey as the straightest path to the NHL. It took a long time for Canadian kids to accept the US college route, a path forged only in the 1990s by Paul Kariya. He's not the first to have eschewed junior for the NCAA, but he's widely credited with popularizing that route.

Even hockey's highest minds haven't embraced analytics, which started its move from basement bloggers to the mainstream media around 2012.

But Matthews was forging his own path. Scouts had fretted he still hadn't played much by way of club hockey in a league with a season-long schedule. He'd been on plenty of teams. He'd played in plenty of tournaments. And had rewritten the record book at the US National Team Development Program.

But getting on a team, getting to know your teammates, getting into a routine, learning to be a pro was really the only thing Matthews hadn't done. And now there was no avoiding it. With his time at the USNTDP over, he'd have to find a team.

Matthews was born the same year as Connor McDavid and competed against him internationally. Had they been in high school together, they'd have been in the same grade. But because Matthews was born September 17, he missed the 2015 draft cutoff date by two days. Only players who would be eighteen by September 15—roughly equating to the start of most training camps—are eligible for the summer draft.

Matthews is what scouts call a "late birth." Notably, John Tavares (September 20) and Alex Ovechkin (September 17) also carried the "late birth" label.

There was no doubt that he was going to go first overall the following June. The only uncertainty was to which team that would be. So the hockey world was wondering how was he going to spend his eighteen-year-old draft season of 2015–16.

The big colleges—Michigan, North Dakota, Boston University, Boston College, Denver, and Wisconsin—all came calling. The year before, Jack Eichel had chosen Boston University heading into his draft year. He went second to Buffalo after Edmonton chose Connor McDavid, of the OHL Erie Otters, first. Some of Matthews's friends such as Zach Werenski, Kyle Connor, Tyler Motte, and J.T. Compher went to Michigan, finishing as that school's top four scorers that 2015–16 season. Matthews would have been absolutely dominant at the collegiate level as Eichel had been, if not more. Eichel was not only the NCAA Rookie of the Year winner, but took home the Hobey Baker Award, given to that season's top player in the NCAA. Eichel was from North Chelmsford, Massachusetts, so going to Boston University would have been something Eichel had always dreamed of.

Matthews? Arizona State had a hockey program and has come a long way the last decade or so. But it was far from a storied hockey college and not at the elite level when Matthews was a teenager, so it was not a school kids would necessarily aspire to attend. His father, Brian, was a college baseball player at Loyola Marymount in California, so the family was well aware what college athletics was all about.

On June 5, 2015, the Matthews camp announced what came as no surprise: Matthews would not be considering a US college.

That put the WHL Everett Silvertips, who controlled his CHL playing rights, on alert. They'd drafted Matthews in the third round of the Bantam Draft in 2012, before he exploded on to the scene at the USNTDP. He wasn't on anybody's top-ten list back then. He was still a bit of an unknown, from a hockey backwater of Scottsdale, Arizona.

The Silvertips had a middling roster for the 2015–16 season and would ultimately finish second in their division, backstopped by goalie Carter Hart. But it was the team that would have trouble scoring. Forward Remi Laurencelle led the team with twenty-eight goals in his final season of junior before joining the Canadian university ranks. He never played pro. Carson Stadnyk was the only other player with more than twenty goals (he had twenty-one) in what was his final year in junior. After four years at the University of Saskatchewan, he played a season with the Fife Flyers of the EIHL.

The Silvertips were anything but a powerhouse and were the kind of team teenage stars tried to avoid. Defenceman Seth Jones had refused in 2012 to report, necessitating a trade before he joined the WHL. Everett was used to such treatment.

But what about Matthews? The family had promised a decision.

Owner Bill Yuill met with Matthews's agent, Pat Brisson, in LA. They had good discussions. They talked about Everett and Yuill's other team, the Bloomington (Illinois) Thunder of the US Hockey League. Matthews had already dominated the USHL when playing head-to-head with the USNTDP. The USHL was a non-starter. But the CHL might provide the right level of competition.

Matthews could have made all the difference for Everett. Davidson was hoping for Matthews and his camp to make up their minds. With the US colleges out of the picture, the path seemed clear.

And then just as suddenly, it wasn't. Stories had been circulating since May about Matthews considering Europe instead, thanks to the connections built in a lifetime in hockey by his agent, Pat Brisson.

Brisson's pro hockey career didn't amount to much after he left the Quebec Major Junior Hockey League, but in the late 1980s, he ended up in Los Angeles, living with his buddy, Hall of Famer Luc Robitaille, his teammate from the Hull Olympiques. He did a little bit of everything, investing in rinks, selling hockey paraphernalia, coaching at just the right time, when hockey exploded in California after the 1998 trade of Wayne Gretzky to the Kings. He got in with the right people and was eventually recruited by baseball agent Tom Reich, who wanted to open a hockey division in 1993. He signed Robitaille as his first client.

Brisson eventually left for International Management Group (IMG). During the 2005–06 NHL lockout, IMG ran a barnstorming tour of Europe, a seven-city trip featuring stars like Mats

Sundin, Joe Thornton, and Dominik Hašek, further entrenching Brisson's ties to Europe.

Eventually, Brisson left IMG to co-found the hockey division for Creative Artists Agency (CAA) with J.P. Barry, and represented some of the biggest names in the game. He had represented three first overall picks in a row (Sidney Crosby in 2005, Erik Johnson in 2006, and Patrick Kane in 2007). Brisson was also the agent for John Tavares, who went first in 2009, and for Nathan MacKinnon, who went first in 2013.

In 2014, Brisson met Matthews.

Auston's coach with the Arizona Bobcats, Ron Filion, was a friend of Brisson's from their junior hockey days and ran one of the Iceoplex rinks Brisson had invested in. Filion brought Matthews and the Bobcats to LA to play the Junior Kings. Filion had been talking up Matthews to Brisson, hoping Brisson might help get Matthews on USA Hockey's radar.

"He was pretty good. Way better than we expected," said Brisson.

They struck up a casual relationship. Brisson and Judd Moldaver, a young agent apprenticing under Brisson, got to know Matthews and his family. Brisson wanted to be his agent when Matthews was old enough and ready to turn pro. A handshake agreement between the Matthewses and Brisson was all it took. And when Matthews emerged from the USNTDP, by the summer of 2015, the relationship was concrete, and they needed to discuss their options.

"We were getting close to doing something with Everett," said Brisson, referring to the WHL Silvertips, "but I had a relationship with Marc Crawford, who was coaching in Zurich. I got the idea to first see if we could send Auston to Switzerland. We thought it was a great idea, but we wanted to make sure if the kid goes there, he's good enough, he's going to play. Is he mature enough to be able to be away from home? There were a lot of questions."

It was an intriguing turn of events. Europeans have been coming to the CHL and American colleges for decades, attuning themselves to North American rinks and the North American style of play, to show themselves off to more scouts, more teams, and to set themselves up for the draft.

In the 2015 draft, the New Jersey Devils took forward Pavel Zacha sixth overall. Though Russian, he'd played for the OHL's Sarnia Sting. The Philadelphia Flyers drafted defenceman Ivan Provorov seventh overall. Again, a Russian playing in Canada for his draft year, in this case the WHL Brandon Wheat Kings. It worked for German Timo Meier as well, drafted ninth overall by San Jose after playing for the QMJHL Halifax Mooseheads. Europeans playing their draft year in North America was a tried-and-true formula.

But could it work the other way around? For Europeans to be drafted from their Euro club teams is one thing. But should a teenage American do it? The answer from the Matthews camp was a resounding yes. For one thing, he'd be paid better: $400,000 for the season as opposed to the $50 a week the junior leagues pay. For another, and perhaps more importantly, he'd learn quickly about playing in a men's league. The European leagues play fewer games. They're big on practice time, a part of the grind Matthews loves. The European schedule would accommodate Matthews playing in the World Juniors for Team USA. There was a lot to like about the decision, a seventeen-year-old free agent choosing his own destiny.

"I guess it's not a traditional move, but I thought for my development that playing pro hockey here in Switzerland is a really great idea," he told the Champions Hockey League website. "It's really going to help me develop and become a pro."

This development required the right program. Some teams have better development reputations than others. The Zurich Lions fit the bill as well as any team. They have a championship pedigree, ownership that cares about hockey and its players, and a coach in Marc Crawford who'd won the Stanley Cup and coached international hockey.

Although Switzerland doesn't produce NHL hockey players at the same rate as the likes of Russia, Sweden, and Finland, the quality of play in its league surpasses that of both Finland and Sweden. In Europe, only Russia's Kontinental Hockey League pays better.

Edgar Salis, the general manager of the Zurich Lions, first knew Matthews was a special player watching him perform in the 2015 World Junior Championships, co-hosted by Montreal and Toronto. Connor McDavid's Team Canada hoisted the trophy that year.

Matthews was a seventeen-year-old at the time playing second fiddle on an American team that featured Jack Eichel and Dylan Larkin at centre ahead of him.

"At that time in Toronto, I didn't think about whether he could ever play for us as a foreigner. It was never before that such young foreigners were signed," said Salis. "That's why I was all the more surprised when I was contacted two months later (to see) if it could be an option to sign a seventeen-year-old as a foreigner."

Fortune was on Zurich's side. The World Under-18 Championships were being held in Zug, Switzerland. Salis would be taking it in, and so would his coach, Stanley Cup champion Marc Crawford.

"We saw him at the World Junior that was in Toronto. He was a good player as a seventeen-year-old playing for that team. But that tournament was filled with great players. It was hard to tell what his level was going to be," Crawford told me. "He was going to be a great player who's going to play in the NHL. But by the end of the year, when he was playing in his age category at the U18s, he was phenomenal."

Matthews was the tournament's leading scorer with eight goals and seven assists, driving the US to gold.

Pat Brisson enlisted another pal from his Hull Olympique days, Doug Honegger, a former defenceman who'd forged a career in hockey in Switzerland, as player, agent, and then businessman. They floated the idea to Salis and Crawford that they were looking for a place for Matthews.

"Everything is always about luck," said Crawford. "Being in the right place at the right time."

Crawford was there more to see Zurich's young players, like future NHLers Denis Malgin and Jonas Siegenthaler. "Auston was so far ahead of them," said Crawford. It helped that Salis was able to meet Brian and Ema. "We were able to meet up and show him and the parents around." It was far from a done deal after initial contact.

"I first had to discuss it with my superiors and convince them, as it was anything but normal to sign such a young foreigner," said Salis.

At that time, there were strict rules for Swiss teams to sign foreign players. Switzerland is not part of the European Union, so it doesn't have to abide by the EU's labour policies. Instead, it limited teams to four foreigners per game (though more could be on the active roster). A foreigner's spot was valuable, generally given to a proven veteran player, not an unproven rookie teenager.

The Swiss league is a terrific landing spot for NHL players whose North American career is coming to an end or who are tired of life in the North American minors. A player like Ryan Shannon, for example.

Shannon was American, from Darien, Connecticut, a centre who'd played four years at Boston College before joining the Anaheim Ducks organization as an undrafted free agent, seeing his name etched on the Stanley Cup in 2007. He eked out a 305-game

NHL career (thirty-five goals, sixty-four assists) that took him to the NHL cities of Anaheim, Vancouver, Ottawa, and Tampa. But he also had trips to the minors: Portland, Cincinnati, Manitoba, and Binghamton. A torn labrum in his final NHL season of 2011–12 with the Tampa Bay Lightning meant he'd require shoulder surgery. It also meant he'd require a less physical league if he wanted to keep playing. The money in Zurich was good. It also meant stability for his young family, with no more trips to the minors. He suited up for Zurich SC in 2012 and played there until he retired in 2017.

And Switzerland is beautiful. Would you rather take a bus from Rochester to Scranton? Or would you rather go to Davos? For tourists, the decision is easy. To get paid to play hockey and also be a tourist, it perhaps should be just as easy a decision.

The Swiss league has even provided a home for top-tier NHLers during lockouts. Doug Gilmour, for example, played for Rapperswil-Jona during the first part of the 1994–95 season, the first lockout. Joe Thornton—Matthews's future teammate—played for Davos HC three times in his lengthy career. He played the full 2004–05 season when the league locked out its players for a full year, meeting his future wife. He did it again for the half-season lockout of 2012–13, and again in 2020–21 when COVID delayed the start of the NHL season.

But this would be new. A draft-eligible player, the likely first-overall pick, was coming. That had never happened before.

Salis worked with Matthews's agents at CAA, Pat Brisson and Judd Moldaver. Salis answered questions from Brian and Ema about how it would all work. There were a lot of phone calls back and forth. And one other group—the one with all the red tape—had a say: the Swiss immigration office.

"The process wasn't easy because the immigration office in

Switzerland initially didn't want to approve the transfer because they thought Auston couldn't be good enough, and they had their doubts," said Salis. Switzerland initially said no, citing that Matthews was only seventeen and that he hadn't finished high school. Lions CEO Peter Zahner passed the decision on to Brisson.

"The Swiss, when they say it's a no, it's a no," said Brisson. "It was rejected. The team president said, 'Unfortunately, this isn't going to work.' And I said, 'I don't understand this.' Do you take no for an answer like that?" Brisson, of course, is an agent. "We never take no for an answer," said Brisson. Switzerland rejected the idea a second, third, and fourth time.

The summer went on, and it looked like Matthews would be in Everett while everybody who was anybody within Swiss hockey and USA Hockey lobbied the Swiss government to change its mind.

Even though he'd rather Matthews play in a US college, the late Jim Johansson—USA Hockey's longtime assistant executive director of hockey operations—was a big voice. He believed Matthews would be a great ambassador for American hockey. Brisson enlisted the help of the US consulate. Doug Honegger had business ties that he worked. The Matthews family started to get antsy.

"It was a lot of money," said Brisson. "More importantly, it wasn't about the money, it was about the development. Brian and Ema wanted to make sure he's in the right place to continue his career." In their minds, that was Zurich, not Everett.

On August 2, Brisson was sitting on the front porch of his house on Lake Wentworth in New Hampshire, vacationing with his wife and two sons and the Hughes family—Jim and Ellen and their hockey-playing sons Quinn, Jack, and Luke—when he received two text messages, one after the other. One was good news; one was bad news.

The bad news had nothing to do with Matthews. That was the

day it was revealed one of his big clients, Patrick Kane, was being investigated for sexual assault in Buffalo. Charges were never issued against him as investigators determined the allegation was groundless.

The good news was about Matthews. The Swiss had changed their minds. He could play, but only after he turned eighteen, and he needed to finish high school first.

Quickly, Brisson's agency found a community college where he could take a high school equivalency test. If he passed, he'd get the diploma. "Brian was teasing, like you better pass that test," said Brisson. "We were nervous." It was such a rush. Matthews had no time to study. "He did fine," said Brisson.

On August 6, diploma in hand, Matthews signed with Zurich. The team released the news the next day. It was a curious decision, an unusual path. But it wasn't wrong. In fact, to most in the hockey world, it felt right.

"I didn't mind it because, at the time, he was physically ready," said Lindsay Hofford, then one of the Maple Leafs' top scouts. "I thought, if anything, he would become emotionally ready because that would be a different hockey climate. I know his mom went with him. But being on your own over there and playing with men. Because he was obviously fast-tracked. And then he had success right out of the gate. And then he had Marc Crawford as a coach. So he had, you know, a Stanley Cup–winning NHL coach there."

The Everett Silvertips were disappointed. The team is not known as a player factory. Matthews would have put it on the map.

"Obviously we're disappointed, as a player of Auston's calibre would have been an outstanding addition to our program for the upcoming season," said Silvertips General Manager Garry Davidson. "Auston and his family have had nothing but positive things to say about our organization and our coaching staff throughout this process, and we're confident that he would be a Silvertip this year if an unprecedented opportunity to play pro hockey overseas had not presented itself. I'd like to wish him the best of luck going forward in his career."

But it was game-on for Matthews in Zurich—back-to-back champion of the National League A (NLA)—to play in front of 11,200 fans at Hallenstadion.

"I think it was important for the whole of Switzerland and also for all the young players to see that you can be so good at the age of seventeen," said Salis. "I think it gave a lot of players hope and the belief that a lot is possible."

After the contract was announced, Matthews said it was the right move for him.

"It's been really good so far," Matthews told Championshockey league.com. "It's not been too hard to adjust, just a different culture, but all the guys have been really welcoming and just helping me get used to everything. The ice is a little bigger than back in the States, but I think it's a good thing. It forces you to skate a little bit more. I try not to take too much advantage of the big ice—especially in the neutral zone I try to push myself in the middle of the ice and make plays from there."

From a family perspective, it was a big deal. There would be no billet family, like the Daniels in Ann Arbor. Instead, it was decided Ema and Auston's older sister, Alexandria, would join him in Zurich. Alexandria took a semester off from Arizona State University.

His father, Brian, and younger sister, Breyana, would stay home. Brian was the chief technology officer for a manufacturing company based in New Jersey. Breyana was still in school in Scottsdale.

"It's hard right now," Brian told ESPN's Scott Burnside in 2015. "But we would do the same thing for Breyana's golf or Alexandria's schooling. Kids first."

Of course, life is never a straight line, and European labour laws had to get in the way. Matthews was just seventeen when training camp opened and the season began. He couldn't actually play until he was eighteen. He could practise, but he couldn't play in the exhibition games or the first two regular-season games, because the Swiss league starts the second week of September.

His birthday was just around the corner, but first there was a team tradition: Street Parade.

Life as a first-year pro, life in another country, and life as a teenager would provide Matthews with some memories for a lifetime, and some chuckles for his teammates. On September 8 that year, Zurich held its annual Street Parade. About a million people show up for an outdoor festival of techno music and everything that goes with it: food, drink, whatever.

Matthews enjoyed the event at least as much as the estimated one million other people who were there to take in headliner Robin Schulz, a German musician and DJ. Matthews was chirped for hiding his beer under his sweatshirt because, back where he was from, it would have been illegal to drink alcohol at that age.

"It's tradition that the team always gets the [Street Parade] weekend off," winger Roman Wick told *The Athletic*. "Of course, we were going to show him that. He was a normal eighteen-year-old kid. He drank a little bit too much alcohol and had to leave."

Crawford put Ryan Shannon in charge of Matthews's well-being that day.

"It's definitely worth seeing," Shannon said of Street Parade. "It was a huge eye-opener for me. I had been there before, so I knew what to expect and definitely knew that I needed to just keep an eye on him the whole day. It's a million people flooding downtown Zurich for an electronic music festival with people barely wearing clothes. Peace, love, and happiness. They have a very open drug understanding. People were openly taking ecstasy and who knows what else."

The team party started at the apartment of veteran forward Robert Nilsson, the son of NHLer Kent Nilsson.

"Auston wasn't jumping in like a rambunctious young teenager, having his first sip of alcohol. He just kind of took it slow. I don't even know if he had drank before," said Shannon.

On top of being a hockey player, Nilsson is a fine-wine connoisseur, and the players started the day drinking some of the best he had to offer before joining Street Parade.

"Three-quarters of the way through the day, Auston had had enough. We had to escort him home. And I'm not a big guy, and he is a big guy. It was tough to keep him upright."

Once he found that it was okay to drink in Switzerland, there was another revelation: He could go to nightclubs, too. His teammates took him to one in Zurich. "He was so excited," defenceman Roger Karrer told *The Athletic*. "I think it was his first time in a club. He went crazy in there with the music. He was smiling all the time and talking to everyone."

But Ema kept an eye on him, and Brian would grill the coach on how his son was doing.

Europe also expanded his taste buds, with a different kind of diversity than Scottsdale or Ann Arbor had offered: kebabs. One place in particular caught his fancy: Ayverdi's Oerlikon, near the arena.

For the Swiss, it was nothing special. For Matthews, it was a new culinary treat. He wanted to go every day. Eventually, everyone in Ayverdi's got to know Auston Matthews.

Kebabs, yes, but drinking and partying were not Matthews's thing. He enjoyed it as far as the European culture went, and team events, but that's as far as it went for him.

"He wasn't a partier," said Shannon. "He was not interested in it. He wanted to hang out with guys, but he was not interested in drinking or getting caught up in nightlife stuff. It seemed like he was enjoying Zurich. He didn't seem stressed. He wasn't quick to smile or to joke, but after a tough practice or a good game, he would. After the first couple of weeks, I didn't feel like I really needed to take care of him. It was like, 'Okay, this kid's got it.'"

What helped was his birthday. On September 17, when Auston turned eighteen, the Matthews family threw a party the likes of which his teammates had never experienced, and it was the moment where he felt he really became part of the team.

It helped that his mother, Ema, was with him. She spent the season with him, something he quite enjoyed, especially her home cooking.

Matthews's teammates gathered at the Hallenstadion restaurant after a morning skate, with Ema overseeing the cooks as they prepared a massive Mexican lunch for the team. They made Auston's favourite meal, including chicken tortilla soup.

"I love Mom's chicken tortilla soup. She made it for the team for my birthday in Zurich, and, afterward, the wives of almost half the players were asking for the recipe. They all liked it a lot. It was pretty neat, and it kind of broke the ice on my birthday," Matthews told Championshockeyleague.com.

Not that there was any doubt, but Matthews really became part of the team.

Afterward, players gathered out in the parking lot. Matthews was blindfolded, and a piñata was hung for him to try his hand at. He kind of went crazy, flailing away at it while one of the coaches was controlling it.

"It was the entire team watching this kid swing blind," said Shannon. "Whoever was [controlling the piñata] was having a lot of fun with him. He was floundering for a bit. But it was like a celebration of where he came from. And it was a really authentic thing.

"We had a lot of fun in the parking lot watching Auston hit the piñata. It kind of gave him the opportunity to have others laugh at him, so it kind of broke any of the hesitation or awkwardness that he may have felt. It probably served him really well, just feeling a part of the guys and not being this seventeen-year-old who's projected to go number one overall. It was just, 'Okay, now you're just one of the guys.'"

Now that he was eighteen—of legal professional hockey-playing age as far as Swiss authorities were concerned—it was time to play the games.

This kid from Arizona, with Mexican roots, playing Canada's game with an American passport could finally get to work in Switzerland. It wasn't so much that he was breaking all the rules, as he was making up his own.

On Friday, September 18—the day after Auston's eighteenth birthday—Zurich hosted Fribourg-Gottéron in NLA play. Matthews was at centre, between Reto Schäppi and former Senators player Ryan Keller. In the second period on the power play, he finished off a give-and-go with winger Chris Baltisberger for a 3–2 lead and his first goal in his first game.

"He broke through the middle, fended off a couple of guys, put the puck in the net," said Crawford. "That was a really spectacular goal."

The following day they traveled to Langnau im Emmental to face the SCL Tigers, and then the Lions flew to Prague, where they opened the Champions Hockey League's Round of 32 on September 22 at O2 Arena against Sparta.

Matthews got off to a hot start. On October 9, Matthews scored twice. His second goal was the game-winner, coming late in the third period to give Zurich a 3–2 win over rival Davos. Fans chanted his name. "It was probably one of the most memorable games of the year because it was the first time Zurich and Davos played since the 2015 National League A final. I was able to score two goals, and the game-winner off a great pass from Robert Nilsson," Matthews said, as recounted by NHLTradeTalk.com. "After the game, the fans began chanting my name and jumping up and down. I was just looking up into the crowd and saying, 'This is crazy.' But what I didn't know was that, when the crowd does that in Switzerland, you're expected to return to the ice by yourself and salute the fans. I had no idea, and everyone was yelling at me that I had to go back. I was so confused as to what was going on, but once I figured it out, it was pretty special."

Matthews had ten goals and seven assists in his first fourteen games. "He was amazing," said Crawford. "The Swiss are a hard group to impress. I don't want to say this the wrong way, but there's a lot of thought there that you've got to earn everything you get. They really challenge any young player, whether they're Swiss or from anywhere, to show them that they're good enough. It was a really big step to give an import spot to an eighteen-year-old. They were very sceptical, to say the least. And by the end of the first practice, I had guys coming to me who said, 'I think he's gonna be really good. Can I play on his line?'"

One of those was veteran forward Robert Nilsson. "I was excited," said Nilsson. "I knew who he was and that he was potentially going first in the draft. When you've been playing for such a long time, you know how good those types of players are. So I was more excited and hoping that we would be on the same line. It took twelve or fifteen games until we played together."

Nilsson was one of those players born to play hockey. A first-round pick of the New York Islanders in 2003, Nilsson was the son of hockey legend Kent Nilsson, known best for his time with the Calgary Flames and later an inductee into both the Swedish and IIHF Hockey Halls of Fame.

Robert didn't quite have the NHL career of his father, playing in 252 NHL games, but he played the sport across the globe. He married Sasha Khabibulin, the daughter of former teammate Nikolai Khabibulin, who was the goaltender for the Phoenix Coyotes when Auston's Uncle Billy started taking the young boy to hockey games.

"He was part of the generation after me," said Nilsson. "They are a different breed. I felt that he as an eighteen-year-old was more mature than I was. And I was probably thirty at the time."

Nilsson said he couldn't stop watching how Matthews played and practised. "You don't see too many players where you're on the same team, where you sit on the bench and it's just fun to see him play. He was doing everything at full speed all the time and still had control over everything. One small thing that I really noticed—and even though people might think it's lucky, but it can't be luck if it happens a lot—the puck followed him around. It could be by his feet, he could lose it, but somehow he always got it back. That was really cool. And obviously his wrist shot was insane."

It takes most teenagers some time, typically a year or two, to get used to the game in the men's league. Not Auston Matthews.

"I did some digging, and then watching the kid play, and it's just like, I wasn't surprised that people were essentially trying to bribe Crow [Marc Crawford] to get on his line," said Shannon. "He just had an incredible sixth sense that always seemed like the puck followed him around. It seemed like he was getting a ton done with very little effort. And after the first month of the season, it was like, because we had Auston, we started every game up 1–0. That's kind of how it felt."

Like Nilsson, Crawford was born into hockey, no stranger to life as a pro in North America, or internationally. His father, Floyd, won gold for Canada at the 1959 World Ice Hockey Championships with the Belleville McFarlands in Prague. Marc and his brothers Bob and Lou would all make the NHL. Marc would stick with it after his playing days, coaching Joe Sakic and Peter Forsberg with the Quebec Nordiques, winning a Stanley Cup with them as the Colorado Avalanche, coaching the Sedin twins when they turned pro in Vancouver, Anže Kopitar in his early days in Los Angeles, and Jamie Benn as a young player in Dallas. And he coached all of Canada's greatest players in 1998 at the Nagano Olympics.

"I've been blessed," said Crawford. "I've seen some really great players come in at a young age, and I can remember Auston coming in those first practices and saying, 'Yes, that's what greatness looks like.' I'd seen it with Peter Forsberg, I'd seen it with Anže Kopitar, I'd seen it with the Sedins, I'd seen it with Jamie Benn. So I'd seen all these guys, really high-end superstar-quality players. And you saw it with Auston right away. Auston just has a presence about him, the way that he handles himself, handles the puck, his skating, his power, his shooting. It really captured you right away."

But Crawford was wrong about one thing. "I said by the end of the year, he'd probably be one of the best players in the league. And I was wrong with that because he was the best player almost right away. He was amazing."

But Matthews suffered a back injury on October 23 when he fell into the boards awkwardly, missing fourteen games.

"He went really awkwardly into the boards, almost headfirst into the boards. It was part check, part fall. Lost his balance," said Crawford. "It looked really serious. But because of his strength and his ability to withstand with his muscularity and all of that sort of thing, it kind of saved him. But he did miss . . . that first part of the season."

When he came back, it was with a vengeance, including an eleven-game points streak that helped Zurich reach the Swiss Cup, an in-season tournament featuring Swiss teams from all levels.

The Swiss Cup is not the biggest hockey trophy in Switzerland but an on-again, off-again in-season tournament initially played from 1957 to 1966, revived for a year in 1972, and revived once more in 2015, just before Matthews got there. It was formative for Matthews's pro career, the first professional club trophy he had won. And he was a big part of the reason why the Lions roared. In the Round of 16, Zurich beat Chur 9–2, Matthews scoring the second goal of the game. In the Round of 8, Zurich beat the Langnau Tigers 4–1, Matthews scoring the second goal of the game, which held up as the winner. In the Round of 4, Zurich beat Ambri-Piotta 5–2, Matthews scoring twice. In the semifinals, Zurich beat Bern 5–3.

Then it was off to Lausanne for the final. The lower seed had home-ice advantage in the winner-take-all single-game championship. Lausanne has some of the loudest, most passionate fans in Europe. It can be an intimidating rink.

And in the final, Zurich beat Lausanne 4–1, Matthews assisting on the final two goals of the game. He won his first professional championship, finishing tied for the lead in points with four goals and three assists in the Swiss Cup. ZSC won for the third time. No team has won it more often.

"Auston was our best player, and he was the best player in the league," said Shannon. "And to see him raise a trophy with the Swiss-style confetti and the music and the strobe lights and things like that, it was great. I think it was well earned. It took incredible courage, putting himself on a different continent in a completely foreign environment. And he was able to win a championship. It definitely is much lower than the Swiss championship. But it was a win."

There was disappointment for Zurich as well, eliminated in the

Pan-European Champions League in the first round of its playoffs, by HC Sparta Prague.

Despite the injury, Matthews finished second in Zurich scoring and fifth in the NLA.

The Lions finished at the top of the regular-season standings with a 31–12–1 record. But they were eliminated in a shocking first-round playoff sweep to SC Bern (21–20–4) in the Swiss National League A playoffs.

Matthews had forty-six points in thirty-six regular-season games. He had three assists in the playoffs against Bern but failed to score a goal in the postseason.

"Zurich was slightly better than Bern in [the] first two games, but the puck did not go their way," said Thomas Roost, who evaluates talent in Switzerland and Germany for NHL Central Scouting (via NHL.com). "Matthews played very well in both games with [Robert Nilsson]. They produced, had great pressure and lots of scoring chances, but Matthews is a bit unlucky right now. He hit the post a few times. Matthews was the best player on the ice in both games, no question about it. He showed top-notch playmaking, excellent stick work, powerful plays along the wall and in the corners, and was even double-shifted toward the end of both games."

By mid-March, Matthews's European adventure was over.

"It was challenging, off the ice, moving to a different country, different language," Matthews told *The Athletic* in 2016. "Looking back on that experience, it's something that I think I gained a lot from. And if I had to do it all over again, I definitely would."

All that was left, hockey-wise, that season was a head-to-head showdown against the only player who had a chance to unseat him as the top pick in the 2016 draft: Patrik Laine. They'd faced each other at the World Juniors, Laine's team Finland winning gold in Helsinki.

Now the two eighteen-year-olds would be key parts of their senior national teams in St. Petersburg, Russia, in May, at which time the NHL would have sorted out the draft order. That little bit of franchise-changing drama was set for April 30.

And Brendan Shanahan didn't have his lucky shamrock.

CHAPTER NINE

Tanking for Matthews

The NHL Draft is an unusual monster. Some years, the players who are selected at number one, such as when the Pittsburgh Penguins got Sidney Crosby in 2005, can alter the course of hockey history, the value of a franchise, the direction it's going to take. Teams lose their minds trying to get that player. Fan bases buy in right away, actively rooting for their team to lose with "Tank for ___" slogans. The media buys in because, hey, who doesn't love a good story and eventually to cover a winning team?

In truth, drafting first overall in the NHL is not that easy. Luck is involved due to the presence of the lottery for the first pick that guarantees nothing. Sometimes a marketing plan is involved, getting the fans on board for a bad season. And the team actually has to lose, not easily done with competitive players who want to win. Getting that first overall pick these days is not like it used to be.

To draft first overall usually means your team is terrible. Sometimes teams come by that naturally, like the Maple Leafs of 1984–85. They tried to be good. They just weren't. They had a no-nonsense coach in Dan Maloney and a captain in Rick Vaive who was coming off three consecutive fifty-goal seasons. They had a number-one centre in Bill Derlago and a number-two in Peter

Ihnačák. They had promising youngsters like Russ Courtnall and Gary Leeman and young defence deep with talent in Jim Benning, Al Iafrate, and Bob McGill supporting veteran Börje Salming.

"I'm convinced that we have enough talent here to get the job done, and this might sound crazy, but I really don't think first place in our division is out of the question this season," Vaive told the *Toronto Star* in training camp that year. "I don't enjoy attending banquets during the off-season and hearing the jokes about how bad the Leafs were. But it's going to be different this season."

It wasn't. It was worse. They finished dead last that season, but the times were simpler. The reward was the first overall pick. No lottery. Last overall picks first overall.

The Leafs selected Wendel Clark, a future captain, a fan favourite, and the heart and soul of a team whose greatest glory in his tenure was a trip to the 1993 Western Conference Final, where they were foiled by Wayne Gretzky and a missed high-sticking call.

The Maple Leafs of 2013–14 thought they were a playoff team, but they were fooling themselves. The 2–12–0 run over the final fourteen games of the season dropped them to eighth from the bottom. They ended up with William Nylander as a result.

The Maple Leafs of 2014–15 started out as a playoff team but had the rug pulled out from under them by management, the lure of trying to get McDavid simply too much. They got Mitch Marner, not a bad consolation prize. The 2015–16 Maple Leafs weren't really that bad, at least on paper. They had to work on it.

Mike Babcock had been hired as coach for the 2015–16 season. He'd guided the Detroit Red Wings to the Stanley Cup in 2007 and was on the bench for Team Canada's Olympic gold medals in 2010 and 2014. He wasn't going to take losing well, unless the price was right. An eight-year, $40 million guaranteed contract helped make the price right. Babcock came aboard amid much fanfare after being lured to Toronto from Detroit by Leaf President Brendan Shanahan, who had played for Babcock.

The same was true for new GM Lou Lamoriello, hired after Babcock in the summer of 2015. He'd managed the New Jersey Devils into three-time Stanley Cup champions (1995, 2000, and 2003) in large part through great goaltending and high draft picks.

"It was more exciting than anything else with two high-profile people in the hockey world coming in with their résumés and what they'd accomplished," recalled longtime Maple Leaf Tyler Bozak. "To have that structure and that direction was good for us. Our team was getting younger."

If nothing else, Lamoriello was ruthless. He didn't mind the comparisons to *The Godfather.* He knew where hockey buried its bodies. It was his way or no way. Lou rules because of Lou's Rules: No facial hair. A strict dress policy. No one is above the team. And he preferred players to wear traditional hockey numbers, from 1 to 35. Nazem Kadri (43) and Morgan Rielly (44) had their numbers before Lamoriello got there, so they were grandfathered in. But Nylander moved from his rookie number, 39, to 29 under Lamoriello, switching to 88 after Lamoriello left. Marner was told by Doug Gilmour that he could use 93. Lamoriello gave him 16.

"I'm trying to create [an atmosphere] where the players are willing to give up their own identity for that logo in front," Lamoriello said in his introductory news conference. "A team is like an orchestra. If the music isn't good, no matter how good each and every one instrument is, everybody leaves. Success doesn't come unless every one of these individuals is committed to each other.

"We want to find players who want to be here, who want to win, and who don't want individual success. They want team success. I can't remember the people who were the leading scorers when we won. But I do remember the names of the people who are on the Cup."

But Lamoriello's ruthlessness was never more on display than with the disappearance of veteran defenceman Stéphane Robidas. During training camp in 2015, Robidas was thirty-eight and well past his prime, but he had still managed to play fifty-two games in a shutdown role the previous season. He had passed his physical and was openly talking on the last day of camp about what his role might be. He was accepting and expecting that he would be in more of a part-time role. A mentor. And he was good with that.

But at 5:00 p.m. on the eve of the season, when rosters had to be compliant to the NHL's restrictive salary cap, Robidas landed on Long-Term Injured Reserve. It was a surprise to the media covering the team. When did he get hurt? How did he get hurt?

Robidas had vanished, unavailable to the media. The team awkwardly explained Robidas was too injured to play, not really explaining what that meant. This was Lou being Lou. A kind of "I'm going to make you an offer you can't refuse" Lou.

Being a fan of the TV show *Lost*, I joked he was lost on Robidas Island. It became the parlance around the team. He was joined the next season by Joffrey Lupul, a talented scoring forward with a history of back and abdominal troubles.

"Haha failed physical? They cheat, everyone lets them," Lupul would post—and then delete—from Instagram.

What was Lamoriello's motive in Robidas's case? Salary cap space? Maybe, but he didn't use it. To sideline players who might help him win at a time when the team needed to draft as highly as possible?

True or not, that one resonated with the Tank Nation that had been forming. Lamoriello not only knew where all the bodies were buried, but he also might have helped dig a few graves.

"There's no question you have to build a foundation before you can go anywhere," Lamoriello said at his introductory news conference. "Yes, it could be slow, there could be more pain, because there could be more subtraction than addition to get that foundation, to get the right culture going forward."

Lamoriello was going to build a winner through the draft. He needed high picks. The Leafs had just drafted Mitch Marner fourth overall in 2015 when Lamoriello took office. Combined with an eighth overall in 2014 (William Nylander) and a fifth overall in 2012 (Morgan Rielly), the seeds were there, but there was a missing piece. With apologies to Tyler Bozak, the Leafs didn't have a bona fide number-one centre. Yet.

Scouts had a pretty good read on Matthews heading into the 2016 draft, since he played against most of the high-end players that got drafted in 2015. In fact, I remember doing a story on the so-called battle between McDavid and Eichel as far as which one was better and which one would go first overall. I spoke with Dan Marr, the chief scout for the NHL's Central Scouting bureau at a Team Canada World Junior camp at the then-named Mastercard Centre. Marr gave his usual spiel about both players. As the interview ended, I put away my tape recorder and threw the name Auston Matthews at him. If he was available in the 2015 draft, where would he go? First, second, or third?

Marr smiled and shrugged with an I-can't-decide look on his face.

Later, at the 2016 World Junior Championship in Finland, I reminded Marr of that conversation. The Americans lost in the semifinal, but Matthews had been terrific. But so had Finns Patrik Laine and Jesse Puljujärvi, each now making a case to dislodge Matthews as the consensus first overall pick.

As if to pour cold water on any discussion like that, Marr told me, "[Matthews] is the real deal. This kid only has an on switch. He's even hard to play against in practice. He'd have been in the mix with Eichel and McDavid."

It's unfair to measure first overall picks against each other.

"Generational" is an overused term, but it could be used to refer to a player who'd change his team's fortunes for a generation. It certainly applies to Alex Ovechkin (2004 to Washington) and Sidney Crosby (2005 to Pittsburgh), but not so much to Erik Johnson (2006 to St. Louis).

Matthews and McDavid are very different players but could change the fortunes of the team that got to pick number one. Having missed out on McDavid, Shanahan was determined not to miss out on Matthews. He put the Shanaplan into action, addressing the media a few days after the mass firings that had been dubbed Bloody Sunday.

"I've often said the plan is not some unique plan that you won't hear twenty-nine other teams say they have to do, which is draft, develop, patience," said Shanahan. "Make good choices. The challenge here in Toronto is not to come up with the plan. The challenge in Toronto is to stick to it. That's the hard part. Our vision is indeed to draft and develop our own players. When a player is ready to come up, he'll come up. If a player needs more time to reach his full potential, we'll leave him down there. Every decision we make is about how do we build a winning organization that can sustain itself year after year in the draft? That is our vision."

It's fair to say the previous regime that ran Maple Leaf Sports & Entertainment under President Richard Peddie and general managers John Ferguson Jr. and Brian Burke misread the market when the Mats Sundin era was ending. It was obvious the team was in decline. Acquiring draft capital and young prospects seemed the obvious way to go, and the fan base seemed ready for it.

Ferguson tried to deal Sundin but was told by the MLSE board they had budgeted for five playoff home dates. Without Sundin, making the playoffs would be impossible. They kept Sundin and missed the playoffs anyway in 2006 and 2007. Ferguson's replacement as interim GM, Cliff Fletcher, also tried to trade Sundin in 2008, but the big Swede invoked his no-trade clause, demonstrating his loyalty not just to wanting to win, but wanting to win in Toronto.

But when Burke took over, he traded away two first-round picks and a second-rounder for Phil Kessel in 2009. Burke's argument for getting Kessel—a dynamic goal scorer—was to get a star to give the folks who pay insane amounts of money to watch the Leafs someone to cheer. Kessel was a good player, the team's top scorer in his tenure, but there was never enough talent to support him. The Leafs were bad then, their ratings declining. New ownership—Bell Media and Rogers Communications—backed the Shanaplan because it promised a good team for a long time, as well as playoffs, which meant good ratings to its new owners.

The draft was the thing. And with Shanahan missing out on McDavid, he set his eyes on Matthews. First, the Leafs had to be worse than fourth from the bottom.

New coach Mike Babcock telegraphed it at his introductory news conference at the then-named Air Canada Centre.

"If you think there's no pain coming, there's pain coming," said Babcock. That meant there was going to be a lot of losing before there'd be any winning.

First out the door was Phil Kessel, the team's leading scorer. The Leafs got a first-round pick and a highly rated prospect in Kasperi Kapanen back from the Pittsburgh Penguins. But now the Leafs didn't have anyone who could score.

Marner and William Nylander had terrific training camps, and any other team might have had them on the roster. But not the Leafs. Those players were young and hungry and talented. They might help the team win. Couldn't have that. Marner was sent back to junior, Nylander to the AHL Marlies.

The Leafs were reasonably good the first half of that season. Perhaps overachieving, at least overachieving the hopes of the front office. They were 16–15–7, five points out of a playoff spot, twenty-fourth overall on January 4, 2016. A long way from last place and the best chance at drafting Auston Matthews. It was around that time that Babcock—a taskmaster as coach—stopped matching lines.

On January 11, a gift for an organization that wants to tank, the team announced that leading scorer James van Riemsdyk would miss six weeks with a broken foot. It was from "friendly fire," too, a Dion Phaneuf slap shot in a 7–0 loss to the Sharks in San Jose.

"We were doing okay. We were still in the mix," said van Riemsdyk. "And then obviously towards the end of the year, things fall off the rails. For me, for me individually and personally, it was a tough year because I had a weird injury. I was out pretty much until like May or June. I had a broken foot that got infected. So I don't vividly remember a lot about that season, maybe trying to block it out. But being in it, the day-to-day of it is definitely tough when things aren't going your way and you kind of know the direction that things look like they're heading."

Players want to win. That's how they're built. Sometimes it's simply because contracts are on the line. Reputations. Egos.

But management has tools it can use to hamstring its team. It's all perfectly legitimate, on the up-and-up. Indeed, in some ways even beneficial for the league. The biggest and easiest way? Trades.

On February 9, the Leafs traded Captain Dion Phaneuf to the Ottawa Senators. On February 27, James Reimer, their best goalie, was traded.

The second easiest? Bring up players from the minors who are not ready for prime time under the guise of seeing what they can do.

A shaky rookie, Garret Sparks, replaced Reimer, playing every second game despite an inflated 3.02 goals-against average and a .892 save percentage.

"We started losing," said Bozak. "That was when Matthews was the number one overall. When it got to the point that we kind of knew we were out, it was almost like the team kind of wanted to finish last. We players obviously didn't. But I think if you know you're not getting in the playoffs and there's a player of Matthews's calibre to go first overall . . . I don't think we were really trying too hard to win at the time, to be honest . . . You never want to lose a game as a player, but I think once we had realized that we weren't going to win the Stanley Cup that year, the focus kind of switched: Can we get this once-in-a-lifetime superstar to be part of our franchise?"

Rookies William Nylander, Zach Hyman, and Connor Brown were among those promoted for a first taste. They did very well and were sent back to the minors quickly.

"It was quite funny," said Bozak. "We called up Hyman and Connor Brown and guys like that, and I think we went out and we won a couple games in a row. And then they miraculously got sent down after we won a couple of games, so that kind of gave me the idea that we weren't really looking to win too many games."

After all, there were still the Oilers to contend with, their run of draft lottery luck not to be taken lightly. Despite the addition of Connor McDavid to a young crew that included Taylor Hall, Ryan Nugent-Hopkins, Jordan Eberle, and Nail Yakupov, the Oilers were also struggling yet again. Both had forty-seven points when the two teams hooked up on February 11, 2016. It was hyped as the Matthews Bowl. Oilers fans called it the Toilet Bowl. By either nickname, the result would be the same: To the loser would go sole possession of last place in the NHL.

Ultimately, the Oilers beat the Leafs convincingly, on a five-point night from McDavid. The final was 5–2 for the Oilers.

"We needed this," McDavid told reporters that night.

Left unsaid was that Leaf management needed it, too. The Leafs would win just ten more games over the final two months of the regular season, to go along with seventeen losses and a pair of points thanks to overtime losses. The Oilers would win only nine more times, to go along with fourteen losses and three points thanks to overtime losses.

The loss in regulation that night ended up being pivotal to the odds in the draft lottery. The Oilers would finish with seventy points, the Leafs—dead last—with sixty-nine.

The Leafs ended up with the best chance to land Matthews.

The Leafs had won very little since 1967. No Stanley Cup. No Presidents' Trophy. No division championship. Very little for hockey's largest fan base to celebrate, until April 30, 2016.

The lottery had changed yet again. This time, for the first time, the first three picks were up for grabs. The Leafs could pick no worse than fourth.

"We're picking one, two, three, or four," Leafs President Brendan Shanahan told *Hockey Night in Canada* host George Stroumboulopoulos that night. "So you're going to get a player that's going to have a big impact on your franchise. It's just a matter of when. And probably, you could argue that those first three are maybe in a situation right now where people think they're going to have that impact next year."

Those first three were Matthews, Laine, and Jesse Puljujärvi, who joined the conversation at the 2016 World Juniors.

Representatives of the fourteen teams that missed the playoffs were in studio, and at the roundtable were Brian Burke, then representing the Calgary Flames, who was in a rambunctious mood and not about to tell Strombo what lucky charm he'd brought; Trevor Linden, representing the Vancouver Canucks, who'd brought a Pat Quinn rookie card for luck; and Shanahan, who told the host he did not bring his lucky shamrock. He didn't have to say why. It obviously hadn't worked in 2015.

But one thing he did do? He went to a website whose sole raison d'être was to predict the outcome of the draft lottery.

"I went online, found it, pressed it once. It worked out well, closed the computer. I have not done it since," said Shanahan.

The top prospects weren't in studio this year. Matthews and Laine were in training camp for their national teams, getting ready for the World Championships. But they were awake—at roughly 3:00 a.m. their time—to be interviewed.

"A little nerve-wracking, but exciting," said Matthews. "It's a unique process to be a part of. I know it's a ways away, and I have a lot of work to do, but to have the opportunity to be drafted and hope to make an NHL club come September time is really exciting."

Unlike the McDavid draft, three draft positions were up for grabs, so the drop of the numbered Ping-Pong balls was held off camera, balls dropping for first overall, then rejigged for second overall, then rejigged for third overall while Strombo did his interviews.

It was revealed later though, and it was close. The first three numbers up the chute were 6, then 8, then 5. The Leafs had gone into the draft with a 20 percent chance of winning first overall. But they were down to 9 percent. Just one number of the remaining 11 Ping-Pong balls could help them: 13. And there it was.

It took fifty-six seconds for the four numbers to be drawn, and another fifty seconds for a pair of accountants to independently verify the Leafs had that combination.

"The Toronto Maple Leafs will have the first selection of the 2016 NHL Draft," NHL Commissioner Gary Bettman confirmed to the cameras in the sequestered room.

The televised drama was left to Deputy NHL Commissioner Bill Daly to reveal the draft order. Winnipeg had moved up from sixth to second. Columbus moved up from fourth to third. Daly ultimately held up a card with the Leaf logo on it representing the first overall pick.

"I'm just a little bit rattled from this whole experience," Shanahan told the TV audience. "That was a pretty tense moment for all of us. Just to get into the final three, even—Columbus, Winnipeg, and us—we just felt we were all going to get a great player."

And the Leafs had actually won something.

"It's a deep draft. There are lots of guys that are going to do very well. But we earned this the hard way. It wasn't a whole lot of fun this year, but our guys and our coaching staff and our management staff did a lot of really good things here in Toronto.

"This will certainly help."

"I felt really that it was something that Maple Leafs fans deserved," Shanahan told me later that season. "There was this mix of happiness and satisfaction that something like that went their way. There have been some good things happening to this organization, with Mike Babcock choosing to come here, Lou Lamoriello. We felt good about the young players that had come up at the end of last season before we sent them back to the Marlies for a playoff run. There was a little bit of momentum. That [lottery win] was a bit of luck and certainly something Leaf fans were waiting for, and hoping for."

GM Lou Lamoriello would never admit he planned for the Leafs to finish last. But he acknowledged, "Some people say we worked pretty hard at it. We knew that there would be some pain to give us the ability to gain. Before gain, there was pain."

Finishing last was pain. Winning the draft lottery was gain. He felt it watching the lottery from his home.

"Excitement. I could give a lot of different adjectives. Chills. All of the above. Because Auston was the player we wanted, unanimously. That was the feeling. I was sitting at home watching TV. And then the phone started ringing.

"There were a lot of people who were excited. I'm talking internal people, scouts, and staff."

That night, Lindsay Hofford, then one of the Leafs' top scouts of amateur talent, held a draft lottery party with Mitch Marner and others linked to the London Knights.

"It was a nerve-wracking kind of exciting thing," said Hofford. "It was really exciting just to get the first pick. You start thinking of all the great things and possibilities that are going to happen for the organization, the city, the province, the country, everything. Being able to get a player like Auston right after getting a player like Mitch, you got that one-two punch, and normally that translates into some pretty positive runs in the playoffs and opportunities to win the Stanley Cup."

If you're a hockey numerologist, the numbers came out in an interesting order on that April night. Out first was 13, the number of retired captain and Hall of Famer Mats Sundin, and to many the greatest Leaf of the post-1967 era. It was followed by 6, then 5. To that point those were the only two numbers the Maple Leafs had retired—Ace Bailey and Bill Barilko. But then it was 8—not a particularly significant number in Leaf history, other than it gave the Maple Leafs the right to draft Matthews two months later.

"I spent close to sixty days in Finland that year, tracking Puljujärvi and Laine," said Hofford. "I don't know if you've ever been to Finland in February and March, but it's dark and not fun. And then we won the lottery. So I'm thinking, 'Oh, I just spent like a sixth of the year in basically darkness and it's for nothing.'"

Well, not for nothing.

"Mitch was happy because he was going to be passing the puck to Auston," said Hofford.

Over in Europe, Crawford was also paying attention. He had grown up a huge Leaf fan and even worked as an assistant coach for the team under Pat Burns in the early 1990s. "They were an older team back then," said Crawford. "I worked in the organization for three years with Cliff Fletcher and Pat Burns, who used to coach. It just oozed greatness. All the people that they had around them at that time, they were such good pros. I have such an affinity for the Leafs in the organization."

Crawford is even old enough to remember the Leafs' 1967 Stanley Cup. "I would have been six years old at the time, and I can remember the empty net goal by George Armstrong," said Crawford.

That goal, of course, clinched the Leafs' last Stanley Cup title.

Even though the European season was over, Crawford had one more lesson to teach Matthews. He handed him a book, one so near and dear to Crawford that a copy sits on his night table. It was *The Glory Years: Memories of a Decade, 1955–65*. It was written by Billy Harris, who won the Stanley Cup three times as a Maple Leaf.

"I said, 'You need to read this book because it's going to be important to you because you're going there,'" Crawford told Matthews. "'You're going to have to know about their history. Read this book. It's going to give you background on it.' I remember giving it to him. So I'm not sure if he ever did, but he's a pretty bright guy. He recognized very quickly how important the Leafs were."

While Matthews did his reading, the Leafs did the final run-through of their homework. The Leafs knew whom they were going to take with the pick. They simply weren't going to announce it until draft night.

CHAPTER TEN

Matthews or Laine?

When the 2015–16 season began, there was no question in any minds that Auston Matthews was going to go first overall in the next NHL Draft.

Pundits called it the Matthews Sweepstakes, with the Toronto Maple Leafs, Carolina Hurricanes, and even his hometown Arizona Coyotes deemed to be the main contenders, each trying to position themselves for that favourable drop of Ping-Pong balls.

But the narrative around the draft is never quite a straight line. There simply has to be drama. If a player has been the presumptive number one overall for more than a year—as Matthews had been—there's always some scout or pundit ready to create some kind of debate surrounding who should "really" go first overall.

In 2009, the debate was John Tavares or Victor Hedman. In 2010, it was Taylor Hall or Tyler Seguin. Even in 2015, there were those who thought Jack Eichel should be chosen over Connor McDavid. And sometimes they're wrong. In 2022, Shane Wright had been the presumptive number-one pick for years but fell to fourth with Montreal taking Slovakian forward Juraj Slafkovský.

And even in the Matthews draft, there were some who said

Patrik Laine deserved to go number one overall, including Laine himself. On April 30, 2016, on *Hockey Night*'s draft lottery show when it was determined the Leafs would pick first, he certainly seemed to embrace the idea.

"I know that the gap is now smaller than when the season started," said Laine. "I've tried to be better every game and every day. And I've played some good games, and it helped me with my game. And I think the gap is now smaller. I hope that I can catch him."

He had one chance left.

"If I can make it to the World Championships, I think it's possible," Laine said.

Over in Canada, and for that matter the United States, the World Hockey Championships don't register a great deal. The championships are always on European time, so it feels sometimes like an afternoon TV time-filler, before the "real" evening games of the Stanley Cup playoffs. And neither Canada nor the US send rosters that are even close to their best. The best players—and the best hockey—are in North America in the middle of the Stanley Cup playoffs.

The World Championships feature the NHLers from the worst teams, the ones who failed to make the Stanley Cup playoffs. But the tournament in St. Petersburg, Russia, May 6–22, 2016, was not one to miss.

The Oilers had missed the playoffs, so Connor McDavid was on Team Canada. Patrik Laine had won just about everything else an eighteen-year-old could win in Finnish hockey, and he was representing his country, trying to make one last push at being considered first overall. And Auston Matthews was on Team USA.

Leafs General Manager Lou Lamoriello and Assistant GM Mark Hunter were not about to miss this, along with others from the Leafs' front office. Besides, they knew just about everything they needed to know from all the remaining NHL teams.

The European tournament offered a different perspective, maybe players playing outside their comfort zones, in different roles, with different teammates and different coaches.

The head-to-head comparison of Matthews vs. Laine was irresistible. Both had been making waves internationally as far back as 2013. The leg injury forced Matthews to miss the U17 2013 Four Nations Tournament in Slovakia in November. Matthews was only getting up to speed at the 2014 World Under-17 Hockey Challenge in Cape Breton, Nova Scotia, where he scored four goals and four assists as the US won gold. But he was front and centre at the 2014 Five Nations Tournament in Sweden in February. Matthews finished third among all skaters in points, with one goal and six assists in four games played, including two assists in a 4–1 win over host Sweden.

Even in 2015, Matthews played an exhibition game with the national team prior to that World Championship. "To be brutally honest, we needed a body for the game, and he was right there," Jim Johansson, then executive director of USA Hockey, told Postmedia on April 30, 2016. "And he scored a goal and our coaches said, 'He's staying, right?' The poise and skill he had in that one game was intriguing."

At various international tournaments, Laine, who was seven months younger than Matthews, had scored hat tricks against both the Czech Republic and the United States. Laine was born in Tampere, Finland, on April 19, 1998. Hockey is by far the most popular sport among the quarter of a million residents in Finland's second-biggest city. The region is filled with lakes that freeze in the minus-thirty temperatures typical of the area's winters. Tampere is home to three professional hockey clubs: Tappara, Ilves, and Koovee. Laine ultimately joined Tappara, following in the footsteps of other Finnish hockey players like Aleksander Barkov, Teppo Numminen, and Jyrki Lumme.

Laine started playing hockey from the age of four, with goaltending being his favourite—and best—position. At the urging of his father, Harri, Laine switched to forward at age twelve. His father would put Coke cans in the corner of nets, giving Laine targets to shoot at, helping him develop his lethal shot. He got into his first games against men in Finland's top league in 2014–15, with one assist in six games for Tappara.

Alex Ovechkin was his favourite player. But Auston Matthews was his target.

When the 2015–16 season began, with Matthews playing against men in Switzerland, Laine was doing the same thing in Finland. Laine was deemed on some scouting lists to be as low as the ninth-best player in the draft, while Matthews held firm at number one. Laine intended to close the gap.

They had first faced each other on April 26, 2015, at the World Under-18 Championships in Switzerland. The Americans prevailed 2–1 in overtime over Finland in that U18 head-to-head game. Matthews had an assist on the game-tying goal in the third period and nine shots on net. Laine registered no points and a lone shot. The Americans would go on to win the tournament.

They were in the same tournament again at the 2016 World Junior Championship in Helsinki in Laine's home country of Finland, though the two teams didn't face each other. Matthews had seven goals and four assists as the Americans finished third, with an 8–3 win over Sweden. Laine, though, helped Finland win U20 gold, leading the tournament with seven goals and six assists. He and

Jesse Puljujärvi both bolstered their standing in the eyes of scouts following their dominating performances.

By then, NHL Central Scouting had Matthews listed at number one, Puljujärvi at number two, with Laine rocketing up to number three. It was Laine whom everyone was talking about. He was six foot four with a shot so lethal he could score from anywhere, as seventeen goals in forty-six games in the SM-Liiga had proved. Laine led Tappara Tampere to the Finnish Liiga championship, scoring a playoff-high ten goals. "He was an absolute monster," Tappara defenceman Nick Plastino told Postmedia. "He was definitely the best player on the ice."

"Laine is a different guy," said Finland's Leo Komarov, Matthews's future teammate in Toronto. "He's a little bit shy and doesn't know us yet, but when you come up to the [senior] team in Finland, you can be yourself. We know who he is. He's got a good shot, and he's going to be a good player."

Now at the World Championships in St. Petersburg, Russia, the two eighteen-year-olds were on their senior national teams with Laine hoping to unseat Matthews as the presumptive first overall pick in the upcoming June draft.

Coming into the Finland-USA clash, Matthews had two goals and three points in his first two games. Canada had held him off the score sheet, but Belarus couldn't. He'd averaged over 18:13 of ice time with six shots on goal over the first two games. Matthews started the tournament skating on a line with Jordan Schroeder and Patrick Maroon. Against Belarus, Frank Vatrano replaced Maroon. Matthews played the left point on the power play.

Laine came into the game as Finland's leading scorer with six points. He had already broken the record for total points by a player eighteen and under at the World Championships set by

Jaromír Jágr in the 1990 tournament in Switzerland with three goals and two assists.

Laine had been put on a line with two NHLers, Aleksander Barkov and Jussi Jokinen, and they performed well as a trio. Three of Laine's four goals were scored on the power play. He was averaging 14:07 minutes per game.

Matthews and the Americans kept Laine off the scoreboard for the first time in the tournament. Laine managed three shots, took a penalty for hooking, and was minus-1 in 13:21 of ice time.

It was Laine's turnover in the first period that led to the USA goal. It was Matthews who stripped him of the puck, setting up Vatrano's goal.

"I was just trying to make a play," said Matthews of that first goal. "They kind of caught us on a fast break, and I poked the puck and Vatrano made a really nice shot coming down the left side." Matthews played 19:09, managed two shots, and was plus-1. Matthews played well, moving the puck but struggling on face-offs against Barkov. But Finland won 3–2.

"This was the worst game for me in a long time," Laine told the Associated Press after the game. "The most important thing is those three points [for winning]."

Canada would go on to win the tournament. Connor McDavid scored the winning goal against Finland, but Laine was named the tournament MVP, with seven goals and five assists.

Laine was named Finnish Player of the Year, and he won the Jari Kurri Award as the Liiga's Best Player in Playoffs. He rewrote the league's record books by soring seventeen goals and thirty-three assists as a rookie. He led the playoffs with ten goals. He was rookie of the year. He had led Finland to World Junior gold, leading the tournament with seven goals, and was named to the World Junior All-Star Team. For good measure, he kept it going with the senior national team, named best forward in the World Championship, posting the most points by a player under twenty years of age. He was the tournament's most valuable player as Finland won silver. In essence, Laine had the best season any eighteen-year-old player ever had.

The Matthews Sweepstakes had turned into a two-horse race. NHL Central Scouting listed Laine as the second-best prospect, supplanting Puljujärvi. But still, Matthews held that number-one position.

As Laine took in the combine in Buffalo in early May, where top prospects are run through a battery of physical and mental tests, he was asked by Sportsnet who should go numbers one, two, and three overall. He didn't hesitate.

"Me, Matthews, and Puljujärvi."

The "this guy or that guy" debate is part of NHL Draft lore. But Laine's attitude, on top of his season, had given it an edge.

"There was a lot of argument about whether or not he was as good," said Marc Crawford, Matthews's coach in Zurich. Crawford had taken in all the tournaments: the U18s, the World Juniors, and the World Championships featuring Laine on the Finnish side and Matthews on the American side.

"That Finnish team was remarkable," Crawford said of the U20 World Junior team. "It was really a great year for fans, the 1997 group. In terms of Auston, I thought the Americans were rolling, but they ended up having a bad game. And in those short-term competitions, that's all it takes. I certainly respected the talent of Laine, seeing them both at the Under-18s. That was the true head-to-head at that age. The US had a great team with all the people that [eventually made] the NHL. Auston was outstanding. I certainly thought he was a much more complete player, where I thought Laine was just pure shooter."

So, despite everything Laine had done and accomplished, it still wouldn't be enough for the skilled and speedy right winger to supplant Matthews in the upcoming draft in Buffalo.

"There had to be discussion about the other players because you have to do that," Lou Lamoriello, then GM of the Maple Leafs, told me. "Auston Matthews was our unanimous number one in our mind." The Leafs didn't have any doubts they would take Matthews. Lamoriello, assistant GMs Mark Hunter and Kyle Dubas, and their top scouts all agreed. Of course, they kept that part private. They wouldn't announce who they were going to pick until the draft itself.

So the "Matthews or Laine?" debate gained traction every time Leaf scouts or management were spotted watching Laine, or for that matter, Puljujärvi, through the regular season. It all makes sense now. They didn't know for sure they would get the first overall pick until April 29, so they had to have a good look at all the top prospects.

"You have to remember, we didn't know where we would pick," says Lindsay Hofford, then an amateur scout for the Leafs, later the director of scouting for eastern regions. "So we had to know who we might take second or third. There was never really a question that we weren't going to draft him. We never really got into a real deep dive through the season because if we won [the lottery], he was the one we were taking."

The Maple Leafs were sold on Matthews, the California-born, Arizona-raised prodigy, as a franchise-altering player.

"It was an easy one," says Mark Hunter, then the assistant GM under Lou Lamoriello. "Everybody agreed. Period. Babcock. Lou, Dubey, Shanny. Everybody."

Hofford thinks about it another way, considering what might

have been over the 2015 and 2016 drafts. Had the Arizona Coyotes taken Marner with that third pick in 2015, the Leafs would have taken Dylan Strome. Had the Leafs fallen to third in 2016, they would have taken Puljujärvi. Neither player has had the kind of career projected for them on draft night in Buffalo in 2016.

"So all of a sudden you could have had Puljujärvi and Strome, as opposed to Matthews and Marner," said Hofford. "It's a big swing. There's some luck that goes into this stuff. The stars were aligned for us."

CHAPTER ELEVEN

Young Guns

At draft night on June 24 in Buffalo, a phalanx of Maple Leafs executives, led by co-owner Larry Tanenbaum and President Brendan Shanahan, paraded to the podium at the KeyBank Center. Commissioner Gary Bettman introduced Leafs General Manager Lou Lamoriello to a chorus of boos from the Leaf-hating Sabres fans, or was it "Lou" from the just-as-many Leaf fans in attendance?

Lamoriello didn't have any last-minute discussions with staff at the draft table. He didn't need to. The team had already made up its mind after taking in the 2016 World Junior tournament. The only question about Matthews in Lamoriello's mind didn't have anything to do with hockey. And it had been answered months before.

"I wanted to meet the family," said Lamoriello, "so I reached out." The company that Brian Matthews worked for had its head office in New Jersey, close to Lamoriello's home. Brian had a meeting there. Ema had joined him.

"So I went to New Jersey," said Lamoriello. "We met at a hotel, and we spent about four hours together, talking about Auston, talking about sports, and just met them, and found out about them. And what they thought about Auston's growth, his commitment. What came through loud and clear was that he wanted to be the best of the best. And he worked hard for that and continued to work hard towards that. He was an all-around athlete. So you knew you were getting something special, but you also knew that the grass roots of the family was impeccable."

Still, in the stands with his family at the draft, Matthews was anxious, not taking anything for granted.

"My heart was beating with them walking up there," he said in the news scrum that followed. "Very nerve-wracking."

As Lamoriello stepped to the podium, he introduced Assistant GM Mark Hunter, who was also the director of player personnel, to make the pick. The cheers from the Leafs faithful in attendance rained down as Hunter called Matthews's name. There were chants of "USA."

"You're excited because you're getting a special player," said Hunter. "Some drafts there isn't that special player. And he was a special player."

Matthews first hugged his mother, Ema. Then he hugged his sisters. Then he turned to his father, Brian, for another long embrace with Brian whispering in Auston's ear.

"He said, 'Congratulations. God bless,'" said Matthews. "They were very emotional. They're very proud of me. I wouldn't be here without them."

Commissioner Gary Bettman greeted Matthews at the stairs up to the podium.

"Number one is a big deal," Bettman said. "Welcome to the NHL."

He wasn't the first American to be drafted first overall. He was the seventh. But he was the first from the Sunbelt, a nod to the progression the league had made thanks to Wayne Gretzky's popularity as a Los Angeles King, and vindication that putting franchises in the south would not just spur fan interest in hockey but also draw top athletes who could easily have excelled in other sports.

For Ema, she saw that little boy who at five told her he was going to play in the NHL see his dream come true. For Brian, whose support for Auston's dream was unquestioned and unequivocal, his faith was rewarded.

"Auston is always going to have fun. But he likes to compete. Whether it's Ping-Pong or hockey, he's going to try to beat you," Brian told Sportsnet before the draft. "Whatever expectations anybody has for him, I can guarantee his expectations far exceed what theirs are. He hates to lose. Absolutely hates to lose. He's going to do whatever it takes. He loves the town. He loves the Leafs. He understands they're starving, and he wants to deliver. He's going to do his part to help them get the Cup back."

It was a harbinger of things to come that, on the draft dais in Buffalo, Auston Matthews donned the Maple Leafs jersey, complete with a new crest that actually told a story. The slogan "Honour. Pride. Courage." was stitched inside the collar of the new jersey that was to go on sale in September, in time for the team's one-hundredth season. Those words came from legendary owner—and war hero—Conn Smythe, who had purchased the Toronto St. Pats in 1927 and rebranded them as the Maple Leafs in a nod to his military background.

"The Maple Leaf to us was the badge of courage," Smythe said then. "It was the badge that meant home. It was a badge that meant more to us than any other badge we could think of. So we chose it, hoping that possession of this badge would mean something to the team that wore it. And they would wear it with honour, pride, and courage."

The logo looked a bit like the logo worn by the Stanley Cup–winning teams of the 1960s. But the Leaf has thirty-one points, a nod to Maple Leaf Gardens' opening in 1931. It features seventeen veins, representing the year the franchise was founded (1917), and thirteen of those veins are at the top of the crest to commemorate the club's thirteen Stanley Cup championships. It was a simple way for the Maple Leafs to convey that things would be different, and that Auston Matthews would lead the charge on that front. Although the first way that he did that came a little bit out of the blue.

After the Maple Leafs picked Matthews first overall in 2016, what followed should have been easy. It wasn't. For whatever reason, a good-news story was turning into a head-scratcher.

This was no fault of Matthews, who did everything that was asked of him, including showing up to a summertime Leafs prospect camp without a contract. Yes, no contract. Somehow that detail seemed to elude the Maple Leafs.

At the time, few paid any attention to it. The assembled media was more tickled that the Leafs had a collection of young, homegrown players unlike any who had been assembled in about thirty years, when the likes of Wendel Clark, Vince Damphousse, and Al Iafrate were starting out. But there weren't these summertime camps back then. These camps were part of the evolution of the salary cap era, when developing your own players mattered a great deal. So along with Matthews those few days in the Gale Centre Arena in Niagara Falls, Ontario, the media were able to familiarize themselves with Mitch Marner, fresh off a Memorial Cup championship with the London Knights.

The Leafs were going to have seven rookies, each impressive in his own way, in the league come fall. And this camp in Niagara Falls was a chance to get to know what Matthews and Marner could bring to the table.

"I just want to learn as much as possible," Matthews said of the team's week. "Soak it all in. We have a lot of different seminars and meetings, nutritionists, trainers, sleep doctors. Then I want to go back home, work out with my trainer, skate, get better in all areas."

It was exciting. Spinaramas. Quick shots. Heads-up playmaking. Speed. The excitement was building.

In head-to-head play Marner's team beat Matthews's team 4–1 before about two hundred oohing and ahhing fans. Matthews emerged with a cut on his chin that required five stitches.

"That's hockey," he said.

Coach Mike Babcock announced that William Nylander would play with Matthews. Marner would not. That was Babcock being Babcock, denying fans the one thing they wanted to see.

Not at the camp were the likes of William Nylander, Zach Hyman, and Connor Brown, who'd been with the Marlies in 2015–16 and had already had cups of coffee with the big team. Nor was Nikita Zaitsev, a defenceman coming over from Russia. The Leafs were assembling an impressive array of rookies.

"Although it appears we'll be a young group again, we'll have an exciting young group," Brendan Shanahan said at a Hockey Hall of Fame event to commemorate the Leafs' one-hundredth year. "It's a matter of growing together."

That camp ended with Matthews still without a deal. This thing about Matthews not having a contract was puzzling. Why? Because he was the first overall pick. His contract was about as cut-and-dried as there could be. It's laid out in the collective bargaining agreement: a three-year entry-level deal at $925,000 a season plus bonuses. It turns out it was the bonuses that were the holdup. Lou Lamoriello was as old school as they come. He hated giving out bonuses, at least individual bonuses. Team-based bonuses were okay, but anything that separates a player from his teammates is a no-no in Lamoriello's eyes.

A few years earlier, he'd convinced the fourth overall pick, Swedish defenceman Adam Larsson, to accept a no-bonus deal, and that didn't sit well with any agent. But Lamoriello's reputation was well known.

After many years helming the New Jersey Devils, Lamoriello had been hired the previous season after the Leafs had drafted Marner fourth overall. The Leafs' Brandon Pridham was in charge of contracts before Lamoriello came aboard and had written up a deal that offered Marner bonuses. There was nothing untoward about that. It's standard practice for high-end picks.

Marner didn't sign right away. Lamoriello was hired as the Leafs' GM on July 23, 2015. There were a few matters to attend to, but as soon as he set his sights on Marner's contract, things started moving. Lamoriello stood by the initial offer to Marner but gave the Marner camp only limited time to accept it. On July 28, 2015, they did. Such was Lamoriello's reputation.

Fast forward a year to Matthews. The Matthews camp was worried that Lamoriello would draw a line. What should be a simple process could become acrimonious.

Matthews's agent, Pat Brisson, and Lamoriello had dealt with each other for years. Brisson, like the rest of the hockey world, respected Lamoriello immensely, but this would be a challenge. Lamoriello was philosophically opposed to handing out performance bonuses. Brisson needed a plan.

"I told Judd [Moldaver, Brisson's assistant] and Brian [Matthews], I said, 'We've got to manage this the right way,'" said Brisson. As Brisson and Lamoriello spoke in the wake of draft night, neither side brought up bonuses, or even talked contract. Instead, Brisson told Lamoriello of a conversation he'd had with legendary college basketball coach Mike Krzyzewski about adapting to stay relevant. Coach K told Brisson and others that brands like Kodak were gone because they'd fail to adapt, and that if he'd recruited basketball players the same way he did twenty-five years ago, he'd be gone, too.

"I was waiting for Lou to come to me," said Brisson. "I didn't want to embarrass Lou because we had all the leverage."

Other agents were talking. It was absurd. "This year's first overall pick gets the same deal as last year's first overall pick." And so on and so on down through the top ten, with the dithering starting beyond that.

Lamoriello was standing in the way of Matthews getting the same contract that Connor McDavid had received from Edmonton a season earlier, signed July 3, 2015, a week after the draft.

The media had started to notice and ask awkward questions like "What's taking so long? How long could this drag out?" It was going to be a shorter summer than usual, with Matthews having accepted an invitation to be part of the World Cup of Hockey, as part of the Under-23 Team North America, who came to be known as the Young Guns. If he was going to play, he needed a deal.

On July 21, 2016, I wrote a story for the *Toronto Star* citing Lamoriello's reluctance to hand out performance bonuses as a reason for the delay. Matthews wanted the same deal that McDavid received (and for that matter, second overall pick Jack Eichel received) the previous year: $2.85 million in signing bonuses that would be easily attainable, such as finishing top five in rookie of the year voting.

The story made the point that it was a needless fight. Matthews was going to win. To make it a war sent the wrong message to Matthews, who'd have even more leverage three years down the road, and to other star players that the Leafs weren't treating players right.

"This one to me feels foolish," an executive from another team told the *Star*. "I don't know what Lou's reward is if he wins for the amount of risk you take going this direction."

In an effort to get Lamoriello's side of the story, the *Star* sent an unpublished version of the story to the Leafs' PR team so they'd have full knowledge of what was to come, argue about any perceived unfairness or errors, and have plenty of time for Lamoriello's side of the story to be told. Lamoriello and the Leafs declined to comment.

Later the same day the story was published, Lamoriello proved he could adapt. A deal was announced that agents said should have been wrapped in a bow by the time the second round of the draft had begun.

"Lou never challenged me on that," said Brisson. "He was cool, basically expecting it. He never said, 'I don't give bonuses.' But I prepared Brian to stay strong in the event he goes there. But he never went there, so we signed a full package."

Matthews is a trailblazer in many ways, an ice hockey prodigy from an arid desert state. But perhaps nothing was more unique than being the first player to whom old-school Lamoriello offered a full bonus package—$2.85 million each year of the three-year deal.

With the deal signed and the future firm, Auston Matthews moved to Toronto, into a condo overlooking Lake Ontario just west of the Air Canada Centre. Brian Matthews helped him move in.

Matthews joked that he was used to moving. He moved from the family home in Scottsdale to Michigan at fifteen to join the US Development Program. And he moved overseas at seventeen to Zurich to play in the Swiss league during his draft year. Then, it was his mother, Ema, and sister Alexandria who lived with him overseas. This year, Brian would be more the fixture as Matthews adjusted to life in Toronto and in the NHL. The move was easy.

"I tried to learn from last year going to Zurich," Matthews told the *Star*. "I think I packed too much, and that's a much longer trip. I slimmed down the suitcases this year."

Given the unusual nature of his road to the NHL—from Arizona via Switzerland—it only goes to follow that his first September in the NHL would be anything but normal.

Typically, just-drafted players head to a rookie camp prior to the main camp. The Leafs were to have theirs in London, Ontario, where former London Knight standout Mitch Marner would star. The main Leaf camp would include five days in Halifax. But Matthews would instead be at the World Cup of Hockey.

It was, well, an interesting concept. Hockey players and hockey fans crave best-on-best international hockey, and the NHL craves making money and trying to be relevant, and it always seems to find a muddy middle ground.

Olympic hockey had been a big hit, at least as far as the fans, especially those in Canada, with gold medals in 2002, 2010, and 2014 for the men's team. But the NHL long fretted it doesn't gain anything from Olympic participation. It can't even use the video highlights of its players.

So the idea of a World Cup was revived. It started as the Canada Cup in 1976, and there have been changes to the name and the format along the way. Unlike soccer's World Cup, which is appointment viewing for the planet like clockwork every four years, the NHL's international tournament is sporadic, probably part of the niche nature of the sport and conservative-minded owners who don't really reap the benefits of their stars playing elsewhere but bear the risks of those same players getting injured.

The event occurred roughly every three to five years. Sometimes not even that. Canada won in 1976. The Soviet Union won in 1981. Canada won the next three in '84, '87, and '91.

The Canada Cup became the World Cup, with the Americans winning, in 1996. Canada won the next one, eight years later, in 2004, the last meaningful hockey before the season-long lockout brought the game the salary cap.

Now the idea was revived, with some oddball twists. Canada, the US, Sweden, Finland, Russia, and the Czech Republic would be represented. But NHL-level talent thinned out after the Big Six hockey countries. Germany had a few players, and Slovakia, too, and Slovenia. What was the point of, say, Latvia in the tournament and losing 8–0 when you could have a team of Pan-European All-Stars? And with the glut of talent in North America, why not put all the kids under the age of twenty-three together?

It seemed absurd, not like a real World Cup. Basically an NHL All-Star event. It was panned by the critics and the fans.

That was, until they saw Team North America actually play.

"I think it's going to be a good learning experience for me," said Matthews at the end of August 2016. "I mean it's the best-on-best tournament. It's going to be the highest level of hockey you can play."

Team North America held its training camps in Montreal, Quebec City, and Pittsburgh. Connor McDavid was named captain. Matthews sat between Sean Couturier and Brandon Saad, who was next to McDavid, who was next to Mark Scheifele.

Excitement was palpable early in training camp when Head Coach Todd McLellan paired the top two picks of the 2015 draft, Connor McDavid and Jack Eichel, with the electric Johnny Gaudreau. Similar electricity was evident when McLellan teamed up Nathan MacKinnon, Auston Matthews, and Ryan Nugent-Hopkins, all number-one picks.

"They're the team that's scary, right," Team Canada forward Tyler Seguin told the Canadian Press. "Because that's a team that really has no pressure."

Connections of this kind might never be seen again for many reasons, including the long-term uncertainty of the tournament and its format.

"There's no question it's been a very interesting exhibition series," Lamoriello said. "First of all, I'm extremely impressed with the young players, North America, as far as their speed. When you see all their talent together, that sticks out."

Matthews was the youngest player on Team North America, with his nineteenth birthday just a few days away when the tournament started. Finland's Patrik Laine, who went second to Matthews in the draft, was the youngest player in the tournament. Most expected Matthews to play as Team North America's thirteenth forward, given his lack of NHL experience. In international hockey, teams dress an extra forward and extra defenceman. Those players usually don't get a lot of ice time, given they're not attached to a line. But, of course, this is Auston Matthews we're talking about.

"He got better every game," North American Coach Todd McLellan told the *Toronto Star*. "We've talked about his maturity level, his skill set, the way he plays the game. He's physical. In baseball, they call it a five-tool player. That's Auston."

That was the stage as he prepared to play his first game at the Air Canada Centre, the rink he would be calling home. Matthews got the biggest cheer of anyone on the ice during the introductions. And if the applause was any metric, Auston Matthews was already beloved.

"There's a lot more hype about him than when I made my debut," said Leafs and North America defenceman Morgan Rielly. "The fans are very happy he's on this team. He has a chance to make a big impact on Team North America, and moving forward, the Leafs as well. He's ready for it. He's very mature. He'll be fine."

The first opponent: Patrik Laine and Team Finland. The Matthews vs. Laine backstory would follow both players around that year. It was probably overblown at the draft, and neither wanted any part of it at the World Cup.

The backstory pitted Matthews, the top pick in the June draft who had just turned nineteen, against Patrik Laine, the number-two pick by the Winnipeg Jets.

"It's Team North America versus Team Finland," Matthews said before the game. "We're not making too much of it."

Laine had been the more colourful of the two, declaring before the draft he should be picked first overall by the Leafs. But that kind of talk had died down from the youngster.

"I don't really care," said Laine. "I just want to have a good tournament. I don't want to think about how other players are going to play."

They dropped the puck. The speed and skill of Team North America trounced that of Finland for a 4–1 win. Team North America went from outlier to tournament challenger to crowd favourite.

"That was amazing, probably the most fun hockey I've ever played," said Winnipeg Jets star Mark Scheifele. "A lot of fun."

Scheifele had been in the NHL a fair bit by then and knew most of the players, either by playing with or against them through the years, sometimes working out with them in the summer. One player he didn't know much about coming into camp was Auston Matthews. He got to know him a lot better.

"You knew he was a talented hockey player," said Scheifele. "You heard the buzz before he was drafted, and you watch him play World Juniors and stuff like that. You can see he's a pretty special player, a fantastic hockey player, fun to watch. And it's kind of cool that his kind of coming-out party was at the World Cup."

It turns out Matthews had the same pregame warm-up routine as Scheifele: stay out on the ice as long as possible before the game to get as many puck touches as possible.

"Auston had just got drafted," said Scheifele. "He and I would stay on the ice, passing. He just never quit. It was fun to see, especially a young kid that just went first overall. Just loved to be on the ice, loved to shoot the puck, pass the puck, work on certain things. Every game, we were just a bunch of young bucks who just loved to play the game. We played fast, we played energetic, we played an offensive-style game, and it was just great."

Auston Matthews (middle row, far right) and the Arizona Jr. Coyotes

PAT MAHAN

Matthews (third from left) with the Arizona Bobcats

PAT MAHAN

Matthews (front row, second from trophy, on the right) and the Bobcats celebrate their U16 Tier 1 Arizona championship.

PAT MAHAN

Matthews dresses for a Ukrainian hockey team at the Quebec International Pee-Wee Hockey Tournament.
QUEBEC INTERNATIONAL PEE-WEE HOCKEY TOURNAMENT

Auston Matthews with his family: older sister Alexandria, younger sister Breyana, parents Ema and Brian, and his skating coach Boris Dorozhenko

BORIS DOROZHENKO

Lawton Courtnall and Auston Matthews in Whistler, BC

RUSS COURTNALL

Auston Matthews (top row, in red, third from right) and fellow skaters at Boris Dorozhenko's Next Generation Hockey camp. They include Lawton Courtnall and Eddy Wong.

BORIS DOROZHENKO

Boris Dorozhenko visits Auston Matthews in Switzerland, where Matthews spent his draft season.

BORIS DOROZHENKO

Matthews wears his number 34 for the Zurich Lions.

ROBERT HRADIL/HOCKEY HALL OF FAME

Matthews raises the U18 World Championship trophy for Team USA.
MATT ZAMBONIN/INTERNATIONAL ICE HOCKEY FEDERATION

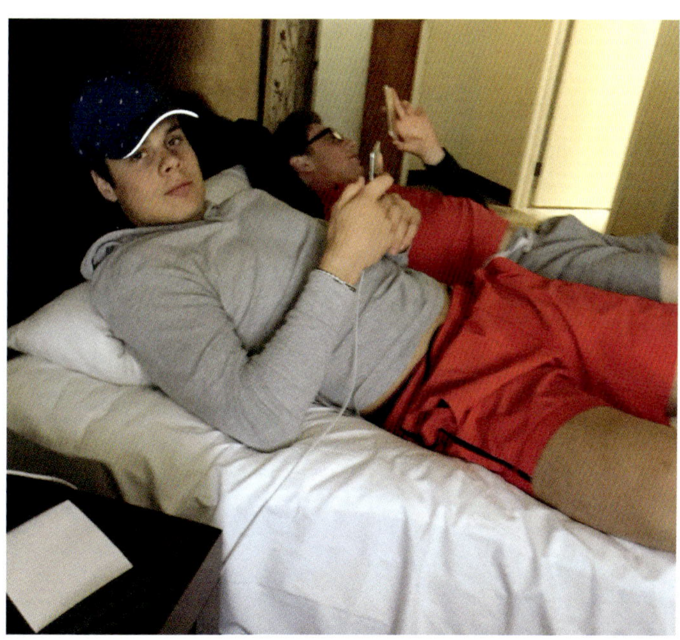

Auston Matthews and Mike Mahan in a hotel room
in Buffalo, New York, the day of the 2016 draft
PAT MAHAN

Matthews and his mother, Ema, pose outside a Mexican restaurant in downtown Toronto.

SPORTSNET

Matthews, put on the top line with McDavid and Scheifele, set the tone early in Team North America's first game, leading a rush that led to the North Americans' first goal. The effort spread throughout the team, with the lineup of young stars displaying an infectious brand of speedy, skilled hockey—dominating puck control—that the crowd at the Air Canada Centre ate up.

The young swashbucklers gained fans with every completed pass and eye-popping play in a wildly entertaining game that gave the tournament some buzz.

Matthews scored the first goal for Team North America in the next two games: a 4–3 loss to Russia and a 4–3 overtime win over Sweden.

"I think everyone in the world was hoping that it was going to be Team North America against Canada in that semifinal," said Scheifele. "We missed out by a point. But it was a blast."

The overtime point gave Sweden first place in the group. Though the Young Guns ended up tied with Russia on points, the Russians had the benefit of the first tiebreak—the win in the head-to-head game—and the Young Guns were eliminated.

"Well, if I get a vote, I'd like to do it again," said McLellan. "We've proven this young generation can play with the older one. I think if you surveyed ninety-nine out of a hundred fans, they'd probably say, 'Put them in again.'"

Some blamed McLellan for the early departure. Had he gambled instead and pulled his goalie to try for a win in regulation, rather than play in overtime and hope that Russia would lose the following day, the Young Guns may have advanced. Either way, Matthews had introduced himself to the professional hockey world and came out on top.

For the players on Team North America, it was a coming-out party. But for Auston Matthews this unique experience—never to be repeated—was only the beginning.

Hockey fans—especially in Toronto—got a taste of what he could do and wanted more. They weren't going to be disappointed.

But first, training camp.

Finally, on September 28, 2016, Matthews (and Morgan Rielly and the rest of the Leafs who were otherwise engaged at the World Cup) joined the team's main camp, which had by then returned to Toronto, with the World Cup teams no longer needing the Air Canada Centre or the Mastercard Centre practice facility in Etobicoke.

Matthews immediately formed a post-practice bond with Mitch Marner, a tradition that would carry over to pregame warm-ups. They stayed out late. "Fooling around" is how some folks might put it. But puck touches are puck touches. Passes are passes. Shots are shots. No matter who is watching.

A Matthews shot in the middle of all that missed its target and hit the glass behind the net at the Mastercard Centre, shattering it.

"Lou's not going to be happy," said Matthews. On the contrary, Lamoriello loved having a player of Matthews's obvious skill.

"I'm really not surprised with what he's done with his peers as far as his age group," Lamoriello said of Matthews's performance at the tournament. "He's going to get better and better."

The most hyped trio of rookies in Leafs history—Matthews, Marner, and Nylander—took to the ice together for the first time in a 3–2 win over the Montreal Canadiens in an exhibition game. "This could be a group together for a long time," Marner said. "I think it's just the beginning of something good."

Said Matthews: "It's encouraging to the whole group to have a lot of young guys coming up, a lot of skill throughout the whole team. It's a really exciting time to be a Toronto Maple Leaf."

It was the first time Matthews wore a Leaf jersey in a game, wearing his trademark number 34. He became the sixteenth player in Maple Leafs history to wear number 34 since Leigh Verstraete first wore it in the 1983–84 season.

Why 34? The stories vary, but they're interlinked.

As Matthews would acknowledge, 34 was more a goaltender's number when he was growing up. John Vanbiesbrouck. Miikka Kiprusoff. James Reimer. The most famous Leaf to have worn it was probably defenceman Jamie Macoun.

But 34 was Matthews's number, no moving off it. And it was low enough—more a traditional hockey number—that Lou Lamoriello approved. William Nylander, for example, wanted 88 but was assigned 39. He had to wait until Lamoriello was replaced by the younger, more progressive Kyle Dubas as GM to make the switch.

Brian Matthews wore number 34 in baseball. Auston was honouring his father. But Matthews's nickname—given to him by his mother—was Papi. It's a term of endearment in the Latino culture. The mother calling a baby "Papi" is her way of conveying pride in her son and the hope that he will grow up to be a strong and responsible man.

There was also a more famous Papi in the sports world when Matthews was growing up: Big Papi. David Ortiz of the Boston Red Sox. He wore 34 as well.

It was almost as if the number was calling him.

CHAPTER TWELVE

The Greatest Maple Leafs

As far as pageantry goes, the Maple Leafs had done very little right between May 2, 1967, and October 15, 2016. That was a total 18,064 days between the time the Maple Leafs last won a Stanley Cup and the night they retired Dave Keon's number 14.

During that time, there were no more Stanley Cup parades. There were a handful of trips to the Stanley Cup semifinals (known these days as conference finals) and a couple of eras remembered fondly by today's Leafs fans, even if captains like Darryl Sittler, Wendel Clark, Doug Gilmour, and Mats Sundin got the Leafs close, but not close enough, to the Stanley Cup Final.

With Matthews now a Leaf, the franchise was celebrating its hundredth season, and Brendan Shanahan wanted to do right by the team, its fans, and its history.

As the centennial season approached, Shanahan and the Maple Leafs had a massive marketing plan in mind, built around the heralded arrivals of William Nylander, Mitch Marner, and Auston Matthews.

The team wanted to find a way to put the past—and all that Stanley Cup drought talk—behind it. That would allow the current group to reset. They wouldn't bear the burden of past playoff failures. They'd simply embark on their own journey.

Shanahan put a massive panel of experts, including hockey writers, together to name the top one hundred Leafs of its first one hundred years. It was both an impossible and joyful task that provides a template to compare a great player from today—Auston Matthews—to those who came before.

It's Keon who holds the mantle of Greatest Maple Leaf, bestowed upon him two days before the 2016–17 home opener, and one day after Auston Matthews's four-goal debut.

Keon was a four-time Stanley Cup champion, a captain, one of the team's all-time leading scorers, a gentleman on and off the ice. He was also among the most decorated Maple Leafs. He won the Calder Memorial Trophy as rookie of the year in 1961, the Lady Byng Memorial Trophy as the league's best defensive forward in 1962 and 1963, and the Conn Smythe Trophy in 1967—the last of his four Stanley Cup triumphs—as most valuable player in the playoffs.

Though he would play in a rival league and retire as a Hartford Whaler, this son of a miner and schoolteacher from Noranda, Quebec, would always be remembered as a Maple Leaf. But that doesn't mean it was easy or that there was always love between him and the Maple Leafs.

"The Toronto Maple Leafs are a distant memory, and not a good one," Keon told the *Star* in a rare interview in 1997. "I could care less about the Maple Leafs."

It's not how it started. *Toronto Star* columnist Jim Proudfoot called Keon the "brightest prospect" the Leafs had landed since Frank Mahovlich. As he was a young hockey player in Noranda, the Detroit Red Wings owned his rights (from ages twelve to fifteen). But he switched to an independent team, the Noranda Lions, coached by a Leaf scout, Vince Thompson. The Leafs took over as sponsor to secure his rights. His parents let him go to Toronto on the proviso he attended St. Mike's College, a prestigious private Catholic school (which was also part of the Leafs feeder system).

His cousin was a former Leaf, Tod Sloan, who advised him, "No matter how bad things look, don't ever get discouraged."

He was small, just five foot nine, but he knew how to play. Always a good offensive player, Keon used his time in junior with the St. Mike's Majors, under the tutelage of Father Dave Bauer and Bob Goldham, to learn how to play defensively. When he got to the NHL, he was a complete two-hundred-foot player, a crafty playmaker and relentless forechecker.

When the game was on the line, especially in the Stanley Cup Final, Keon was typically out against the other team's best centre: Jean Béliveau of the Habs or Stan Mikita for the Blackhawks or Alex Delvecchio of the Red Wings.

Ultimately, he would win the Stanley Cup four times in Toronto, with George Armstrong as captain and Punch Imlach as the coach and GM, in the last great heyday of the Maple Leafs: the 1960s.

But all good things come to an end. Imlach was fired. Armstrong retired. Team ownership was in flux.

On October 31, 1969, at age twenty-eight, Keon was named captain of the Toronto Maple Leafs. It turned out to be a tumultuous reign, one that pitted Keon against Harold Ballard, who would assume full control of the team in 1971 in the wake of the death of co-owner Stafford Smythe, son of the franchise founder Conn Smythe, and with the rival WHA just getting under way.

Ballard was a notorious skinflint and headline-seeker. He would insult and berate his players publicly for their performance, would get into contract squabbles, and ultimately would deplete the franchise's talent pool. Keon was among the first to feel Ballard's wrath.

Through the post–Stanley Cup 1970s, cantankerous owner Harold Ballard gutted the team. Captains were shipped away. Keon was chief among them, Ballard unwilling to sign him or trade his rights to an NHL team that wanted him. It was out of spite more than anything.

Leafs President Brendan Shanahan, named to the post in 2014, had some bridges to mend. He had a plan to take the team out of the doldrums of the Phil Kessel–Dion Phaneuf years. He gathered young talent. He changed the logo, one that had a story to tell beyond "Toronto Maple Leafs."

If there's something different about today's breed of young players, they expect to be treated well. First-class travel. Their own rooms on the road. Gyms at the ready. Nutritionists on staff. Masseurs. Not only do they expect to be treated well; they expect their team to treat everybody well. Do what's right.

Shanahan needed Keon back in the fold. He needed to do what was right.

The groundwork had been laid when the team approached Keon to allow his likeness to be unveiled outside the Air Canada Centre along Legends Row in time for the 2016–17 season. But Shanahan had something else in mind, something he wanted his new young players to see. And Keon's participation was at the heart of it.

Keon had many good reasons to eschew the Maple Leafs franchise. Ballard had sent him into exile in the WHA, going so far as to nix a trade for his playing rights in 1979. The Islanders wanted him. They got Butch Goring instead, starting a run of four straight Stanley Cup championships that perhaps Keon might have instead been a part of.

When he came back as a Hartford Whaler after the NHL absorbed four WHA teams for the 1979–80 season, he scored a goal and received a standing ovation from the Maple Leaf Gardens crowd. When the Gardens closed in 1999, he declined to be part of the ceremonies.

"I will have nothing to do with the Toronto Maple Leafs," Keon told the *Toronto Star.* "I won't have anything to do with any event involving the Toronto Maple Leafs."

Keon was also irked that the Leafs had long retired Bill Barilko's number 5 and Ace Bailey's number 6, but no others. Instead, the playing greats were honoured—their names and sweaters hung in the rafters—but their numbers were kept in circulation.

The idea was that the number would go to a player worthy of it. It just didn't work out that way. Peter Ing and Mark Laforest were among those who wore the heralded number 1 of Johnny Bower and Turk Broda. Zdeněk Nedvěd and Aaron Gavey wore the number 10 of George Armstrong and Teeder Kennedy. Miroslav Ihnačák wore the number 27 of Darryl Sittler and Frank Mahovlich. The list goes on.

Each of those players, or their surviving family members, took part in a celebration to raise those "honoured" numbers to the rafters.

Keon said no, and the few times he would participate in Leaf-related events—he would always support nights that honoured the Cup-winning teams he was part of—the issue of the honoured number vs. retired number would come up.

"You go around the league, and the players that made this game, their numbers are retired," Keon's longtime teammate Ron Ellis said January 25, 2007, at an evening honouring the fortieth anniversary of the 1967 team. "Davey is a true traditionalist. The Leafs were his team. That was the team that he wanted to play with, and he was proud of being able to bring them to the top again and win those four Cups in the 1960s.

"He believed in the tradition of the Leafs."

At the time, Keon's 14 was being worn by Matt Stajan.

"One of the things that gets us old-timers a little concerned is when you see a sweater like Frank Mahovlich's [number 27], and then another player, who certainly deserves to be in the NHL but doesn't have the same credentials as Frank Mahovlich, is wearing it," Ellis continued. "I think that takes something away from the number."

On that Saturday night home opener against Boston—a day after Keon had been named the Greatest Leaf—came Shanahan's ultimate showpiece, with current players like Matthews and Marner watching.

All those previously "honoured" numbers were officially retired. The last one still in use was Börje Salming's number 21. James van Riemsdyk had worn it since he became a Leaf in 2011, and wore it through training camp and the first road game of the season. He switched to 25 that night.

"When you asked questions, people really didn't have an answer as to why we weren't [retiring numbers]," said Shanahan to reporters that night. "I like the story of players handing numbers down, honoured numbers, and handing them down to another player. But I don't remember Börje handing a sweater to JVR. It wasn't happening. It's a great story, but if you're not doing it, then let's do the right thing."

Suddenly, all the "honoured" numbers were instantly retired: number 1 (Turk Broda, Johnny Bower), number 4 (Hap Day, Red Kelly), number 7 (King Clancy, Tim Horton), number 9 (Ted Kennedy, Charlie Conacher), number 10 (Syl Apps, George Armstrong), number 13 (Mats Sundin), number 17 (Wendel Clark), number 27 (Frank Mahovlich, Darryl Sittler), and number 93 (Doug Gilmour). They joined long-ago retired numbers, number 5 (Bill Barilko) and number 6 (Ace Bailey).

The ceremony was massively well received. But what about number 14?

"Leaf Nation, we have one more player to honour this evening," the in-house announcer told the crowd.

The Air Canada Centre was brought to its knees with what happened next. Dave Keon walked out onto the ice surface to deafening applause to watch his number 14 raised to the rafters. Finally, and properly, retired.

"I was pleased they made the decision," Keon told reporters that night. "All great franchises retired numbers of players who brought glory to their franchises. I just didn't think the Leafs should be any different."

This time they got it right.

And for the next generation of players, Auston Matthews included, the bar was set.

CHAPTER THIRTEEN

The Calder

For a franchise that was celebrating its hundredth season in Matthews's rookie campaign, the Maple Leafs hadn't won a lot of individual trophies. Nine had won the Calder Trophy, which goes to the NHL's rookie of the year, all of them in the Original Six era or earlier. The last was Brit Selby in 1966. He scored twenty-seven points in his rookie season—the fewest by any Calder-winning forward since 1937–38—and was ultimately lost in the expansion draft in the summer of 1967 to the Philadelphia Flyers.

As the goals poured in for Matthews's first game, the world took notice, pride beaming from Phoenix, his former Arizona Bobcats coach Ron Filion chiming in. "I know it's already creating a big buzz," Filion told ArizonaSports.com. "At our rink, it was crazy. I'm sure it was on everybody's lips at every rink in town. Everybody's embracing Papi as their own."

Matthews's four-goal debut instantly made him a candidate for the Calder, and indeed, everybody seemed to want a piece of Matthews. There was a real buzz around hockey, so much so that something almost unheard of happened: NBC Sports, the American broadcaster that fed US eyes a steady diet of Chicago Blackhawks, New York Rangers, and Detroit Red Wings games, changed its schedule on the fly just so Americans could watch the Maple Leafs play the Bruins in the second game of the season.

"He can absolutely be a star here in the US," NBC Sports Executive Producer Sam Flood told the *Star*. "A record four goals in his NHL debut and the chance to showcase his home debut was too good to pass up."

Matthews was becoming big news down south, with the likes of ESPN and *The New York Times* interested in the impression this kid from the desert was making on Canada's game.

The day after he scored those four goals was a practice day. The enormity of what he'd done had started to sink in, with texts, tweets, and well-wishes headed his way. He was asked the next day how he'd slept.

"It took me a while to finally settle down and get to bed," Matthews said. "There were a lot of congratulations from a lot of guys. It's just one game, but your first one is always special."

Name recognition and good first impressions help with the people who vote for the Calder. The voters are members of the Professional Hockey Writers Association and a few select broadcasters.

But, of course, that was just game one of eighty-two—more precisely, game one of a 1,230-game regular-season schedule because there's more than just the Maple Leafs in the league.

And there were more than just Matthews among high-profile rookies, as the Leafs would discover in their third game of the season. Matthews had gone without a point his second game, a home win over the Boston Bruins. Then came a head-to-head match with Patrik Laine and the Jets in Winnipeg.

Matthews actually took a moment before the game to reflect on the circle of life. This was the second version of the Winnipeg Jets, having relocated from Atlanta where they were born the Thrashers. The original Jets had moved to Phoenix all those years before, with

Matthews seeing his first game at age two with Uncle Billy and falling in love with the game.

"If [the Jets] didn't move down there in 1996–97, or whatever it was, I probably wouldn't be playing hockey," Matthews told the *Toronto Star.* "So I guess I was fortunate for that to happen."

Matthews got an assist as the Leafs jumped off to a 4–0 lead. But those Leafs had trouble holding leads, and Laine whittled it away. One goal, then another as the Jets built confidence and tied the game, and the fun-loving fans chanted "Laine's better."

Then finally, in overtime, Matthews was stopped on a breakaway by Winnipeg goaltender Michael Hutchinson, then Laine led a rush and beat Frederik Andersen for the game-winner. Laine was the hero. A hat trick. The Jets won 5–4. Now Laine tied Matthews at four goals for the rookie scoring race. In just one week, the Calder conversation moved from Matthews to Laine.

"Everybody is talking about it," Finnish hockey reporter Juha Hiitelä told the *National Post.* "You look at social media and parliament members and politicians are tweeting about it. It's like déjà vu from last year, except it's happening in the NHL."

Teemu Selänne, known as the Finnish Flash in his playing days, got in on the action, tweeting his pride after Laine's hat trick, writing "new sheriff in town" followed by three hat symbols and the words "congrats" and "wow." Selänne started his career with those original Jets, scoring seventy-six goals on his way to the Calder in 1993.

It wasn't only a "Matthews vs. Laine" scenario that was brewing. There were other serious Calder contenders on his own team: Mitch Marner and William Nylander. They got off to solid starts to their careers as well.

Marner was the local boy from Thornhill, a product of the Greater Toronto Hockey League, which produces more NHLers than any other league and most other countries. The Leafs chose Marner fourth overall in 2015 out of the London Knights. Though Marner probably could have played in the NHL the following season, the Leafs returned him to the OHL, where he led the Knights to the Memorial Cup and collected the Red Tilson Trophy as the Ontario Hockey League's outstanding player.

Marner grew up admiring the Leafs and played hockey thanks to the devotion of his father, Paul, who sold auto parts, and his mother, Bonnie, who worked at Ontario Power Generation. Marner also competed with his older brother Chris in road hockey.

Paul Marner told the *Star* in the summer of 2015 that he figured the family spent between $600,000 and $700,000 on hockey—on both boys—when the all-in price tag was considered, from registration fees to new equipment to private lessons, hotels, and gas money to get to tournaments for both sons.

"It's staggering when you think what most hockey parents spend," said Paul at the time. "We're one of the lucky ones where at the end of it hopefully Mitch is going to have a career out of it. That's not why you do it. But it's an expensive sport, very expensive at the upper level."

Though fans would clamour for years when Mike Babcock was coach to see the magical Marner and goal-scoring Matthews play on the same line together, it wasn't to be in that first season. Marner drew the right wing assignment on what was then the first line, with Tyler Bozak and James van Riemsdyk. "You like to play him with guys with hockey sense," said Coach Mike Babcock in October. "[Marner] generates a lot. I think he's been really good. He's good defensively, way better than I thought." Marner scored his first goal in the Leafs home opener against Boston, a Toronto win.

Matthews centred an all-rookie line, with Zach Hyman on his left wing and Nylander on his right.

The Leafs used an unprecedented number of rookies that season, with seven of them going on to become NHL regulars: Matthews, Marner, Hyman, Nylander, Connor Brown, Nikita Zaitsev, and Kasperi Kapanen, who joined the party late.

Nylander was almost as intriguing a player as Matthews and Marner. His father, Michael, was a longtime NHLer, and William had many of his father's attributes in terms of skill and speed. Born in Calgary, Nylander nonetheless was a proud Swede.

The Leafs' choice of Nylander eighth overall in 2014 was the true beginning of the Shanaplan. Had Brian Burke still been running the show, it would have been likely the Leafs would have chosen the more brutish Nick Ritchie at eight. Ritchie went tenth to the Anaheim Ducks. He would later—and briefly—join the Maple Leafs as a free agent, though it was not a good fit, as it turned out.

Nylander played part of the 2014–15 season in Sweden with MoDo, then joined the Marlies at nineteen to play for future Leaf coach Sheldon Keefe.

Like Marner, Nylander probably could have made the 2015–16 Leafs, but that might have meant too much winning. So it was another year with the Marlies, though he did get a twenty-two-game NHL call-up (six goals, seven assists) that gave the world a taste of what he could do.

With three top centres—Bozak, Matthews, and Nazem Kadri (playing mostly with Brown and Leo Komarov)—the Leafs were able to create mismatches against the opposition, and it was Nylander who benefited the most early on.

Nylander—not Matthews, nor Marner, nor Laine—was named Rookie of the Month that October. He had eleven points (four goals, seven assists) in nine games to lead all rookies, and he had the most power-play points in the league with seven.

Broadcasters weren't the only ones changing their schedules.

Wayne Gretzky changed his, too, just so he could be at the game to watch number-one overall picks from back-to-back years play each other: Connor McDavid vs. Auston Matthews.

If Matthews vs. Laine didn't pan out, then maybe Matthews vs. McDavid would. It was almost a sin that McDavid didn't win the Calder in his rookie year, voters holding it against him that he missed nearly half the season with an injury. Still, many believed McDavid was on his way to establishing himself as the heir apparent to Sidney Crosby as the best player in the game, with Matthews cast as the Ovechkin-like goal-scoring foil.

"All eyes will be on those two kids, no doubt about it," said Gretzky before Connor McDavid's Oilers played Auston Matthews and the Toronto Maple Leafs. "I'll be watching. That's why I flew in. I'm excited to see the game. I think it's great for our sport.

"Both of those kids seem to understand their scenario and their responsibility to not only the team but to the league. They are both really good, young, mature kids. It's great for hockey. It is great to see."

In a way, Wayne Gretzky was responsible for Auston Matthews.

It's only partly because Gretzky raised the interest level in Arizona as coach of the Coyotes around the time Matthews was honing his skills as a young hockey player. It's more because Gretzky played in Los Angeles, a superstar in a city that demands superstars, and put hockey on the map in parts of America where it had been only a curiosity. Even Gretzky acknowledged Matthews is part of that emerging group of players from hockey's former netherworlds.

"It is one of the things that has changed a little bit in the Southwest," Gretzky said. "The best athletes at eight, nine, ten, eleven play baseball, tennis, golf, or whatever. And now some of the best ones are saying: 'I want to play ice hockey.' That opens doors for a lot of other kids. And gives everybody opportunities. And exposure. What [Matthews] has done is really something special."

When Gretzky joined the league at eighteen, folks compared him to Marcel Dionne and Guy Lafleur, the best players of the day. By the time his career was over, he was generally considered the best of all time. Matthews and McDavid were on that kind of trajectory.

"It's not like they just got thrown into the frying pan and then told, 'Okay, you are the new faces of the league,'" said Gretzky. "These kids were good at fourteen and fifteen. Auston went to play in Europe as a seventeen-year-old. That was a good thing for him. You play against men, and that makes you that much better. For Connor, he has been in the limelight since he was a young boy. He handles himself very well."

The Leafs won that game, 3–2 in overtime, Nazem Kadri scoring the winner.

They were just 2–4–3 through October, a team of promising rookies offering highlights and hope, but not victories. But that win over Edmonton was the start of something bigger, an 8–5–1 run that had folks wondering just how good the team could be. By the end of November, they were a single point out of a wild-card spot, though New Jersey, Boston, and Philadelphia were all tied for that second wild card. Not only was Matthews in the hunt for the Calder, but the Leafs were in an unlikely hunt for the playoffs.

It was December 23, and the NHL schedule-maker gave Matthews an early Christmas present: his first road trip to his hometown, Leafs vs. Arizona, to face the Coyotes at Gila River Arena in Glendale, Arizona. It was front-page news.

"It'll kind of be like full circle," Brian Matthews told *The Arizona Republic* in its December 23 edition. "The fact that he's now going to be stepping on that ice and actually playing, knowing fifteen, sixteen years ago he was the one sitting on my knee watching."

"It's a huge day for Arizona hockey," Boris Dorozhenko, Matthews's old skating coach, told the *Toronto Sun* in its December 23 edition.

Matthews had scored a couple of weeks before against the Coyotes in Toronto, a 3–2 overtime win by Arizona. It was clear Matthews was looking forward to the rematch, perhaps more so for being home. He was experiencing his first eighty-two-game season, and he was still learning how much of a grind that could be.

"It's a different lifestyle, you're travelling so much, and you have a lot of downtime," Matthews said heading into the game. "The NHL is a different animal. It's an eighty-two-game schedule, and the last couple of weeks we've been playing almost every other day. It's definitely a grind, but it's something that you embrace and enjoy. It's a blast."

At game time, Leaf fans were out in full force, as usual for the NHL's best travelling fan base. Even non-Leaf fans were wearing number 34. A crew in yellow Arizona Bobcats gear held a sign: "#34 Matthews is our Bobcats brother."

Matthews took the opening draw for the Leafs, across from none other than Shane Doan, his boyhood hero. Matthews earned an assist in the Leafs' 4–1 win. But the game was special for Doan across many fronts. It was his fifteen-hundredth game. All for the same franchise, the one that started in Winnipeg, where he had his rookie season. And Doan scored career goal number four hundred.

"It's an unbelievable accomplishment. I'm happy for him, but happy we got the win as well," Matthews said. "It would have been nice if I wasn't on the ice for that one. He's been so amazing . . . not only as a hockey player for this team, but in the community."

The NHL makes a big deal about its outdoor games. The first outdoor game, dubbed the Heritage Classic, was played in 2003 in Edmonton's Commonwealth Stadium, pitting the Montreal Canadiens against the Oilers. Despite freezing temperatures, it was a massive hit. It felt like a one-off, though, an idea not broached again until January 1, 2008. The NHL noticed that college football, which once owned viewership that day with various bowls, had moved off that day. A national holiday was awaiting a sports league to fill the vacuum.

Sidney Crosby and the Pittsburgh Penguins moved in. It was Penguins vs. the Buffalo Sabres on a snowy—almost too perfect—afternoon at the home stadium of the Buffalo Bills. Crosby scored the picturesque overtime goal.

The idea became annual, with more outdoor games—about two or three each year—bringing the league's "hyper local" strategy across North America.

The Leafs would be a natural partner given the big fan base would always help fill a football-sized or baseball-sized stadium. But in the early days of the league's foray into outdoor game, the Leafs were simply not a good team.

Finally, the Leafs were pegged for a game in The Big House, the home of Michigan football in Ann Arbor, to play the Red Wings before 105,000 people on January 1, 2014. The Leafs won in a shoot-out.

In Matthews's rookie season, a rematch was set for January 1, 2017. The Centennial Classic, they called it, since both the Leafs and the NHL were celebrating their centennial season.

The city of Toronto added seating to the BMO Field (home of MLSE's soccer property, Toronto FC, as well as the Toronto Argonauts). Because BMO was not an NHL sponsor, the league and the Leafs referred to the field of play as Exhibition Stadium, since it was on the grounds of the Canadian National Exhibition, the former home of both the Blue Jays and Argonauts. More than 40,000 saw the Leafs beat the Red Wings 5–4 in overtime in what was a massive learning-curve game for Matthews.

The Leafs were up 4–3 with a minute to go when Babcock put his rookies out—Matthews, Zach Hyman, and Connor Brown—to hold the lead. They didn't. "Why don't I put the veteran guys out? Because [the kids] have got to learn," said the coach. "We had an opportunity to do it here in a big game."

Matthews was overpowered by Detroit's Henrik Zetterberg in the face-off circle. The Leafs failed to clear the puck. The Leafs had a 4–1 lead—memories of that 4–1 meltdown in Boston in 2013—in a big game, and now were tied 4–4 going into overtime.

But it was Matthews with the winner. "It was a blast out there under the sun, the setting, a couple of Original Six teams going at it against each other. Definitely one of the best moments in hockey I've ever experienced. It's pretty special."

The game-winner was Matthews's twentieth of the season. He took over the rookie goal-scoring lead from Laine with that goal and hit a $212,500 signing bonus. More importantly, the Leafs were 18–10–7, winners of five in a row, and in third place—a playoff spot—in the Atlantic Division.

There was still a lot of hockey to be played, but the Shanaplan appeared to be ahead of schedule. A team of rookies, led by the league's best rookie in Matthews, was over-performing. And everyone loved it. Everyone except TV interviewers. The prized rookies were kept off pregame, in-game, and postgame TV interviews. That was one of Lou's rules. They were still part of postgame scrums around their lockers. But they were not to be put on a pedestal with special TV appearances.

"They were going to be sheltered," former Leafs GM Lou Lamoriello told me. "When I say 'sheltered,' they weren't going to be allowed to have any distractions."

That was a conversation Lamoriello actually had with Brian and

Ema prior to the season, that Lamoriello didn't want NHL success to go to the heads of young players, that their overall development would be better if they just focused on hockey early in their careers.

"They were 100 percent on board with everything," said Lamoriello.

Though Matthews and Marner were leapfrogging each other for top spot in the team's scoring race, it was Matthews who got the nod to go to the January 29 All-Star Game in Los Angeles.

As far as All-Star Games go, it was a big deal. The league put on a show, naming the top one hundred players of the league's first one hundred years, and the biggest names in the game—Sidney Crosby and Alex Ovechkin—showed up to play.

Matthews went head-to-head against Crosby in Saturday's skills competition, losing both times. And Matthews was out whenever Crosby was out in the three-on-three games on Sunday, which pitted division against division. Crosby had a goal and an assist to Matthews's goal as Crosby's Metropolitan Division beat Matthews's Atlantic Division 10–6.

It was fun, sure, but a weekend for a nineteen-year-old Matthews to learn from the best.

"He doesn't like to lose," Matthews said of Crosby to the *Star*. "It got pretty competitive out there. He's the best player in the world. You've got to watch him. I have watched him ever since I was a young kid, so getting to play against him is the best."

There was one more impressive rookie that Matthews and the Maple Leafs had yet to face: his friend Zach Werenski. The defenceman was chosen eighth overall in the 2015 NHL Entry Draft. There was some talk then that Coach Mike Babcock urged the front office to take Werenski—a six-two left-handed defenceman—instead of Mitch Marner that year. Werenski was from Grosse Pointe,

Michigan, and played with Matthews in the US National Team Development Program, and even earlier than that, in summer hockey tournaments set up by Boris Dorozhenko.

Werenski was seventh in rookie scoring when his Blue Jackets beat Matthews's Leafs in their first head-to-head game, 5–2. Werenski had two assists. Matthews was held off the board.

Werenski was a nineteen-year-old playing top-pair minutes. Voters for postseason awards take note of that. It's not always about goals and assists, but often how important a role a player has carved out for himself.

"You don't see people control the puck the way he does," Matthews said of Werenski. "He's a big body, he's got a long stick, and he's tough to play against."

The Leafs had two more meetings with Columbus. Matthews scored in their next meeting a month later, this time Toronto winning 5–2. Werenski had an assist. Their last meeting was the final game of the season.

Matthews and company had more business to attend to before then.

Despite that loss on February 17, the Leafs stood at 26–19–11. That was fourth in the Atlantic Division, the second wild card in the playoff race.

The rebuild era—which had really only started two years prior with the drafting of Marner and the hiring of Babcock and Lamoriello—was already over. They had leapfrogged other teams that were in rebuild mode, like the Buffalo Sabres. "If in September, when we started training camp, somebody said we would find ourselves where we are today, with the number of young players we have and the number of changes that transpired, we'd sign on that dotted line," Lamoriello told the *Star*. "You have to be pleased with not only the development, but the success up to this point we have had."

This team of rookies had to learn what a playoff race was all about. Lamoriello rewarded them with the acquisition of veteran centre Brian Boyle at the cost of little-used Byron Froese and a second-round pick. The veteran acquisition went over well. That he came from the Tampa Bay Lightning—the team on the Leafs' tail—was even sweeter. They were throwing in the towel.

A playoff spot, however unlikely it might have seemed at the beginning of the season, was in their sights.

That goal in Columbus was Matthews's thirty-third of the season, the start of a hot streak. Two games later, he scored again: thirty-four for Number 34, and in doing so, tied Maple Leafs legend Wendel Clark's thirty-one-year-old record for most goals by a Leaf in his rookie season. On March 28, against Florida and ex-Leaf goalie James Reimer, he scored on a wrist shot from forty-three feet. That was his thirty-fifth goal. The team record for most goals by a rookie was his alone. He was in the midst of six goals over five games to get to thirty-nine by the seventy-eighth game of the season, the Leafs having won seven of their last eight. He went scoreless over the next two games, to Washington and Tampa. That loss to Tampa was crushing. A Leaf win would have clinched a playoff berth. As it was, the Leafs had two more games to go and had to win one of them to secure a playoff spot, the Lightning still within striking distance.

But the angst in game eighty-one was palpable, especially when goalie Frederik Andersen had to leave the game against the star-studded Pittsburgh Penguins, having taken a hit from Tom Sestito.

Andersen had gotten off to a slow start that season, but from November forward he was easily one of the best goalies in the NHL. He stole games. For a team filled with young players, Andersen was just what they needed in net, making sure their vast and many mistakes didn't end up behind him. But when the Leafs needed him most—to clinch a playoff spot—he was hurt. It was up to backup goalie Curtis McElhinney.

There was a storybook feel to the game, though. Longtime Leaf Phil Kessel was now a Penguin. He seemed to laugh when he scored the game's first goal. The player the Leafs got in return for Kessel, Kasperi Kapanen, scored a more important goal, tying the game at 14:30 of the third period. Connor Brown got the go-ahead goal at 17:12, tipping in a shot from Jake Gardiner. And McElhinney came up big, with a pad save on Sidney Crosby, who almost tied the game with forty-nine seconds to go.

It was remarkable that Coach Mike Babcock trusted the rookie to play in the final minute—against Crosby—to preserve the lead. He repaid the trust, sealing the 5–3 win with four seconds left: Matthews into the empty net. His fortieth goal. And the Leafs were back in the playoffs.

"It means everything," Matthews said of making the playoffs. "It's been our goal since the beginning of the year, to make it. We've done better each game, each segment, each month. That's been the goal for everybody. It's a big night for us, a huge clinch."

Matthews put up the greatest single season a Maple Leafs rookie had ever accomplished. He set new franchise bests by a rookie with forty goals and sixty-nine points (Peter Ihnačák had sixty-six in 1982–83). Matthews was also the only NHL player that season to record at least one shot on goal in each and every one of the eighty-two regular-season games. Teemu Selänne in 1992–93 was the last first-year player to accomplish the feat.

He didn't do it alone, of course. Toronto was to that point the only team to have had three different players (Matthews, Mitch Marner, and William Nylander) be named the NHL's Rookie of the Month in the same season. Marner's forty-two assists bettered the long-standing Leafs rookie record of forty by Gus Bodnar in

1940–41. Nylander set team rookie records with nine power-play goals and the longest point streak, which reached twelve consecutive games. Zach Hyman earned the record for most shorthanded goals by a Leafs rookie with four. Nikita Zaitsev put up thirty-six points, second only to Börje Salming's thirty-nine in 1973–74 for the highest total by a Leafs rookie defenceman.

The ballots for the NHL's postseason awards had been emailed to voters in the final week of the season. They had until the eve of the first playoff game to get their ballots in. Matthews looked like a lock for the Calder. When the tally was finally revealed, Matthews had 164 first-place votes out of 167 cast. Patrik Laine had three first-place votes. Matthews was rewarded for the best season a Leaf rookie had had in the team's hundred-year existence. The Leafs had a bona fide star, a player worthy of awards. Someone who could compete in name recognition with the likes of Sidney Crosby, Alex Ovechkin, and Connor McDavid. Someone who could be the face of hockey's most iconic franchise.

CHAPTER FOURTEEN

A Body of Work

It caused quite a stir when Auston Matthews showed up at the NHL Awards with a new tattoo of a lion, crowned as a king, on his right bicep, from shoulder to elbow, as he was about to collect the Calder Trophy as rookie of the year. It took a five-hour session with Bubba Irwin at Old Town Ink in Old Scottsdale.

What did it mean? Well, one thing it didn't mean was that Matthews wanted to play for the Los Angeles Kings, though the folks running that team's social media account didn't mind making it seem so. The Kings' mascot is that of a lion named Bailey (after late scout Garnet "Ace" Bailey, who was killed in the 9/11 terror attacks).

"Honored @AM34 got a tattoo of me on his arm," read the tweet. "Don't tell Carlton."

Of course Matthews didn't want out, but what did the lion represent? "It's got personal significance for my family," said Matthews. "That's about it. That's all I'm going to say about it."

Over the years, Matthews would add to his tattoos, including a crucifix. And emblazoned across his right side near his chest some words made famous by Martin Luther King: "The ultimate measure of a man is not where he stands in moments of comfort and convenience, but where he stands at times of challenge and controversy."

He's added the number 34, some flowers, petals, and other designs.

But the king theme stands out—the king of the jungle, the king of kings, and the social activist.

It belies his humility. Around hockey players, he's just another hockey player. Around people, he's just another person. In a hospital fundraiser or awareness campaign, he's just someone who's trying to help. With his family, he's a son or a brother. He's Papi.

But to himself, perhaps, he wants to be the king of hockey. He is driven to be the absolute best. It doesn't bother him to hear someone else being called the best. It motivates him. Far from being a negative, it's another hill to climb. Something else yet to prove.

In Las Vegas, the night before the Golden Knights would have their expansion draft, Matthews sat on the aisle, his father to his right, his mother next, his two sisters beside Ema. It was not quite a mirror image of 362 days earlier as he waited to hear his name called first overall. But it was close, given he was surrounded by family.

This was the NHL Awards, and Matthews was a finalist for the Calder, as rookie of the year. Patrik Laine of the Winnipeg Jets and Zach Werenski of the Columbus Blue Jackets were finalists as well. It wasn't close.

He was the tenth Leaf to win the Calder but the first in fifty-one years. With apologies to Alexander Mogilny's 2002–03 Lady Byng Trophy, Matthews was also the first Leaf since Doug Gilmour in 1993 to win one of the big five individual awards. (Gilmour won the Frank Selke Trophy as the best defensive forward.)

It was a recognition of a whirlwind year, one that changed Matthews's life and the course of a historic franchise. From being drafted first overall to a four-goal debut and a forty-goal season, the wunderkind gave himself a tough act to follow but promised to be better.

"Individually, you want to take a step forward," Matthews said that night.

He spoke of getting back to work, getting back to training, getting better. It was ever thus for him.

If he allowed his body to be used as a canvas to send messages about his intentions, it had to start with adding to his body of work on the ice. Many players heading into their second season have to worry about the sophomore jinx. Great rookies often stub their toes in their second season in the professional ranks. Some, because they don't train quite as hard as they did the year before. Some, perhaps because they take life as a professional for granted. Some, because the rest of the league has caught up to them, know what to expect, and play them differently.

"Let's look at it realistically, you should get better," Maple Leafs General Manager Lou Lamoriello said to the *Toronto Star* on the eve of the 2017–18 season. "But you're also now not going to sneak up on anybody. People are going to be ready for you. First time around a batting order is a little different than the second. Attention is going to be different. There are going to be a lot of things different."

Even some Hall of Famers felt the effect of the sophomore jinx. Calgary Flames forward Jarome Iginla, who would go on to win two Maurice "Rocket" Richard Trophies, went from twenty-one goals in his first season to thirteen in his second season. New York Rangers defenceman Brian Leetch scored twenty-three times in a Calder-winning rookie season, dropping to eleven the following season. The great Winnipeg Jet Teemu Selänne set an NHL rookie record of seventy-six his first season, dropping to twenty-five the following year.

But if there was a sophomore jinx, it wasn't about talent, ability, or production. It was injuries. Auston Matthews played all eighty-two games in his rookie season. It was the only time he ever did that in his first nine seasons.

As for any hockey player, injuries take their toll. Matthews played heavy minutes, usually against the other team's best offensive players, or best defensive players and top defensive defencemen.

Given his goal-scoring prowess, he was a moving target for all kinds of cheap shots. And in the hockey world, teams have come to believe if they reveal the actual injury of a player, then that part of the body is going to be targeted even more.

Folks believed Matthews was playing through some kind of injury through the early part of the 2017–18 season. There were telltale signs, like missing practises and leaving morning skates early. Finally, on November 8, 2017, Matthews missed three games to a mysterious injury. The Leafs called it "upper body." He'd been slashed that week in a game against St. Louis, so it could have been an arm, wrist, or hand injury. Those count as "upper body." But most believed it was his back.

"Just watching sucks. You want to be out there. You want to contribute," Matthews said, suggesting he could have played if it was the postseason. "But it's early in the season, you don't want to make it worse. If it's not fully recovered, if you tweak it again, you're back to square one. Be cautious."

By mid-December, Matthews was sidelined again. He had collided with Morgan Rielly in a game against the Pittsburgh Penguins, leading many to believe he had suffered a concussion. But the Leafs simply called it "upper body." In all, Matthews missed twenty games that second season. He still managed thirty-four goals and twenty-nine assists in sixty-two games, second to Mitch Marner in points and second to James van Riemsdyk in goals. But on a goals-per-game and points-per-game basis, Matthews was on a planet of his own.

There would be a great deal of drama in his third season, in 2018–19, though very little of it had to do with him. Although in some ways, it all had to do with him.

The summer of 2018 would alter the franchise. The mere fact that the Leafs had so many young players, all coming to the end of their three-year entry-level deals at roughly the same time, was now going to put pressure on management dealing with the league's restrictive salary cap.

The Leafs had had plenty of salary cap wiggle room to this point. The idea of the collective bargaining agreement, at least from the owners' point of view, was to keep young players under contract at bargain prices. For first contracts, the price was mandated (though franchises often provided performance bonuses). Second contracts were typically shorter in term, expiring in one, two, or three years—all designed to keep the players as "restricted" free agents. It was the third contract, a year or two before players hit unrestricted free agency, where they would get duly rewarded as teams "bought" their free agency years. Or, the player could wait until he hit free agency to sign a big-term deal.

But the market was changing, especially for high-end players. Connor McDavid signed an eight-year, $100 million deal, a deal that set the benchmark for NHL stars. Jack Eichel re-upped with Buffalo for eight years at $80 million. These were huge numbers for players with just three years' experience. For the Leafs, it was not just one or two players they had to worry about, but three, all of them looking at the precedents that had been set.

William Nylander was first up, his entry-level contract expiring on July 1, 2018. Auston Matthews and Mitch Marner were eligible to sign extensions starting that same day.

For Maple Leafs President Brendan Shanahan, there were other elements at play.

The Colorado Avalanche had tried to poach Assistant GM Kyle Dubas earlier that season to become their GM. Shanahan balked at letting go of one of the brightest young minds in hockey and needed to follow through on a promise to make him GM of the Maple Leafs. Lou Lamoriello's three-year deal to be GM of the Leafs was expiring, so the opportunity presented itself. On May 11, 2018, Dubas was named GM. Lamoriello was named senior advisor. But Lamoriello was soon out the door, on his way to become president of hockey operations for the New York Islanders. And assistant GM Mark Hunter, who'd also hoped to become GM of the Maple Leafs, also left, returning to run the OHL London Knights, a team he co-owned with his brother Dale.

It was an odd series of developments, almost unnecessary. The team was at a crossroads, at least as far as how its roster was going to be constructed salary-wise, which is an important element in a salary-capped league.

Two key people who had helped Shanahan get the Shanaplan up and running were gone. And now a new front office was running it.

Dubas was amiable, with an analytics mind and who understood the value of talent. But he was hardly cutthroat. His chief assistants were now-promoted Brandon Pridham, who executed the contracts and made the Leafs into leaders in the labyrinthian rules around the collective bargaining agreement, and Laurence Gilman, a well-connected hockey mind who'd paid his dues in Vancouver and Arizona. Their focus wasn't so much on getting Nylander under contract or getting Matthews and Marner to sign extensions. They wanted to make a big splash. And did they ever, landing New York Islanders captain John Tavares as a free agent, seven years at $11 million a year. The Oakville native tweeted a picture of himself as a boy, sleeping in Maple Leafs bedsheets. It was his dream come true to play for the team he loved growing up.

That deal changed the marketplace, most notably in Toronto. Tavares was a point-a-game player, an Olympic gold medallist, a number-one overall pick in 2009 who'd lived up to the billing. Even so, he knew he'd be taking a back seat to the other three. Their agents knew it, too.

The media started asking uncomfortable questions: How could the Leafs afford all four in a cap world? Dubas's answer would ring through the ages: "We can and we will."

Nylander became the next big order of business. And it wasn't easy. Nylander didn't sign at any point in the summer, and he stayed away from training camp in September. He wasn't on the ice for the opener in October, nor November.

Nylander's contract situation was loud, and it was messy. There were "Willie Watches": He's in Sweden. He's in an airport. He's in Switzerland. There were apparently no talks. No conversations.

The new GM had never dealt with such a situation. Few GMs, to be fair, ever had. There were calls to trade Nylander. There were calls to let him sit the year out. Anger was directed at his father, Michael, an ex-NHL player, who had shopped himself around routinely in his playing days.

It was a wild ride that came to an end right up to the deadline for Nylander's ability to play that season. On December 1, about a half hour before the deadline, Nylander signed a six-year, $45 million contract. There were cries that Dubas had overpaid, that Tavares's contract inflated Nylander's worth, that Lou Lamoriello would have done things differently. But the circus was over. The player was signed.

It was a scene that Matthews would do his best to avoid, a tack his new agent, Judd Moldaver, fully endorsed.

Judd Moldaver was born and raised in Toronto, coming from a family of lawyers. His father, his older brother, and his sister are lawyers. But unlike them, he wanted to be a hockey player. He was a pretty good one, too. A bit undersized at five seven, he played for the Vaughan Vipers in the Ontario Junior Hockey League, as well as for the Blues of Upper Canada College, a prestigious private school.

"Let me for the record state that I am not a lawyer. I'm the only dumb one in the family," Moldaver told Craig Custance on his podcast.

Hockey—not law, not business administration, nor medicine—was his path. Moldaver was en route to becoming one of the biggest, most powerful agents in sports. He spent four seasons playing hockey at Colby College, a liberal arts college in New England, graduating in 2004 with a degree in government. "You know, government structures, international politics, domestic politics, things that I've always found super interesting, mixed with some history. I didn't really academically do anything in the sports realm," Moldaver told Custance.

The summer after his junior year, thanks to a friend, he got an internship in New York City at the agency IMG, where he got the agent bug. He headed to LA in 2004 to join CAA, becoming an agent in 2006, apprenticing under the likes of Pat Brisson and J.P. Barry.

Moldaver's time with Brisson allowed Moldaver to become close to Matthews and family. Moldaver certainly has a self-deprecating sense of humour, something he has in common with Auston Matthews. Moldaver also liked the feeling of being one of the guys. He liked Auston's family. And he was good at his job.

"I didn't learn how to be an agent in a book or in a classroom. I think it's been the collection of being around good people, great experiences, playing the game myself at a low level, but trying to understand the culture and looking at myself in the mirror and saying, 'Well, what would I do?' And try and give that advice to the guys," Moldaver told Custance's podcast.

In June 2018, though, Moldaver took a big leap. Matthews leapt with him. Much like the deals he had worked out for Matthews, Moldaver kept his own movements a secret right up until the moment they happened. Moldaver left Brisson and CAA to join the fledgling hockey division at Wasserman, which had acquired a significant equity stake in Bobby Orr's ORR Hockey. That group has about forty NHL players, including Connor McDavid.

Moldaver basically seemed to be following the same advice he gave his players. "Someone's going to be the lucky person who gets to represent great athletes, great families, and be in these situations. If I have an opportunity, I've got to seize it and I've got to push through and I've got to be myself. In life, whether it's against clients, friends, anyone, the key is to be yourself and plough through.

"And I think once I started to feel good in my own . . . skin and that I could be myself, I think that really enabled me to feel free."

As things worked out, Moldaver began representing McDavid as well in 2023, when McDavid's agent, ex-Leaf Jeff Jackson, left the agency business behind to become president of the Edmonton Oilers.

Moldaver is one of the biggest names in the hockey agency game now. One thing about Moldaver, he does not deal in headlines. His clients have typically been drama-averse.

And Matthews is a team-first kind of player. Scoring goals is his job. He's aware that a fourth liner who blocks a shot is just as valuable on any given shift. And he likes being a Maple Leaf.

"He's embraced the challenge and the honour of being a Toronto Maple Leaf and what that comes with," Moldaver told *The Arizona Republic* in Matthews's rookie year.

Folks may have had their doubts, may have thought that an American kid would want to make his way to an American team. Maybe the Arizona kid would want to play for that Arizona team he grew up admiring the same way Tavares engineered his way to Toronto.

But no. Very quietly and without fanfare, Moldaver, aided by Jackson, met with Dubas in February and emerged with a deal that should have been more team-friendly than the way it worked out. On February 5, 2019, Matthews signed a five-year, $58.17 million extension that would kick in July 1, 2019. It made him the Leafs' highest-paid player, which was only fitting since he was their best player. With Tavares's $11 million as a benchmark, Matthews's average annual value (AAV) came in at $11.634 million (the 34 being meaningful to him).

He took less money than McDavid, whose AAV worked out to $12.5 million a year. When McDavid signed, his AAV used up 16.67 percent of the cap available at the time. Matthews's deal was taking up less as a percentage, just 14.64 percent. It was a no-fuss, no-muss, good-news-all-around story. Matthews made a long-term commitment, and he left money on the table. The cap—the amount teams were allowed to spend on players on an annual basis—was at $79.5 million when Matthews signed. It was projected to go to $100 million during the next few years based on exploding NHL revenues. There'd be more than enough money for Dubas to keep his collection of young players happy in that scenario.

The way things unfolded, however, may have changed the public perception of the dollars given to the group who became known as the Core Four: Matthews at $11.634 million, Tavares at $11 million, Mitch Marner at a shade under $11 million, and Nylander at roughly $7 million. But a pandemic was only a season away. It would flatten the cap at $81.5 million for three seasons. Dubas had counted on a rising cap, but with revenues depressed due to the pandemic and with the cap not rising, the Leafs couldn't keep all the players they wanted to. Dubas was forced to trade players the team had developed, like Andreas Johnsson and Kasperi Kapanen, just for cap space in 2020. And they couldn't find enough to match an offer for Zach Hyman, who signed with Edmonton in 2022.

But the day Matthews signed was a good day for the Maple Leafs.

Matthews had produced in his first three seasons: forty, thirty-four, and thirty-seven goals. He had 111 goals in three seasons, tied with the legendary Ace Bailey for forty-ninth all time among the 884 skaters who had laced up to that point in the iconic franchise's history.

And folks outside of hockey were noticing. It helped that with Lamoriello gone and Dubas in charge, the old-school shackles were off.

Lamoriello's belief is that the logo is the face of the franchise, not any particular player. Players were all part of one big orchestra, each performing its role. Matthews understood that better than most. His goal-scoring prowess, individual trophies, and media accolades never inflated his ego. Or if they did, he never showed it publicly.

But Matthews was also part of a different generation of players. The whole idea of a hockey player showing off any part of his personality was an affront to the sport, at least in the minds of old-school thinkers. That's why Don Cherry called the Carolina Hurricanes "a bunch of jerks" for their post-win celebrations. The old school didn't like "cellys" after goals. But that's how most hockey players were raised.

But Matthews, of course, was not raised in a hockey market.

Matthews's cellys are a thing of beauty. Going down on one leg. Fist pumps. Arms raised. And on the road, holding his hand to ear pointing out that his goal has silenced the crowd.

That happened the night of October 7, 2018, at the United Center. It was the home opener for the Chicago Blackhawks, whose star player was Patrick Kane, one of the greatest players in US hockey history, who liked his cellys, too. Matthews had long admired Kane, nine years his elder.

But this game was crazy. The Blackhawks scored the first two, the Leafs the next three, including one by Matthews. The Blackhawks tied it in the second, then John Tavares scored his second of the game to make it 4–3 going into the third.

The Blackhawks tied it. Tavares completed the hat trick to make it 5–4. Then Kane tied it at 18:36, and 21,000 die-hards at the United Center smelled blood.

But Matthews scored for a 6–5 lead just twenty-two seconds after Kane.

"It was so loud in there, and I scored and it got quiet," said Matthews to EA Sports.

He put his hand to his ear, as if to ask what happened to all the noise. The crowd hated him for it. Kane hated to be shown up in his own building.

The Blackhawks pulled their goalie, and Kane scored with twenty-nine seconds left.

"He scores and he does like the same thing," said Matthews. "I was dying laughing on the bench. And then he came by the bench, screamed at me. I can't remember what he said, something like, maybe like, 'Respect your elders,' or something like that. I was like, 'Oh, this is so cool.' I didn't even care either. This was so fun. And then, I was like, 'We need to win this game.'"

Morgan Rielly won it for the Leafs in overtime.

Against Colorado on January 22, 2018, Matthews scored the go-ahead goal, but it was disallowed for the play being offside after a video review. So he scored again, the next shift, and showed everyone watching he thought it was a good goal by pointing at the net with his arm, the way referees do to signal a good goal. "Just made sure the puck was in this time. Was pretty excited about that one."

The All-Star Game was just a few days away, and Matthews was teamed up with his Team USA friend Jack Eichel on the Team Atlantic Division in a three-on-three tournament. When Eichel scored, both he and Matthews pointed at the net Matthews-style to indicate that was a good goal.

"Just keeping it light out there," said Matthews. Matthews's personality was showing. With Lamoriello gone, it was time to show it off a little. When the 2018–19 season started, Matthews looked a bit different. His clothes. His accoutrements. Gucci. Givenchy. Louis Vuitton. A Rolex Submariner on his wrist. For fragrance, Saint Laurent or Tom Ford.

That was all in a *GQ* article about Matthews. Imagine that: a hockey player in a *GQ* article. With everything that goes with *GQ*: "Coat by Belstaff / Sweater by Givenchy at Saks Fifth Avenue / Pants by Frame Denim."

He wasn't talking about getting pucks deep, or how to fix the power play. A hockey player was talking about fashion. He'd picked up the fashion bug in Switzerland.

P.K. Subban was among the first hockey players to appear in the pages of *GQ*. He was also one of the first hockey players to display a sense of fashion. Tyler Seguin showed off his tattoos to *GQ*. Connor McDavid talked about growing out his hair with the magazine. Matthews was next, riding that influential wave. Maybe even leading it.

Hockey players traditionally wear suits to games. This is true even of Triple A players, who wear suits to high school on the day of games. Matthews is part of an evolution away from that thinking. Matthews's hope was that hockey players would be free to be more like football and basketball players, wear what they want. "Get creative and make things a little more interesting," he told *GQ*. "I don't mind at all wearing a suit. I actually kind of like it. . . . But at the same time, I wouldn't hate being able to wear street clothes and something different than a suit."

Matthews continued to push his sense of self out there. He showed up wearing a moustache on the eve of the 2019 season at the team's season-launching golf outing at Rattlesnake Point.

"I think it's awesome," said forward Nic Petan. "It represents his style. It's Mexican-*Narcos* style."

"I love the show, the *Narcos* one. Without the beer belly," Matthews said. "I figured why not try this moustache thing. I've never done it. Feel a little greasy. Just kind of stuck with it." But the moustache's biggest fan was his mother, Ema.

"That surprised me," Matthews told reporters that day. "She made fun of me when I tried to grow a beard a couple of years ago. She likes the moustache. I started it when I went to Mexico. Had to blend in a little bit there. She was loving it when we were down there."

A few days later, Coach Mike Babcock announced the team would be naming a captain before the 2018–19 season began. The team had played without a captain since Dion Phaneuf was traded on February 9, 2016. Matthews was the obvious choice, though there were worthy contenders in Morgan Rielly and John Tavares. Rielly was the longest-serving Maple Leaf and carried himself with ease. He seemed to be the conscience of the team, especially after he handled a controversy in which he was accused of yelling a homophobic slur on the ice. He apologized. Tavares would be a safer choice, the Toronto kid who grew up loving the Leafs. He'd been captain already with the Islanders. And he had been used to the limelight since he was fifteen.

The odds were on Matthews, with the self-confident persona he'd revealed and that had been ever-evolving. His new five-year contract was kicking in. He was the team's best player.

But the laughs about the moustache, and any talk that Matthews was going to be the next captain of the Toronto Maple Leafs, would soon vanish.

CHAPTER FIFTEEN

The Scottsdale Affair

Fayola Dozithee always carried a blade, she told police. She had served in Iraq and suffers from post-traumatic stress disorder. She worked as a security guard in a luxury condo complex just off North Scottsdale Road, near a picturesque canal that cuts through Scottsdale, Arizona. She had the overnight shift, spent mostly outside in her car in the parking lot near a roundabout by the front entrance. She worried, understandably, about her own security. She didn't want a gun. She didn't want to kill anyone. But the knife gave her that sense of security. She could hurt someone just enough to force them to run away. As she would tell police later, she has that mindset every time she went on shift.

The job was never boring. She once witnessed a suicide attempt. She mostly witnesses drunks coming home at night, but she can handle herself, being former military. Four times an hour she did rounds, checking on things. Then she'd retreat to her car and fill out her paperwork. For the most part, she ignored the drunk and disorderly residents as they returned from a night out. As long as they got into the building without causing a ruckus or disturbing anybody else, all was good.

Around 2:30 a.m. on May 26, 2019, three young and very drunk men arrived outside the condo complex and tried to get into Dozithee's car in the outdoor parking lot.

Auston Matthews, who lived in the building, started pulling on the handle on the back-seat passenger side. It was locked, thankfully. But Dozithee was stunned, angry, and a little frightened. It actually took her some time to process what she was seeing. The war veteran was back in the States, but as she told police, she still processed information like she was in a war zone. What was happening? Was this right? How did it all feel?

Knife or not, military service or not, it was three against one, three men against one woman. And at least one of them, Matthews, was quite big, six three, 220 pounds.

The last thing she wanted was a fight, or worse. She knew they were drunk because she'd seen them earlier, around 11:00, and asked them to move their car. They appeared drunk then. They'd gone out, drunk more in her estimation, and now were back, and for whatever reason had decided to harass her.

That boys will be boys, and drunk boys will be even more so, is hardly comforting to a woman alone with three of them in an outdoor parking lot in the middle of the night. She was worried for her security. She decided to stay calm and just try to find out what they thought they were doing.

Turns out, they thought it was funny. They told her they thought she'd laugh. As she told police, they said, "We thought it would be funny to see how you'd react if we got in your car." She didn't like it one bit, and she told them so. It took some encouraging, but they finally took the hint and left.

One of the men stayed behind. He apologized. He said, "We're sorry."

He knew his friend was a big-time hockey star, earning millions of dollars, and was just trying to let off some steam, step outside himself for a night. He tried to convince the security guard not to file a report with the condo board that employed her. The friend was looking out for his friend. He didn't want this huge misstep to get out and cause a black mark on his public profile. The spotlight was always on him, after all.

It was roughly at that moment that Matthews, while walking away, dropped his pants. He kept his boxers up. But as he got to the apartment building door, he bent over, grabbed his cheeks, and mooned her.

Matthews's friend tried to laugh it off, saying he'd been doing that all up and down North Scottsdale Road, despite being told by his buddies to cut it out in case he got arrested. Any goodwill disappeared. Dozithee looked away and told the friend that she was going to make a report, and that the sooner Matthews pulled up his pants, the better. If any of the residents were awake, none wanted to see this. Besides, there were video cameras everywhere, including in the elevator. The video cameras, she said, would support the report she would file before she went off duty.

It might all have ended there, or the next day, if the three had apologized. But now the condo manager and the board were involved and were in touch with the Matthews family.

According to her statement to police, her manager relayed to Dozithee that their initial defence was that Matthews didn't do it.

This was family looking out for family. The Matthewses are a close bunch, and they'd gone through a lot. Brian wasn't going to let anything happen to his son if he could help it. He didn't want this huge misstep to get out and stain his son's public profile. Any son would appreciate this unconditional support.

Unfortunately, Brian's efforts failed.

When the security guard heard that Matthews had denied trying to get into her car, and mooning her, she became angry at being called a liar. Now, instead of defending her person, she had to defend her own honour, her own reputation. She went to the police to file a complaint.

She thought he might be charged with public indecency. Instead, the police charged Matthews with disorderly conduct. It's designated a Class 1 misdemeanour in Arizona, punishable by up to six months in jail and up to a $2,500 fine.

Again, it might have ended there, too. But neither Matthews, nor his agent, Judd Moldaver, informed the Maple Leafs in late May that this charge was outstanding. Maybe Auston hoped it would go away on its own, or that he and his family could handle it by themselves.

Matthews was soon to move into a new house and leave that condo anyway, thanks in part to his big extension.

Brian and Ema Matthews used a trust to purchase a $3.2 million contemporary-style mansion in Phoenix's Red Rock community, near Camelback Mountain. The 7,319-square-foot, single-storey estate nestled at the base of Mummy Mountain has five bedrooms and six and a half bathrooms, according to a story published August 12, 2019, by *The Arizona Republic*'s real-estate section. The home had been remodelled in 2018 with upgrades that included twenty-seven feet of glass pocket doors, a separate guest apartment, and a kitchen with Binova cabinets manufactured in Italy.

Around the time Dozithee filed her police report, the hockey media would largely be focused on the Stanley Cup playoffs, the draft, and free agency—usually. Then it would be the summer off. No one would think or talk hockey until September. No one would wonder if there was a police report filed against a star player. When those things do happen, they usually blow up right away.

Auston Taylour Matthews was arrested on July 23, 2019, for a misdemeanor disorderly conduct offence. There were no immediate media reports. Neither Matthews nor his agent told the Leafs.

Matthews had talked it over with a confidant, veteran teammate Patrick Marleau, during the summer. "I don't think he thought it was going to be as big an issue as it has become," Marleau told the *Star.*

What became clear was the public didn't like one bit that a drunk Matthews and two friends were trying to get into a locked car at 2:30 a.m. with a woman inside.

By the end of September, with the Leafs on the cusp of deciding on a captain, all hell broke loose.

The first reports came out of social media on September 24, internet sleuths tagging hockey reporters on Reddit and Twitter to alert them. The *Toronto Star* and the CBC were the first mainstream media with stories.

The team was caught flat-footed. My initial call to the Leafs' PR department for comment went unanswered, the team needing to verify the initial reports. GM Kyle Dubas would later admit he'd learned about the incident from Twitter, where the story quickly trended. Under Brendan Shanahan, sensitivity to the brand was paramount. Dubas was trying to get the Leafs to be the team that helped hockey evolve from its knuckle-dragging past.

The organization hires a security team to help keep players out of trouble. They have a massive public relations department to help gloss things over. But no one had any idea that their star player had put himself in hot water.

The next day, Matthews was clearly uncomfortable, rambling somewhat as he did his best to apologize. "Obviously not something that I don't think any of us really wish we were talking about today, but I know unfortunately [the] situation [I'm] in. I, you know, regret, you know, any of my actions that would ever, you know, put a distraction on the team or distressing an individual," said Matthews. "I take a lot of pride and, you know, preparing myself for the season, you know, representing the Toronto Maple Leafs as well as I can. So unfortunately, due to the situation, I can't make any other comments, but that's all I have. And, you know, thank you guys for coming out."

Matthews was not the first hockey player to get in trouble with the police, not by a far stretch, but he was by far the most high-profile at that moment.

"We want to support [Auston] and make sure all is okay with him," John Tavares told reporters that day. "He's obviously addressed it. He doesn't want to cause any distraction. I think he just wants to play and carry on like he always has and focus on playing and being himself."

It can be a particularly hot spotlight if there's the mere suggestion a Maple Leaf has stepped over a line, since the franchise itself sets a high bar.

"The Toronto Maple Leafs, we really pride ourselves on doing things right, on the ice, off the ice, and treating people (well). It's an unfortunate situation," said Head Coach Mike Babcock. "Anything that goes bad, what you do is you take it, and you get better as an organization. We got a close family inside. We're going to look after Auston, and we're going to look after our actions."

A previous generation might have chalked it up to boys will be boys. But this happened at a time when people of privilege—and young millionaire hockey players are privileged—are scrutinized for their actions and on a team that was trying to change hockey.

"We don't take this job for granted, and I think that applies to Auston as well," Morgan Rielly said in a scrum in the story's immediate aftermath. "We feel very lucky to play here in Toronto. We feel very lucky to have the jobs that we do. We try not to take it for granted, try to treat people with respect, carry ourselves in a manner to be proud of. Auston is no different than that. We know Auston, we know what kind of person he is. He's been a leader since day one since he walked into this room. He's going to handle this maturely, he's going to deal with it as it comes, and we're his teammates and we're going to support him."

To many, it seemed the front office was simply waiting for Matthews to mature enough to become captain, not wanting to put too much on his plate. Connor McDavid had been made captain of the Edmonton Oilers on October 5, 2016. He was nineteen years, 266 days old, the youngest captain in NHL history. Like McDavid was to the Oilers, the twenty-two-year-old Matthews was to the Maple Leafs: the face of the franchise. The Maple Leafs captaincy seemed a logical next step.

But if Matthews was more than just in the mix, his drunken actions that frightened a female security guard in the middle of the night in Scottsdale eliminated him from consideration. As Bruce Arthur wrote in the *Toronto Star* on September 26, 2019, it would "mean handing the official leadership keys to a young man who displayed judgment this poor, whose apology was clumsy at best, who didn't tell the team, and whose reputation has been tarnished."

Before the puck dropped on the 2019–20 season, Tavares was handed the C on October 2, 2019.

If Matthews was bothered by the attacks on his reputation, or the legal ramifications of what he had done, he didn't show it as the season started. Known as a fast starter, he had five goals in his first three games, and seven by the ten-game mark. Not quite the eight and ten of the two previous seasons, but enough to think he was able to put it all behind him.

By November 15, the charges were dropped, with an agreement reached by lawyers representing both sides. The Arizona justice system promotes such action. He paid a $500 fine. Dozithee never spoke to a member of the media about the incident.

"I just want to reiterate again just how truly sorry I am for my actions and my behaviour," Matthews said in a scrum after the charges were dropped. "I never meant to cause any distress to this woman, and I can assure you that I've learned from my mistakes and my actions, and now it's something for myself to strive every day to be better in every aspect of my life."

"The Toronto Maple Leafs are committed to developing and promoting the qualities of good character, respect, and equality in our organization, including our players, and we recognize and embrace the role we serve in the community," said Leaf President Brendan Shanahan in a statement. "While Auston has been an exceptional ambassador for the Leafs in representing those values, his conduct in this incident last May failed to meet expectations."

Six days after the court dismissed charges against Matthews, the Maple Leafs dismissed Coach Mike Babcock, who was replaced by Sheldon Keefe. Eventually, stories of Babcock's malfeasance and mistreatment of his players followed him out the door, shining a light on hockey's culture.

It was revealed shortly after Babcock's firing that the head coach asked Mitch Marner in his rookie season to rank his teammates based on work ethic, from hardest workers down. Babcock then revealed Marner's opinions to his teammates. Babcock would later apologize. Marner moved on. But there was a real sense that "old-school" approaches by coaches toward players would no longer be tolerated.

Leaf fans were already upset with Babcock for scratching Jason Spezza from the first game of the 2019–20 season for what should have been a triumphant appearance for the hometown player. Some of Babcock's former players with the Red Wings also spoke up about mistreatment. Winger Johan Franzén told *Expressen* that during a playoff game against Nashville in April 2012, Babcock verbally assaulted him.

"I get the shivers when I think about it," he told the Swedish paper. "But that was just one out of a hundred things he did. The tip of the iceberg . . . He's a terrible person, the worst I have ever met. He's a bully who was attacking people. It could be a cleaner at the arena in Detroit or anybody. He would lay into people without any reason."

He had benched Mike Modano to keep him from playing his fifteen-hundredth game late in the 2010–11 season. He tried to keep Chris Chelios out of the lineup when the Wings played the Blackhawks in an outdoor game in Chicago, Chelios's hometown.

Keefe was a Kyle Dubas favourite who'd won the Calder Cup as the bench boss of the Toronto Marlies in 2018. Dubas had previously hired him as coach of the OHL Sault Ste. Marie Greyhounds.

The program Keefe was trying to help build with his progressive boss, Kyle Dubas, allowed for growth from mistakes.

"We're trying to put together a program that celebrates the positives in people," Keefe told Rosie DiManno. "Also, pinpointing and working on the areas where we need to grow. While staying positive and showing us at our best, still being realistic about where we need to go and what we're capable of."

Matthews had addressed his youthful shortcomings publicly, and in Toronto, where hockey was king, he was able to move on.

The Leafs were in the midst of a Jekyll and Hyde season, with some great nights, some terrible, when something more monstrous appeared: the coronavirus pandemic.

The season was called prematurely. The Leafs had played seventy of eighty-two games and had rounded into form. Everyone was sent home to self-isolate.

Matthews had moved into his new digs. Goalie Frederik

Andersen, one of Matthews's best friends on the team, joined him. It was better to be in Arizona in a palatial house with a swimming pool and a gym than in Andersen's downtown Toronto condo.

For a while, it looked as if Matthews would get an advantage over other shooters, given he and Andersen were permitted to play road hockey, and he had an actual NHL goalie to shoot on as the league was concocting a plan to play an expanded playoffs in the summer.

Reports surfaced in late June that Matthews had contracted COVID, one of the first top athletes in the world to get it. Andersen did not get it, one of those head-scratching turns of events that continue to puzzle families in similar situations. Matthews had to self-isolate.

Panic swept Leaf Nation. Little was known about the science of the virus at the time. What the world knew was that to get it was mostly bad. It was potentially fatal. The world was only beginning to learn about COVID's potential long-term effects on daily health. Or you could simply recuperate, as from any virus. Or you could simply have it without experiencing any effects. That, it turns out, was the version that struck Matthews.

Despite the pandemic, the business of the NHL had to carry on. The regular season was declared over. Matthews finished with forty-seven goals and eighty points, both career highs. He only took eight minutes in penalties all season long. He almost certainly would have scored fifty—that scoring mark of a superstar—had the full eighty-two games been played. He'd have been the first Leaf to do so since Dave Andreychuk scored fifty-three in 1993–94.

Regardless of the points total, Matthews had established himself as a bona fide star. Leaf fans might not have liked that at six feet, three inches he rarely delivered punishing checks. He had the frame to do so, and Leaf fans like things rough-and-tumble. Wendel Clark and Tie Domi are revered by Leaf Nation.

But Matthews was elite at those small things that most barely notice, like lifting a stick to get the puck back. He often did so without getting called for hooking or high-sticking, which can go with the territory. He'd give a small bump along the boards, just enough to bump the opposition off the puck, not a bruising hit that could be called boarding. He was aggressive without the puck and, more importantly, without getting penalized.

So when the time came for the members of the Professional Hockey Writers Association to vote on their postseason awards, Matthews was top of mind for many. He didn't have a Hart-worthy season because the Leafs weren't good enough. His sublime defensive game had yet to capture the imagination of Selke voters. But those penalty minutes—just eight—for a guy who plays as much as he does, that was something.

Matthews didn't win any trophies that season, but enough voters thought strongly enough about his play that he was a finalist for the Lady Byng, given to the "player adjudged to have exhibited the best type of sportsmanship and gentlemanly conduct combined with a high standard of playing ability."

Twitter being Twitter, many of those who voted for him were reminded—after they voted—of Matthews's transgressions. Most of them failed to consider his less-than-gentlemanly actions toward Dozithee the previous summer when casting their ballots. Some didn't think it was an issue, since the trophy is awarded for what happens on the ice.

The Lady Byng was given out September 20, 2020, following the summertime Stanley Cup playoffs, one week shy of a year since the story first broke. So much had happened to the Leafs and to hockey and to the world that if the transgression was not necessarily forgiven, it was certainly forgotten.

CHAPTER SIXTEEN

Zero to Sixty

Auston Matthews tapes his stick heel to toe, meticulously. Superstition is part of being a professional hockey player. His stick is a blue-and-white CCM JetSpeed, usually switching between FT4 Pro and FT6. It has a P29 curve—a "mid" curve, halfway between a heel curve and a toe curve. It's one of the most popular curves, made famous by Sidney Crosby, because it allows for great stickhandling and puck control. Its open face provides maximum lift on shots.

Matthews prefers a very whippy stick. He uses an 80 flex, meaning it takes eighty pounds of pressure to bend by one inch. Defencemen with big slap shots prefer rigidity, meaning a flex over one hundred. But for shooters like Matthews—a player who likes to lean into the shot—the flexibility of the stick is paramount. He can get a shot off hard and quickly by letting the natural flex of the stick whip the puck. The flex turns the stick into a spring, storing up potential energy that is released when the stick snaps back into its original shape. There's more force into a shot, causing the puck to travel faster. The stick is textured for better grip. The Toronto skyline is featured on the shaft. On the name bar, his sticks read "Papi 34."

"I just want to make [the defenceman] move," Matthews explained to Paul Bissonnette in a 2022 promotional video for EA

Sports. "I want to make him think I'm going one way and then take it and go another. If I'm shooting, I want him to think I'm shooting here, then flip the other way and change the angle so it not only messes up the D-man, but also the goalie. That's what's going through my head, to make him make the first move."

As respected a talent as he was, he still hadn't accomplished much as a player. A few team records, a few league records, and a Calder Trophy was more than most, but not enough. Playoff success had eluded Matthews and the Leafs, dogged by an inability to get out of the first round.

It particularly stung that the Leafs had just lost to the Montreal Canadiens in seven games in 2021 after leading the series three games to one. It was a year that had been set up for Leaf success, the team playing only Canadian teams in a rebranded "North Division," created due to COVID travel restrictions.

Most believed the Leafs would steamroll through the division in the playoffs, but instead, the season ended again in a first-round exit. Matthews scored only one goal in seven games against the great Carey Price. Matthews was, perhaps, done in by a lingering wrist injury that would require surgery.

Matthews doesn't set personal goals. Or if he does, he keeps them to himself, more worried about team success than personal success. Pat Mahan, one of Matthews's coaches when he was a youngster, said if Auston is told that he can't achieve something, he'll do everything he can to achieve it. "Whatever you want to say about him as far as the phenom that he is, he didn't just show up," said Mahan. "The kid works, and he still works. He is committed. And it's never enough. And it's never been enough. Tell him he can't do it. Tell him he's not as good as McDavid. Tell him he's not as good as MacKinnon. Tell him he's from Arizona, so he's not good enough. Just keep telling him that. See how that works out."

Still, if the Toronto Maple Leafs are to have any success, Matthews will have to score goals. He'd been scoring at a pretty good rate since he entered the league. He scored forty-one in fifty-two games in 2021 to win the Rocket Richard Trophy for the first time in his career, the first American to lead the league in goals since Keith Tkachuk scored fifty-two in 1996–97. And he was the first Maple Leaf to do so since Gaye Stewart scored thirty-seven goals in a fifty-game season in 1945–46. It was an achievement, for sure, but it did feel like it came with an asterisk. Matthews, after all, faced only the six other Canadian teams. He didn't score all those goals against all the goalies, and the Canadian teams were generally deemed to be among the weakest opponents. He had scored forty-seven in 2019–20 in a seventy-game season, missing the Rocket Richard Trophy by one goal. Both seasons were shortened by COVID, robbing him of a chance to score that magical number: fifty.

To score goals, he'd need healthy hands. And to that end, Matthews had surgery on his left wrist on August 13, 2021. A six-week recovery period correlated well with an October 13 start to the season. He'd miss all the training camp games. Not exactly a heartache, but it was less than ideal.

All the talk from the prognosticators was whether he would finally score fifty. The consensus was yes. Boy, were they wrong, at least for the moment.

As it turned out, Matthews's wrist hadn't healed enough for him to start the season. The Leafs played the first three games of the 2021–22 season without him, winning twice. He joined them for the fourth game of the season, a 2–1 overtime loss to the New York Rangers. They lost the next three as well, with Matthews scoring only once. It was his worst start to any season to that point. He had one goal, one assist for the month of October.

The Leafs turned the tide in November, reeling off a pair of five-game winning streaks as the team descended on Los Angeles for a November 24 bout with the Kings. For the Leafs, the wins were coming around, but not the offence.

The Leafs were 13–6–1 but were one of the lowest-scoring teams in the NHL, scoring a mere 2.55 goals a game in that stretch. Their defence and goaltending were winning games. They were known to be a high-octane team offensively, but they were sputtering.

For Matthews, the numbers were even worse. He had seven goals through twenty games, a thirty-three-goal pace. This from the player who had scored forty-one the season prior to win the Rocket in a COVID-shortened season.

There was no shortage of theories. Mitch Marner, his main winger and a gifted passer, was having a slump himself. Some put that up to a sort of hangover from the team's disappointing playoff loss to Montreal the previous spring.

Matthews also had a new left winger in Nick Ritchie. Zach Hyman, who had mostly played with Matthews since their rookie season, had left as a free agent for Edmonton. He was a hard player to replace. He was a big body with speed who hounded the puck, caused havoc in front of the net, and had a knack for playing with players far more talented than himself.

Nick Ritchie, shall we say, was a big body. But that was about it. Though he was highly touted as a junior and was chosen just two spots behind William Nylander in the 2014 draft, he had trouble fitting in with the speed and skill of Matthews and Marner. Neither would ever criticize a teammate, but through November, Keefe had seen enough and experimented with an unheralded player, Michael Bunting, with Matthews and Marner, instead of Ritchie.

Bunting was a local kid, from Scarborough, who—like Matthews—didn't play hockey at a high level until later in life. Matthews didn't because Triple A hockey wasn't really available. Bunting didn't because Triple A hockey was too expensive. He had played for Keefe (and GM Kyle Dubas) in Sault Ste. Marie and came to the Leafs on a bargain contract. Bunting shared a September 17 birthday with Matthews but was two years older. And at twenty-six, he was officially considered a rookie, with just twenty-six games of experience in the NHL before he came to the Leafs.

Hope was not that high. But Keefe was willing to try anything to get his dynamic duo of Matthews and Marner going.

The early-season offensive struggles were paired with predictable whispers that Matthews built Rocket Richard–winning numbers against weaker opponents in the COVID-shortened season and now faced real competition. He offered an alternative view. He pointed out that the off-season wrist surgery that kept him out of training camp and the season's opening three games wreaked havoc on his "touch, feel, and timing," adding he felt only now—twenty games into the season—he was finding his legs.

"[Spending] six weeks off the ice or so with no pucks [after recovering from surgery], you have to play a little catch-up," Matthews told the *Toronto Star*. "But it's all good. I think that the chances, if they continue to come, they're going to drop. So I think it's just a matter of time, just staying positive. We're winning games, and that's all that matters." He scored that night in a 6–2 win over the Kings. He scored two nights later in a 4–1 win over the Sharks. And in two more days, he scored again in a 5–1 win in Anaheim. The team returned home to an 8–3 win over Colorado that featured a Matthews hat trick. They went right back out on the road to see Matthews score on back-to-back nights in Minnesota and Winnipeg, returning home and Matthews scoring twice against Columbus.

That was ten goals in seven games, seventeen in all, four behind league-leader Leon Draisaitl. Suddenly a thirty-three-goal pace had become a fifty-eight-goal pace. He couldn't keep that up, could he?

As his defenceman teammate Travis Dermott put it: "When he's hot like this, you just want to put the puck, not even on his tape, you can put it on his backhand, and he'll make magic out of that."

The Leafs had a date December 14 in Edmonton, the must-watch nature of the game only raised since the two teams faced each other nine times in the North Division. The Leafs won six times. There was a bit more spice because the Winter Olympics were only a few months away. Connor McDavid was a shoo-in for Canada, and Matthews was already named to Team USA (along with Patrick Kane and Seth Jones). USA Hockey had taken care of that business on the eve of the season.

"I've represented the US before. But obviously the Olympics is as big a stage as it gets," Matthews told me when his name had been announced. "It's been a bit since the US sat on that podium at the top, so hopefully we can obviously change that. It's always fun to watch. You get the best players in the world from so many different countries, and you get them all together. It usually makes for some pretty fun hockey."

Matthews picked up his nineteenth and twentieth goals of the season in a 5–1 win over Connor McDavid and the Edmonton Oilers at Rogers Place on December 14. That meant he had scored at least twenty goals in each of his first six seasons. Only one other Leaf had ever done that: Dave Keon. "I know what he means to this organization and to the city of Toronto," Matthews said that night. "So just to be in the same sentence as him is very humbling." But the talk of Matthews equalling another Keon achievement wasn't dominating the conversation, nor was any talk of Matthews catching Draisaitl. The COVID conversation was back.

While two COVID-shortened seasons were behind them, the virus itself wasn't. A new strain of the virus, Omicron, had emerged, and as a result, the hockey World Junior Championship in Edmonton and Red Deer was postponed until summer.

Right after that game, the Oilers put Coach Dave Tippett into COVID protocol. The Leafs were supposed to play Calgary after Edmonton, but the game against the Flames had already been postponed because at least six Flames had tested positive for the virus. So it was off to Vancouver, but John Tavares, Alex Kerfoot, Jason Spezza, and Wayne Simmonds had to enter COVID protocols. That game was postponed, too. Hanging in the balance wasn't so much a record-scoring pace, but the Olympics.

The Winter Games were certain to go on in February in Beijing. The bigger question was whether NHL players would participate. As part of a six-year extension to the collective bargaining agreement that saw players accede to a relatively flat salary cap that would keep salaries low, the players had convinced the NHL to agree to let them play in the Olympics. They hadn't since 2014, Canada winning gold in Sochi, Russia.

The Russians won in 2018, but it was hardly best-on-best with NHLers not participating. So in 2022, the NHL was supposed to be back.

With the league having to postpone games in December, Commissioner Gary Bettman argued the only possible makeup dates were the time set aside for Beijing. The Leafs had two unscheduled weeks off after that December 14 game in Edmonton.

Players all over were testing positive. Matthews did. So did McDavid, who missed the January 5 rematch in Toronto.

In the middle of it, on December 21, the NHL and the NHL Players' Association pulled the plug on NHL players' participation in the Olympics.

For hockey fans of the best-on-best competition, and the players who were looking forward to representing their countries, it was bleak. COVID was ruining everything. When the Leafs played home games in early January, against Ottawa and a McDavid-less Edmonton, it was again in an empty building. Matthews didn't score in either game.

"It's been tough going from what we did last year with no fans and then getting the fans back. You can just tell how much of a difference it made and just how much fun it was to feel the energy and the excitement in the arena and just the buzz of everybody. And so I guess it's taking one step forward, two steps back. It's too bad," said Matthews.

"But we're going on the road, and we travel pretty well. So, hopefully, maybe some of these away games feel like home games and we can kind of get that buzz back. Hopefully, it's not too long that we're going without fans here because they honestly make a huge difference, and it's not the same without them."

Leaf fans travel well. They show up in every city to cheer on their team. And the Leafs were heading out on a six-game road trip. (There should have been a game in Toronto to break it up, but it was postponed due to COVID.) True to form, Matthews started the trip with a pair of goals in Colorado, with one more each in Vegas, Arizona, and St. Louis. His slow start of twenty-five goals in the first thirty-five games up to January 16 still meant he trailed league co-leaders Leon Draisaitl and Alex Ovechkin, each at twenty-six. He went on a four-game goalless drought and started up again with a hat trick January 31 against the Devils, sparking a run of eight goals over seven games. After a two-game break, it was four goals in three games. Two more goalless games were followed by nine goals in six games. He was steering the conversation away from COVID and the Olympic disappointment, and fans, the media, and his teammates were talking about that magic number: fifty.

Matthews at the NHL Global Series in Stockholm in the 2023–24 season

KEVIN McGRAN

Matthews scrums outside a practice rink in Anaheim, California, in 2024.

KEVIN McGRAN

Number 34's name on the Hart Trophy
KEVIN McGRAN

Matthews and the Make-A-Wish Foundation at the 2024 NHL All-Star Weekend
KEVIN McGRAN

Signing autographs after a Leafs outdoor practice at Nathan Phillips Square in downtown Toronto

KEVIN McGRAN

Number 34 (third from left) and his NHL buddies at the NHL All-Star Weekend in Toronto

KEVIN McGRAN

With his family on the red carpet at the 2024 NHL Awards in Las Vegas

KEVIN McGRAN

Auston Matthews accepts the captaincy of the Maple Leafs in August 2023 at an event at Real Sports.
KEVIN McGRAN

Thanks, Mitch: Auston Matthews would be the first to credit his linemate Mitch Marner for their success together. Marner has assisted on more Matthews goals than anyone else.
GERRY ANGUS/ ICON SPORTSWIRE VIA GETTY IMAGES

That's a celly! Auston Matthews celebrates his goal against the Florida Panthers, January 17, 2023. His emotion comes out in big moments. And scoring against Florida is big.

KEVIN SOUSA/NHLI VIA GETTY IMAGES

A flexible stick, such as the one Auston Matthews uses, helps with the speed and power of the shot, like this one from game one of the first round of the 2022 Stanley Cup playoffs against Tampa.

CLAUS ANDERSEN/GETTY IMAGES

It's been a long time since the Toronto Maple Leafs had players as talented as these five: John Tavares, Auston Matthews, William Nylander, Morgan Rielly, and Mitch Marner.

JULIAN AVRAM/ICON SPORTSWIRE VIA GETTY IMAGES

Maurice "Rocket" Richard himself was the first to hit that magical number in a season, and he did so in fifty games in 1944–45. Richard was as fiery a player as the league has ever seen, a hero in Quebec. Montreal Canadiens famously rioted when league president Clarence Campbell suspended Richard in the heat of a playoff race for deliberately injuring Bruins defenceman Hal Laycoe and punching linesman Cliff Thompson. This decision came when the Rocket was leading the NHL in scoring and the Habs were battling for first place in the standings. Campbell was pelted with eggs when he tried to take his seat at the Forum for a game against Detroit the following St. Patrick's Day. The crowd became so unruly that the game was forfeited to the Red Wings and the building evacuated. A riot ensued outside, causing $500,000 in damage and leaving some deep wounds, particularly among the francophone community.

I would argue that hockey players don't enjoy that level of fan loyalty anymore, but for generations Richard was the player by whom all scorers were measured. He was the first to score eight points in a game, finally bested by Darryl Sittler's ten in 1976. Richard was the first to hit five hundred career goals. He led the league in goal-scoring five times, though the trophy awarded for such prowess—the one that bears his name—wasn't created until the Montreal Canadiens donated the trophy for the 1998–99 season. Matthews was still a toddler then.

After Richard hit fifty in a season in 1944–45, the record stood for sixteen seasons. Bernie Geoffrion hit fifty in 1960–61, then Bobby Hull did it in 1961–62 (the first of five fifty-goal seasons for the Golden Jet). It became de rigueur in the league for elite scorers to hit that mark—or go beyond. Johnny Bucyk, Phil Esposito, Vic Hadfield, Rick MacLeish, Mickey Redmond, Ken Hodge, Rick Martin, Danny Grant, Guy Lafleur, Danny Gare, Bill Barber. The list goes on.

Notice any Leaf names in there? No. Frank Mahovlich was painfully close, scoring forty-eight in 1960–61.

After Richard hit fifty, the number was reached or eclipsed fifty-seven more times before the Leafs had a player worthy to join the club. Rick Vaive scored fifty-four in 1981–82.

"I guess I had forty-five or forty-six goals and [reporters] were telling me, 'You could be the first player to score fifty goals as a Maple Leaf.' And I was shocked," Vaive recalled to the *Toronto Star*. "I couldn't believe with all the great players over sixty-some years the franchise had existed at that time, nobody had done it. So for the couple of weeks leading up to it, it was like, 'Wow, I'm right there. I could do this.' And it's all anybody wanted to talk about. There was pressure that year, no doubt about it."

Scoring was so much more predominant back then that fifty-four didn't even lead the league. Wayne Gretzky set the all-time record with ninety-two that year, 1981–82, a pace that included getting his fiftieth goal in thirty-nine games, obliterating Richard's record of fifty in fifty. Nine players had at least fifty that season.

Vaive was a consistent scorer, potting fifty-one the following season and fifty-two the year after that. The dam had broken. Gary Leeman (fifty-one in 1989–90) and Dave Andreychuk (fifty-three, 1993–94) also managed fifty-goal seasons in the blue and white.

The pace of scoring, and the number of fifty-goal seasons, dropped considerably from the mid-1990s onward. In the salary cap era (from 2005–06 on), players topped fifty just twenty-two times up until Matthews's magical 2021–22 run. Alex Ovechkin was responsible for eight of those times.

The beat went on. Matthews scored goals thirty-five and thirty-six in a win over Minnesota. For those counting—and Leaf fans were—that was seventy-seven goals in his last hundred games, dating back to the previous season.

He scored a hat trick against Seattle to reach forty-three goals in the season. He had just scored ten in his last ten games, thirty-six in his last thirty-seven. It was March 8, still more than a month's worth of hockey to be played.

The conversation wasn't about whether he could get to fifty. It turned to, could he beat Rick Vaive's team record of fifty-four? Or, oh my, could he score *sixty* in a single season?

He scored his forty-fifth goal in just his fifty-sixth game against the Buffalo Sabres, in an outdoor game in Hamilton's Tim Hortons Field, home of the CFL's Tiger-Cats. It came at a price, though.

The game had a vicious edge to it. Matthews was targeted all game. It finally got to him, and he cross-checked Rasmus Dahlin in the face. The league suspended him for two games, his first run-in with the Department of Player Safety in his career.

"I was a little bit disappointed, a bit more than I was expecting," Matthews said at a practice the day after his suspension was over. "I think as a player I've got to be in control of my stick . . . My intent was never to touch the guy up high, but I did. I made a mistake, and I recognize there's got to be some kind of punishment. I just thought two games was kind of a lot."

The Leafs won both games without him, and when he returned, he still led the Rocket Richard race by five goals. And he scored in his next game to sit at forty-six, when Canadian entertainer and mega–Leaf fan Justin Bieber made his presence known. The two were developing a burgeoning friendship.

It was clear that the association between Bieber and Matthews benefited the Maple Leafs. Star power with star power does that. Bieber's former design company, Drew House, designed a special jersey for the Leafs (and for fans) that they wore against New Jersey, a black-and-blue design that reversed to show a second black-and-yellow design. Matthews didn't score, but he clearly had fun seeing Bieber after the game.

"I thought it was awesome, I thought it looked good," Matthews said. "I like the black. I think when you wear black on the ice, it's pretty intimidating, it kind of makes you look bigger, so it kind of helps us out in that department. I thought it was cool and unique to flip them inside out. The jerseys looked great, and I thought they turned out well."

The scoring resumed the next game, and the game after, and the game after. Heading into a showdown against the Winnipeg Jets, Matthews stood at forty-nine. The whole Matthews vs. Laine thing had run its course. Laine wasn't even a Jet anymore, having been traded to the Columbus Blue Jackets. He wasn't much of a scoring threat either anymore. Clearly, Matthews was the best of the best from the 2016 draft—and moving on to other plateaus.

"That kind of stuff, I think, just has a way of working itself out," Matthews told Dave Feschuk, speaking of statistics. "As long as I'm just taking care of myself, making sure I'm playing the right way on both sides of the puck, obviously we have some really good players, and our chemistry has gotten better and better as the season's gone on. And we've just found, I guess, a recipe for success within our work ethic and competitiveness on both sides of the puck. So as far as [fifty goals] goes, it's not really something I'm too focused in on. It's not an easy feat, I don't think," Matthews said, speaking of fifty. "But the most important part is that we're winning games. And I think the rest of that stuff takes care of itself."

In all, ninety-two NHL players had managed a fifty-goal season before Matthews completed the feat on March 31, 2022. His shot drifted down the ice into the Winnipeg Jets' empty net, the Leafs' sixth goal in a 7–3 win. When Matthews's effort crossed the goal line, the Leafs and more than eighteen thousand fans went into a frenzy, cheering the historic moment.

"It's just pretty special to do it here, in front of our fans, all the energy and atmosphere, all that kind of goes into it," an appreciative Matthews said afterward. "I didn't envision [the fiftieth goal] going into an empty net, but I'll take it. I had so many chances tonight, but they just didn't go in."

He was the first player to reach fifty that season, moving one goal ahead of Edmonton's Leon Draisaitl in the race for the Rocket Richard Trophy.

"This is special, but this won't be the last time we see special things from Auston," said his coach, Sheldon Keefe.

How about Vaive's record of fifty-four? Or another elite plateau: sixty? His scoring pace was amazing, scoring on average four goals every five games. No one had scored sixty since Steven Stamkos did it in 2012. Matthews and the Leafs had twelve games to go.

Matthews scored a hat trick on April 4 against the best goalie in the game, Andrei Vasilevskiy and the Tampa Bay Lightning, giving him fifty-four, tying Rick Vaive's team record. It was also his forty-seventh goal in his last forty-seven games. He, too, was on track for fifty goals in a fifty-game span.

Two games later in Dallas, Matthews had another two-goal night. He scored on the power play at 18:58 of the second period for his fifty-fifth goal to break Rick Vaive's single-season record on a one-timer from the circle that beat Scott Wedgewood. Then he kept going, scoring number fifty-six in overtime, driving the net, for a 4–3 victory over the Stars. Leaf fans in the Dallas building chanted "MVP!"

"It hasn't really weighed on me too much. I take it game by game, and obviously every game I'm trying to create offence and try to score and try to produce and help the team win," Matthews said modestly that night.

He'd passed Vaive. Matthews stood alone among Maple Leafs goal scorers in the then 105-year history of the franchise.

Vaive was watching and rooting for Matthews.

"I'm actually enjoying it. He's a hell of a player and obviously a magnificent goal scorer. It's not a problem for me. I've had [the record] for forty years, and it's probably time for a generational player like him to take over that crown. He's worked extremely hard in the off-season to become a better player every year. That's important. For him to do what he's doing, I think that's great."

Vaive was surprised his record stood for so long. "It's been forty years. I'm surprised because of some of the good players they brought in here like [Mats] Sundin. He's the team's all-time scoring leader and never got there."

With Rick Vaive in attendance posing for pictures with Toronto's new single-season goal-scoring king in a home game against Montreal, Matthews potted two more, goals fifty-seven and fifty-eight, but also had fifty-one goals in fifty games. He became the first Maple Leaf, and thirteenth player of all time, to do so.

Richard, Mike Bossy, Wayne Gretzky (three times), Mario Lemieux, and Brett Hull (twice) scored fifty in their team's first fifty games. Lemieux, Jari Kurri, Alexander Mogilny, and Cam Neely scored fifty in their first fifty games of the season, but not in their team's first fifty. Teemu Selänne, Bernie Nicholls, Charlie Simmer, Phil Esposito, and now Matthews have fifty-in-fifty stretches in one season.

Matthews was the first fifty-in-fifty player since Mario Lemieux, who accomplished the feat for a third time from October 26, 1995, to March 7, 1996.

He wasn't in the conversation with just Leaf greats anymore. He was now in the conversation with all-time greats.

Matthews had ten games to score two goals to get to sixty. It turned out to be a rougher-than-anticipated ride. He didn't score a goal in his next three games, but he did pick up three assists and surpassed the hundred-point total. He became the third Leaf, behind Darryl Sittler and Doug Gilmour, to hit that plateau.

But he was hurt and missed three games. The team called it "minor." Everyone was reminded the playoffs were around the corner and a healthy Matthews for the playoffs took precedence.

When he came back, he failed to score in his next two games. There were only two games left in the season, and he was stuck on fifty-eight.

What was he thinking? His answers were always of the team-first variety. But Steven Stamkos, who'd scored sixty in 2011–12, chimed in with how he felt as he closed in on sixty that year.

"I did not want to finish at fifty-nine, that's for sure," said Stamkos. "People were like, 'Oh, it doesn't matter.' It matters when you get to that number, I mean, forty-nine or fifty-nine. That would haunt you, I think, if you got stuck at that number. I was pressing. It certainly gave me something to shoot for down the stretch, a little different situation. We weren't as good a team as Toronto is, so at that time, it was something that the guys were really going out of their way to do, but it was special getting the sixtieth."

Matthews was not to be denied on home ice against the Detroit Red Wings, ending his longest goal-scoring drought of the season, having gone five games and sixteen days without lighting the lamp.

Matthews opened the scoring in the second period of the 3–0 win, then closed it with a wicked snap shot to the top corner from the high slot. It came after he curled at the blue line, barely keeping the puck in the zone, and found a seam in the middle of the ice.

"I was nervous about it a bit," Matthews said. "I got the puck, I had some room there, and I just shot it." He got a water dousing from his teammates and a two-minute ovation from fans chanting "MVP" and "Aus-ton Mat-thews."

If there was ever any lingering doubt that an American hockey player from the desert could be beloved in hard-nosed hockey Toronto, it was all erased.

"It was pretty special, honestly," he said after the game. "The receptions from my teammates, from the fans, it kind of sends chills down your bones."

His reward: He got game eighty-two off.

He became the twenty-first player to score sixty in a season. He earned his second Rocket Richard Trophy.

The voting for the Hart Trophy as most valuable player to his team wasn't even close. He scored 119 first-place votes and 1,630 total points based on votes, among the 195 ballots cast, to easily surpass second-place Connor McDavid, who had twenty-nine first-place votes, 1,111 points based on votes.

Only two Leafs had ever won the Hart before, and you had to go back a few generations: Babe Pratt in 1943–44 and Teeder Kennedy in 1954–55. On top of that, Matthews became the first Leaf to win the Ted Lindsay Award, the most valuable player as chosen by his peers—his fellow players.

As the goals mounted for Matthews en route to sixty, Tampa Coach Jon Cooper had gone one further. "I wouldn't be surprised if some time in his career he gets seventy. That's how good a scorer he is."

CHAPTER SEVENTEEN

Winter of 69

By May 2023, it felt as if the Auston Matthews–led Maple Leafs had run their course.

Matthews had a subpar—only for him—seventh season, amassing just forty goals. He had his best playoffs, with five goals and six assists in eleven games. The team had only a modicum of success. They won a round in the playoffs for the first time since this group got together, and indeed for the first time as a franchise since 2004. There was a great deal of optimism when they ousted Tampa in six games, only to see themselves be outplayed and out-goaltended by the Florida Panthers.

"You get out of the first round and it's a big talking point," Matthews said in his final postseason availability. "But obviously the main goal every year is to challenge, and win. We still haven't met that. But I think throughout the season, there's obviously ups and downs and adversity that gets thrown your way and lessons and experiences that are really important in the evolution of being a person, a player, organization, and team." But the evolution of the team seemed to be flatlining.

Changes seemed inevitable. The team might have to move on from one or more of its Core Four—Matthews, John Tavares, Mitch

Marner, and William Nylander—to go with a different look, a different makeup. Maybe just change for the sake of change. Maybe free up some cap space, which hadn't grown by much due to the pandemic, and there were needs at goaltending and defence. The general manager, Kyle Dubas, said as much about three hours after Matthews spoke.

"The goal remains the same, but perhaps the path needs to shift slightly," said Dubas. "I would consider anything with our group here that would allow us a better chance to win the Stanley Cup. I would take nothing off the table at all." Dubas had never spoken like that about his team, especially with the Core Four involved. The "We Can and We Will" rhetoric was gone.

As part of his answer, he praised the work done by the Florida Panthers that year. They had won the Presidents' Trophy in 2022, and lost in the second round of the playoffs, then traded two of their core players, Jonathan Huberdeau and MacKenzie Weegar, for Matthew Tkachuk, a power forward with snarl who could score and who led them to the Stanley Cup Final.

Suddenly the idea of one of the Leafs Core Four moving was on the table.

There were all kinds of issues with them. Notably, Tavares was on a full no-movement clause. Similar clauses were to kick in July 1 for Matthews and Marner. Nylander had a limited list of teams he could not be traded to. In addition, Matthews and Nylander were heading into the final year of their contracts, each eligible to sign extensions come July 1.

There was always some sort of speculation that followed Matthews around. He was American, and wouldn't he prefer to play for a big American team, like the Rangers or the Kings? Or why wouldn't he want to play for his hometown Coyotes, the same way Tavares had left the Islanders to play for his hometown team, the Maple Leafs?

Matthews was always steadfast in his commitment to the Maple Leafs. In that same press conference, Matthews expressed his desire to stay.

"My intention is to be here," said Matthews. "I've [said] that before, how much I enjoyed playing here and what it means to me and the organization, my teammates, and how much I just enjoy being here. It will work itself out in due time."

Dubas's ensuing press conference threw a little grenade into that notion. But a bigger bomb was to come.

Dubas's contract itself was coming to an end, and by the end of that week he'd had a stunning falling-out with Leafs President Brendan Shanahan. Dubas was fired. The biggest change wasn't going to come on the ice. It was happening off the ice.

The Leafs looked in complete disarray. The draft was only a month away. Free agency was right behind it. Management had to peruse scouting reports. They needed to make decisions. May, June, and July are the most critical months imaginable to prepare a hockey team for the following season. On top of that, Matthews and Nylander were at crossroads as far as their future as Leafs were concerned. And Shanahan suddenly didn't have a general manager.

By June 1, he turned to Brad Treliving, who had recently been fired by the Calgary Flames.

It was Treliving who had dealt Tkachuk to Florida for Huberdeau, proving he had what it took to make big trades of name players. It backfired, however. The Flames failed to make the playoffs. To be fair, though, the Flames had more points (ninety-three) than the Panthers (ninety-two). But ninety-two points were good enough for Florida to make the playoffs in the Eastern Conference, and Calgary's ninety-three weren't enough in the West. Winnipeg took the Western Conference's final playoff spot with ninety-five.

If there was a notion that Treliving was going to come in and shake things up, he telegraphed in his first meeting with the media that wasn't going to happen.

"This is a really good team," he said. "It's led by world-class players. It's hard to get talent. They've got talent. I know there's been heartache, and there's been some frustration in terms of where we've been in the playoffs lately. It's a hard league, but this team has put themselves in a position, and we're going to try to keep putting ourselves in a position to keep knocking on the door, keep knocking on the door, keep knocking on the door, and eventually push through."

Then he said it: Auston is the priority.

"Auston is one of the elite players in the world. We're not talking about a good player in the league. We're talking about an elite player in the world. Getting to Auston is a priority. But outside of the contract stuff, number one is just getting to build that relationship. It's not walking down and trying to arm wrestle about contracts. It's getting down and getting a chance to meet him, but more importantly, having Auston get a chance to meet me, know what we're about. And just talk a little bit."

And in a cagey move that was all kinds of smart, Treliving hired none other than Shane Doan to be his special assistant. Doan had been Matthews's favourite player growing up in Arizona and now was part of the Maple Leafs front office.

"He's somebody that I really enjoy and admire," Doan said of Matthews. "We joked when he got drafted that he's entering an NHL that's different than what I played in. He's going in as a first overall pick in the largest hockey market in the world. And he's going to be the premier player there. That's unique. And the way he's handled himself has been incredible. We've got a great relationship. He comes and skates down here, he's skated with me since he was sixteen. And we've continued those skates. It's been fun and I enjoy that. And we have a good relationship."

Doan, of course, offered his assistance in any way he could with Matthews's contract negotiations. But Treliving also had another ace in the hole that perhaps other general manager candidates didn't; it's that he knew Arizona.

Treliving had cofounded the Western Professional Hockey League in 1996 and merged it with the Central Hockey League in 2001 to become the new league's commissioner, a post he left in 2007 to join the front office of the Phoenix Coyotes. Treliving, his wife, Julie, and daughters, Ryann and Reese, resided in Scottsdale.

And he was already used to dealing with players from the Arizona hockey system, scouting centre Dusty Collins. Collins was born in Gilbert, Arizona, in 1985. He had been playing hockey since he was five. He was good enough to join the USNTDP's Under-18 roster in 2001, was drafted by the Tampa Bay Lightning in the fifth round in 2004, played four years at Northern Michigan University, and eked out a five-year professional career that included a twenty-three-goal season with the CHL's Arizona Sundogs. Collins never did get a deal with the Coyotes.

But David Spina did. He was never drafted but played his youth hockey in Arizona, born in Mesa in 1983. Four years at Boston College led to a minor league career that included time with the San Antonio Rampage, the Coyotes' top farm team, which Treliving was the general manager of.

If any manager was prepared to talk to Matthews about life in Scottsdale, living in the desert, or the trials and tribulations of hockey in Arizona, it was Treliving. The two hit it off. Treliving came away impressed.

"He's going to score goals. He's one of the world's best players. But when you get time with Auston he doesn't talk about that, he talks about team success. Everything for him is about taking responsibility for wins and losses, driving the group forward. How can *we* be better, not how *he* can be better. That's just the evolution, that's just the step that great players take. He's special-special. And those players have an aura around them. And he certainly does."

So the fact that on August 27—in the middle of a John Tavares charity hockey appearance—Auston Matthews posted to social media his own contract extension probably shouldn't have been the surprise it was.

Matthews had said he'd always wanted to stay. The new GM had said keeping him was his top priority. And both knew that going into the season without an extension would have created a team-distracting circus unto itself. They got the job done.

Matthews signed a four-year extension that came with an average annual value of $13.25 million. He would become the highest-paid player on a yearly basis starting in 2024–25. He'd pushed the bar beyond McDavid's $12.5 million AAV, signed in 2018, and Nathan MacKinnon's $12.6 million AAV, which kicked in for the 2023–24 season.

His agent, Judd Moldaver, had pulled off another Matthews quiet, harmonious contract coup, a month before the 2023–24 season kicked off.

"Like I've expressed before, my passion, my belief in this team and loving playing here in the city of Toronto and for these great fans and for the Maple Leafs," said Matthews. "Like I've expressed before, I take a lot of pride in that, and I've really enjoyed my time here. So getting it done is obviously very exciting. I can put it behind me now and continue to focus on myself, on the next couple of weeks here leading up to training camp and just going from there."

And boy did Matthews go in the 2023–24 season, with a hat trick in the season opener in a 6–5 shoot-out win over the Montreal Canadiens. He scored a hat trick again in his second game, a 7–4 win over the Minnesota Wild. He was just the fifth player in NHL history to open a campaign with consecutive three-goal performances, joining Alex Ovechkin (2017–18), Cy Denneny (1917–18), Joe Malone (1917–18), and Reg Noble (1917–18).

And he was the first Leaf to record hat tricks in consecutive games since Wendel Clark in 1994.

"He's just excited to be great and lead the way," said Tavares.

There was another hat trick against Buffalo on November 4. Goals were coming in bunches. Another Rocket Richard Trophy seemed inevitable. It's not like Matthews was ever deluged with questions regarding "just" scoring forty goals in 2022–23, but if he had been, he was answering them.

"You don't expect back-to-back hat tricks, of course, but I have gotten somewhat comfortable and used to Auston having big nights and making a big impact," Coach Sheldon Keefe said of Matthews's start. "To do so on back-to-back nights to start a season is terrific. He looks like he is having lots of fun."

Keefe's comments that night after a 7–4 win over Minnesota hinted at what was to come that season for Matthews.

"Auston is focused on the big picture here. He is looking to really drive our team. He knows his job is to score, but I really don't think he cares how many goals he gets or what the number is in the end. It is about how many wins we have, how good our team is, what we are building towards, and how he can lead us there. That is where his focus is. All of the other stuff comes with that. I don't know how many times he picked off pucks on the back-check tonight and turned it around the other way. To me, all of those things are connected. When Auston is feeling it like that and making such an impact on the game in all areas, the goals just seem to come.

"The year he got sixty, defensively, I thought he was

outstanding. The year before that, defensively, he was outstanding. He just has way more jump in all areas of the game on all sides of the puck."

One thing that is true of Auston Matthews: He accepts the spotlight that comes with being an elite goal scorer on the most important team in hockey history. But he doesn't necessarily seek it. He'll avoid it as much as possible. He'll speak to the media when the moment requires it—a big goal, a big win, a big loss. But he'd rather avoid the idle chitchat that contributes to the white noise that can accompany life with a professional sports team.

He has frequently left the team's dressing room in Scotiabank Arena or the team's practice facility before the media enters. Unless specifically requested, of course. Which happens a lot.

The effect of signing his extension for the 2024–25 season before the 2023–24 season even began is evidence of that. He didn't want the contract discussion to be the focus it would have been.

Instead that focus switched to William Nylander, whose contract also expired at the end of the 2023–24 season. Of the members of the Core Four, Nylander had been a relative bargain at an AAV of $6.9 million, compared to Marner, Tavares, and Matthews.

There were rumblings he wanted too much money, as much as $10 million a year.

Nylander's personality was different from Matthews, though the two were alike in many ways. Nylander was cool as a cucumber. They called him "Willie Styles." If he was ever frayed, he never showed it.

But who was best dressed? One night it might be Nylander, the next it might be Matthews. Both in Euro-style.

Of the two, Matthews was the better conversationalist with the media, though he doesn't really like talking about himself. Nylander seemed a little more comfortable with people talking about him.

Nylander was off to his best-ever start, actually leading the Leafs in points when the team headed off for a European adventure, two games in Nylander's hometown of Stockholm.

Nylander was a hockey hero in Sweden, a world champion, son of Michael Nylander, a great hockey player in his own right.

William Nylander was on fire at the Globe Arena, the prime reason the Leafs won both games.

Nylander appeared on Swedish TV shows and on the red carpet for the premiere of a miniseries about Börje Salming. He scored the biggest goals in front of an adoring crowd, his grandmother watching him play as a professional for the first time.

Matthews took a back seat. Understandably so.

"We all love Willie. He's a special guy," Matthews said. "He's a special player. And I have no doubt that this is a trip that we'll all remember. But it's I think especially special for him . . . being here for two games in Sweden."

While Nylander was in the midst of a career year—at just the right time with his contract expiring—it didn't take long for the numerologists to start looking at Matthews's goal numbers. With twelve goals during a seven-game scoring streak, he was at twenty-eight goals by Christmas, in just thirty games.

There were a lot of issues with the Leafs at that time that had drawn attention away, primarily about goaltending. Goalie Ilya Samsonov was struggling. Backup Joseph Woll was injured. Free-agent forwards Tyler Bertuzzi and Max Domi weren't living up to their billing. Defencemen were getting injured. Even Captain John Tavares and winger Mitch Marner were having off years.

And though it looked at mid-season as if the Leafs were flirting with missing the playoffs, Matthews kept scoring. He was flirting with a seventy-goal pace.

By the time the All-Star break rolled around, he had forty goals in forty-six games.

Matthews kept the momentum going through the 2024 All-Star Game, held in Toronto, as he and teammates Mitch Marner, Morgan Rielly, and William Nylander won the team event and shared $1 milllion. Matthews had two goals, including the winner.

"The whole weekend in itself was special for all of us, especially the host city and the hometown guys," said Matthews. "Nice to cap it off with a win, and everyone goes home happy."

It was a feel-good story that set up the stretch drive. The Leafs still hadn't asserted themselves in the standings, sitting on fifty-eight points, tied with Detroit for a wild card.

But Matthews was about to get hot, and so would the Leafs. Matthews would score back-to-back hat tricks against Philadelphia as part of a run of a season-best seven wins in a row. Matthews would score ten times over six games in that run, getting to a landmark fiftieth goal—and fifty-first—in his hometown.

Goal fifty was on the power play, a pass from Timothy Liljegren followed by a hard, tight-in-the-corner, bad-angle, deceptive wrist shot. Other than a big smile, the celebration was muted. Up in the stands, Brian and Ema were far more effusive, jumping, hands in the air, sharing high fives.

He reached fifty in just fifty-four games, the fastest Maple Leaf to the mark, and the fastest American player to do so, beating Kevin Stevens's record by eight games.

"It's great, it's a small step in a long season," he said after the game. "But playing at home, and playing against a team that's had our number the last couple of seasons, it was a good win and a good effort throughout the lineup."

It happened on the NHL's smallest stage: the five-thousand-seat

Mullett Arena, a college rink in Tempe, Arizona, an embarrassingly small rink for the pro league. Brian and Ema Matthews were in the stands that night with some cousins from Mexico.

What none knew then was that this could quite likely have been Matthews's last game in his hometown. The Coyotes were like vagabonds in their own city. They had moved from America West Arena—the place Auston's Uncle Billy brought him to for his first game in 2003. They moved to Glendale, the suburb on the western edge of the region, and where Matthews saw Ovechkin score "The Goal," until 2022.

Their original home had been turned into a basketball-only venue. They lobbied the city of Tempe to build a new arena. They failed.

Unwilling to move to another city, Alex Meruelo, who'd become majority owner in 2019, made a deal with Arizona State University to let the team play in the college rink, Mullett Arena. The NHL, quite reluctantly, allowed the Coyotes to play in a rink built for five thousand fans. It was by far the smallest rink in the NHL, and truly not up to league standards.

"Selfishly growing up there and them being a big part of me getting into hockey, I hope they can figure it out," said Matthews. "But you can understand the position of the NHL as well. It is what it is. It's out of my control."

At the time, though, the Leafs were on a roll. Next stop was goal number sixty—unlike in 2022, when Matthews needed the eighty-first game of the season to get there (his seventy-third), it came much earlier, in game seventy-two. And it happened against one of his favourite victims, the Buffalo Sabres, in their building, KeyBank Center, the place where he'd been drafted first overall in 2016. The place was filled with Leaf fans. The seats are an easy mark for the

Leafs travelling fans. Buffalo is close to home, just ninety minutes away (in good traffic). Seats are cheaper than at Scotiabank Arena. Sabres fans, whose team has been in the dumpster, are always happy to sell Leaf game seats at a premium to help offset the cost of the season subscription.

The decked-out Leaf fans that night chanted "we want sixty" and "MVP" when Matthews was on the ice.

With 5:37 remaining in the game, Matthews put a rebound into the Sabres net, and he let loose an emotional fist pump.

"It means a lot, obviously," said Matthews. "It's as much of a team accomplishment in my opinion as an individual one. It's always a fun atmosphere here with all the blue and white in the stands, so it was pretty cool."

He became the only active player with two sixty-goal seasons, and the first American-born player to register two sixty-goal seasons. (Brett Hull had three such seasons, but though he represented the US internationally, he was born in Belleville, Ontario, and played youth hockey in British Columbia.)

The goal was the nineteenth goal he'd scored against Buffalo. Only Montreal (twenty-six) and Ottawa (twenty-four) had been victimized more to that point by Matthews, and he ran up some of those numbers playing both teams nine times in the 2020–21 season, one in which temporary realignment was necessary due to COVID.

"He's had an incredible season, scored in different ways," Coach Sheldon Keefe said of Matthews. "Happy for him to get that accomplishment again. He does so much for our team. It's more than just the goals. For him to get it is great. If you're not going to get it at home, [Buffalo] is second best. I loved the fans acknowledged it, too."

Matthews became the ninth player to register at least sixty goals in two seasons, and the first since Mario Lemieux registered his fourth sixty-goal season in 1995–96. Matthews had joined elite company.

The big question was, could he get to seventy?

He scored two the next game against Florida, one three nights later in Montreal, one more two nights later against Pittsburgh.

He was in the midst of an eight-game goal streak. He passed Connor McDavid's sixty-four-goal plateau from the 2023–24 season. He joined Alex Ovechkin as the only active players with sixty-five-goal seasons.

"You're watching history," marvelled teammate Ryan Reaves. "You're watching Maple Leafs history."

He reached sixty-six—the most among active players—in New Jersey. And he scored two more at home against the Devils. That they were sixty-seven and sixty-eight mattered somewhat less.

What mattered more: They were the 366th and 367th goals of his career. He had passed the legendary Dave Keon for third on the team's all-time scoring list. Keon had amassed 365 goals in a 1,062-game career with Toronto. Matthews beat it in 559 games. Only Darryl Sittler (389) and Mats Sundin (420) had scored more often as a Leaf. And they were now in his sights.

"It's remarkable what he's doing," said Captain John Tavares. "There's no question that we're seeing something truly special."

That scoring streak got him right to sixty-nine—against Detroit, at home in Scotiabank Arena—in game eighty. Again, fans were chanting "MVP" and "we want seventy." They gasped every time he touched the puck. Halfway through the game, he took a pass from Mitch Marner and beat James Reimer on the short side. He might have scored his seventieth that night, only he hit the crossbar. He was trying not to think too much about it.

"I just try to take the same approach to the game every night," said Matthews. "I just try not to really overthink anything, just go out and play my game and compete."

There were two games left in the regular season: in Florida and in Tampa. He had five shots in Florida, twelve in Tampa. And no goals.

"I wanted it for sure," he said of that elusive seventieth goal. "But it just wasn't meant to be."

As the season wrapped up, there was a lot he had accomplished that put him in rarefied air. Matthews had eighteen multi-goal nights that season, the most by any player since Alexander Mogilny in 1992–93. At twenty-six, he wrapped up his third Rocket Richard Trophy.

But there was more. He was nominated for three more awards: the Ted Lindsay, as MVP as voted by the players, the Lady Byng for gentlemanly play, and, impressively, the Frank Selke. Imagine that: The best goal scorer in the league was also deemed to be one of the game's three best defensive forwards.

It was a level his coach, Sheldon Keefe, had seen coming. Sometime around Christmas 2019, Keefe had taken Auston Matthews aside for a conversation.

It was about Matthews's future, what kind of player he wanted to be. At the time, Matthews was still just twenty-two, a proven goal scorer, a legitimate star. But Keefe had a point to make. Matthews had sixteen goals in his first twenty-five games, en route to a forty-seven-goal season (in seventy games).

"'The pace is less than one goal a game, and you're going to get twenty-some shifts per game,'" Keefe said he told him. "'So how are you impacting the game in those [other shifts]? That's what really being great is. And that's what can drive our team.' He really bought into that."

It may fly in the face of reason that the greatest goal scorer of his generation could be also great defensively, but he is.

"He's right there with anyone defensively in my opinion as a forward," said teammate Mark Giordano, a Norris Trophy winner as top defenceman. "He wins face-offs, he plays the right way. He blocks a lot of shots, too. People don't give him enough credit for that. He gets a lot of blocks in there because he reads the play so well. He's a great two-way player. He doesn't get enough credit because he scores so many goals. Everyone talks about his offence all the time."

The 2023–24 season saw Matthews mature into a complete two-hundred-foot player. A disrupter in his own end. A takeaway artist. Bump and get the puck. Block shots. Win face-offs. Get the puck and go the other way.

"As he's gotten older, more experienced, he's shown great passion for winning puck battles and defending hard, limiting time spent in the defensive zone, valuing the puck," said Coach Sheldon Keefe. "All these kinds of things make up a complete game."

Matthews was the Maple Leafs' most decorated player as far as individual awards go. Dave Keon had three: the Lady Byng, the Selke, and the Conn Smythe, given to the most valuable player in the playoffs.

Though he didn't win any of the three he was up for that year, Matthews already had six: the Calder, three Rockets, one Hart, one Ted Lindsay.

Something bigger was on the way.

CHAPTER EIGHTEEN

Beyond Hockey

When the story is told of how Auston Matthews became a hockey fan, the central character in that story is Uncle Billy.

Uncle Billy, nicknamed Dollar Bill, was the hockey fan, the one with the Coyotes season tickets, the one who took his toddler nephew to his first NHL game. But that's not the full story.

There's a sadder version. Bill died when Auston was quite young. Bill was just thirty when he died of cystic fibrosis on October 11, 2000, a genetically inherited disease. Auston had only just turned three.

"He was the only one in our family who has had it," Auston Matthews told *The Athletic*'s James Mirtle in 2017. "It was a lot different back then, with the stuff that you've got to do to stay alive and treatments. It's a pretty tough disease."

Bill and Brian Matthews were quite close. Bill's life in Arizona is one of the reasons Brian and Ema left California after Auston was born.

Bill's memory—understandably—looms large in the Matthews family lore. As far as Auston's place in hockey goes, Uncle Billy will always be a part of it. And so will cystic fibrosis.

Auston may not fully remember his first game with Uncle Bill, being just a toddler. Apparently it was the Zamboni cleaning the ice surface between periods that really transfixed him that first game.

"He had season tickets to Coyotes games, so he would always bring me and my dad," Matthews said in a YouTube video posted by CCM in 2024. "Without him and without that connection, I'm not sure I'd be playing hockey."

But the story of Uncle Billy was one that has never left him. His attachment to his uncle is a story that resonated even more strongly when he got to Toronto and started immersing himself in the local community. An involvement with the Hospital for Sick Children was perhaps inevitable, since the Maple Leafs make regular charitable visits there.

But for Auston, something else resonated, something beyond the usual.

Only a few years earlier, in 1989, Dr. Lap-Chee Tsui and his team at the Hospital for Sick Children in Toronto, together with Dr. Francis Collins at the University of Michigan, made history as they became the first to discover the gene responsible for cystic fibrosis.

It was more than hockey calling Auston Matthews to Toronto. When he found out SickKids' leading role internationally in finding a cure for cystic fibrosis, he knew he would have to help. No, not "have" to help. He'd love to help. Auston talked things over with his dad, dove right in, and called the hospital.

"Auston gives back in ways that he feels will honour my brother," Brian told Sportsnet for a documentary called *I Am: Auston Matthews*. "We tried to raise our kids in a certain way with certain values. And one of the things we told them: The best way to judge character is to see how people treat other people who can do nothing for them."

Cystic fibrosis is inherited genetically from parents. It impairs the normal clearance of mucus from the lungs, but can also affect the pancreas, liver, kidneys, and intestine. Thick mucus accumulates. Long-term issues include difficulty breathing and coughing up mucus as a result of frequent lung infections. Other signs and symptoms may include sinus infections, poor growth, fatty stool, clubbing of the fingers and toes, and infertility in most males.

Quality of life is affected. Lung disease eventually worsens to the point where the person is disabled. Today, the average lifespan for people with CF who live to adulthood is about forty-four years. Death is most often caused by lung complications.

It is a very isolating disease. Germs can spread as far as six feet when someone coughs or sneezes, landing on surfaces or in another person's eyes, nose, or mouth. That's why it's important for people with CF to stay at least six feet away from others with CF and anyone with a cold, flu, or infection.

That's the world Stephanie Stavros was born into, feeling like she lived her life at SickKids. Thanks to the work of SickKids hospital, she survived. And thanks to the genetic breakthrough of doctors Tsui and Collins, some groundbreaking gene-modification therapy is helping her live a more normal life.

Maple Leafs used to come for frequent visits.

"I wasn't a big Leaf fan as a kid, so I really think I humbled them, because I could care less when I saw them wandering through the halls," said Stavros.

She's a fan now, of one in particular: Auston Matthews.

As an adult, she's an ambassador for SickKids, drawing attention to rare disorders and diseases, to help raise money to find cures and treatments. She says no celebrity has done more for cystic fibrosis than Matthews.

"When you meet him, you never feel rushed," said Stavros. "I've never felt like I was wasting his time. He has extreme eye connection. He's very gracious. He gives out lots of big hugs. Like he just lifts kids up in the air and embraces them. He is a truly humble, wonderful human being. You almost forget you're speaking to this legend."

The kids, of course, love him. Not just because he's a great hockey player.

"They know he's the legend that he is," said Stavros. "But also I think they think of him as a big buddy. I've talked to moms in the CF community, and I've talked to the kids. And I really feel like he has a reputation almost like a big brother or favourite uncle vibe with the CF community. Auston doesn't walk into the room and make you feel less than. It feels like you're meeting an old friend. He really has a gift when it comes to just connecting with people."

This is a part of Auston's life that does not get widely reported. That's because it's never about the player; it's about the kids.

"The parents want to see their kids smile," said Lisa Charendoff to *The Athletic* in 2017. "They have to go through so much with their cystic fibrosis treatments. They miss a lot of school. So to be able to meet somebody who's really giving them that kind of focused attention just makes them feel special."

One thing Auston did was perform in a video that showed how a particular breathing device worked.

"Kids who have breathing disorders like cystic fibrosis come, and one of their regular tests to see what their baseline is and how they're doing is they have to really have a huge breath in and breathe out as hard as possible for as long as possible into a tube," said Charendoff. "The kids don't like doing that. So the director of that area asked him, 'Would you consider doing this? We think it's going to inspire and motivate the kids and make them not feel upset about having to do it.' He very graciously said yes to it."

The video remains in use with the hospital.

"My impression, from the minute I met him, was that he was an extremely respectful, dignified, mature young man," Charendoff said. "It's hard to believe that he was at the time nineteen. He was so down-to-earth, did not walk in with any kind of attitude or strut, and that first impression was borne out with every subsequent time he came into the hospital. He's very natural with these kids and families."

Matthews's connection with SickKids has never waned. And though he was able to keep things private in the early years, now his face is far more widely known, so it's a little more difficult to remain incognito.

That's what happens when you become a superstar hockey player in the world's largest hockey market, your very arrival to work televised for the masses with the fashion critics dissecting what you're wearing.

There are other, shall we say, benefits, too.

For example, he's not the most famous person in his own friend group. That would be pop star and manic Leaf fan Justin Bieber.

It's a friendship that seemed to naturally grow, the two crossing paths at the 2017 All-Star Game in Los Angeles. Matthews was representing the Leafs. Bieber, a huge Leafs fan, played in the celebrity game that was part of the All-Star festivities.

Bieber grew up in Stratford, Ontario, a pretty good hockey player, but obviously a much better singer and entertainer. Despite his fame, he never lost interest in his beloved Maple Leafs.

He was there in Boston for Game 7 in 2019, posting on Instagram: "Dear lord, please be with Auston Mathews [*sic*], Mitch Marner, and all the Toronto Maple Leafs as they play game 7 against the Boston Bruins."

The friendship took off the next season, during a 4–1 win over the San Jose Sharks featuring this loud fan in a white knit hat yelling behind the bench and banging on the glass.

Matthews turned to a teammate: "Is Justin Bieber behind us?"

Indeed, he was. With his father, both having the time of their lives.

The next time Matthews skated to the bench, he made eye contact with the pop star.

"Yo," Bieber said. "What's up?"

Matthews told ESPN that Bieber spent the rest of the game pumping him up, then slid into his DMs that night. They messaged as the Leafs were whisked away on the team charter. "I was sitting next to Tyson Barrie, and we were both tweaking out," Matthews said. "Like, 'No way, this is so cool.'"

Within two months, Matthews, Barrie, and Mitch Marner were invited to play shinny with Bieber's childhood buddies in Stratford.

"He's small, but he's pretty fast, and he's got good hands," Matthews told NHL.com in 2019. "He loves to score goals. He doesn't believe in assists."

Matthews invited Bieber to a private box to watch a game with his family. During the pandemic, they vacationed together on a tropical island and co-starred in Instagram live sessions. Both had an affinity for chess. Each had the other to talk to about the fleetingness and perils of fame. Both are family-oriented.

"I didn't know him back in the day when he was a little bit younger and a little bit wilder, but now you just see he's very family-oriented, and he spends lots of time with his cousins, his dad, his mom," Matthews told ESPN. "He's very much involved in all of their lives and takes time out of his day to call them and make sure that they know he's thinking about them and stuff like that. I think that was just, for me, really cool to see because I try to be that way as well, but I think you can always get lost in that. Your life gets busy, but you can't forget about your family and the people that you truly care about."

They did things together, like go to UFC 264 in Las Vegas in July 2021 to see Conor McGregor fight Dustin Poirier.

"We were just like, 'Let's make a little trip of it, and maybe we'll just watch the fights and do the whole Vegas thing,'" Matthews told Canadian Press. "It was an incredible experience."

And on this night, Matthews and teammate Joe Thornton appeared in an Instagram story posted by model Kendall Jenner to her 190 million followers. Matthews was beginning that crossover from hockey star to much, much more.

People who travelled in Matthews's world also travelled in Bieber's world, at least in the off-season.

"Definitely some fun experiences," said former Leaf goalie Frederik Andersen, one of Matthews's closest friends when they were teammates. "It's like some pinch-your-arm kind of moment and that's heavy stuff. Justin, obviously he grew up being a hockey guy. Like he wanted to play hockey like any Canadian boy, and obviously Auston looked up to Justin, totally. It's a very unique situation where two guys at their level, at the very best of their worlds, look up to each other."

Andersen was one of those drawn into the Bieber–Matthews world, going to UFC fights, hanging with celebrities. He saw Auston walking through that world, but he was still just Auston.

"It was pretty exciting," said Andersen. "There's a big energy in the building, especially the ones in Vegas where you see the most celebrities. It's a big buzz. It's fun to get to meet so many celebrities and see how down-to-earth they can also be. Not everyone gets to see that. There are so many teenage kids that put them on a pedestal because they never get to meet them, and they think they're greater than life. But they're good people who are really good at what they do and have passion for it."

Auston Matthews's unusual path—certainly in his early

years—may explain some of his so-called non-hockey character traits. He has broken the mould of what people think about a hockey player.

That is, he's not afraid to show his personality, to make fun of himself, to stand out in ways hockey players don't normally stand out. And he does it in a way that's not really boastful, just showing a quiet confidence in being himself: The way he dresses. His moustache. His friendships with celebrities like Justin Bieber. He doesn't make a big deal about any of it, but others around him do.

In Canada there's this hockey mentality that no player is above the team. It dominates the Canadian sports fan's mentality. The personality-driven NBA can drive Canadian hockey fans crazy. Here was a star on a Canadian team getting attention for facial hair.

Granted, that pales in comparison to some of the antics of say, Dennis Rodman of the Chicago Bulls, or Philadelphia 76er Allen Iverson complaining about practice.

But it was a side of Auston Matthews that he didn't mind sharing. It opened a small window into him. It certainly helped that Lou Lamoriello—and his strict "no facial hair" policy—had been long gone. New GM Kyle Dubas was, to put it politely, far closer to the players' ages than Lamoriello and relaxed many of the policies.

It wasn't just Matthews. The other Young Guns—William Nylander and Mitch Marner—wanted to break the mould of a hockey player in their own ways. Old school was giving way to new school.

Auston Matthews developed a taste for clothing that year in Zurich. He arrived like a typical American teenager, in sweatpants. He left completely comfortable in the Euro-style, clothing that fit tight to the body, pants tapered tight to the leg. No socks.

Clothes and moustache aside, Matthews is one of the few players—and they're growing in numbers perhaps because of him—who's unafraid to show his personality on the ice. Usually, through the celly—the post-goal celebration.

The game is about winning, and it's a team sport, of course. But there's nothing wrong with a little individuality, a little personality, a little fun. In Matthews's mind, that will make the sport more accessible, especially to Americans who've enjoyed the showboating—both behind the scenes and on the court—of the NBA.

Players are their own brands.

The celly has been derided by conservative hockey purists, who'd rather see a player head to straight to the bench after scoring.

But Matthews is unafraid of breaking those norms.

"I talk about it a lot with my family and my agent, who is one of my best friends, just kind of being like transcendent in the game," Matthews said in an interview with Paul Bissonnette in the video produced by EA Sports to promote Matthews on the cover. "Just not being like everybody else. Being different and not just following the herd. Paving my own way. And I think that's kind of how I've always done it. That's how my parents raised me. To be myself and not really worry about what everybody else is doing or what everybody else thinks. Be yourself and have fun and don't be a sheep." His hockey star and celebrity status has made Matthews a natural spokesman. Over the years he's been part of campaigns for lesser-known companies like off-ice training technology company Marsblade and sleep-aid company Dream Water, and big-name companies like Apple, Nike, CCM, McDonald's, Uber Eats, Upper Deck, and Fanatics.

His worlds all collided at the 2024 All-Star Game in Toronto, where hockey, celebrity, fashion, music, and philanthropy met in the same place.

The NHL All-Star event had hit hard times. It had come across as too gimmicky in recent years, trying too hard. The real stars often preferred to skip it. And the game was typically played without hitting. Hockey purists pooh-poohed it. It never had a feel that it was truly an event, at least not the way the NBA All-Star event took over cities.

The NHL desperately wanted it to work, and so did its emerging young stars. The 2024 All-Star Weekend in Toronto was a case in point.

The biggest names not only came out but were heavily invested in it. Oilers Captain Connor McDavid, for example, designed a skills competition that was easy to understand and fun to watch. He won it, of course.

Matthews and his All-Star Leaf teammates Mitch Marner, William Nylander, and Morgan Rielly all wanted to make sure the rest of the All-Stars had a good time in Toronto.

Celebrities like singer Michael Bublé, actor Will Arnett, and, of course, Matthews's good friend Justin Bieber were a big part of the event. They were honorary coaches, and Bieber's oversized winter coat stole the show. He even took the ice for the pregame skate, as the All-Stars stopped him—not the other way around—for selfies at centre ice at Scotiabank Arena.

Bieber was a big presence. He'd designed the All-Star jerseys. And he put on a show in Toronto's famous Beach neighbourhood.

But there was more to it, of course. All-Star is a big networking event, and Matthews did his share with his sponsors. One that made a louder statement than Bieber's jacket was a crossover with CCM and SickKids. One patient in particular, eight-year-old Finnegan Sposito, was diagnosed with cystic fibrosis at five weeks of age.

Matthews met Finn when he was three and a half. It was December 23, 2019, and the Leafs beat the Carolina Hurricanes 8–6 in an afternoon game the team calls "Next Generation Games." As he typically does, Matthews invited children from the hospital to the box he and his family rent.

The Spositos got the call. Kids with CF cannot sit close to other kids with CF, but there were other families—kids with cancer—who were in the private box as well.

After the game, Finn and his parents got a one-on-one with Matthews. Among the things that Matthews learned about Finn, the youngster liked to draw.

"It was a phenomenal experience. He was such a down-to-earth guy. My son just absolutely adored him," said Matthew Sposito.

A connection grew and one day in December 2023, the Spositos got a call. Matthews wanted Finn to make a drawing for him so CCM could customize skates that Matthews could wear at the All-Star Game.

Finn was ecstatic. He drew a green dragon on one side, a teal dragon on the other, and a blue maple leaf on the back.

"That's supposed to be me and him," Matthews said on his Instagram post promoting the skates.

But there was more: a big media appearance with other kids from the hospital, cameras everywhere. It could be a lot for a seven-year-old. Matthews's focus, though, wasn't the media. He was focused entirely on the children.

"We did the promo for the skates, and all the CCM crew were there," said Sposito. "There were a lot of cameras, and it was like, I was overwhelmed. So I can only imagine my son. But with Auston, it's like none of that was even there. And he was just really in the moment, hanging out with Finn and talking with Finn and just really good with kids. You know how people are just really good at engaging, and just getting them to open up and be active in the conversation? He's just really good at relating to children. I definitely didn't know how amazing he is with kids. He's been fantastic every time we've met him and have done things with him. He's very focused on the child, and my son in particular when we're there, and just makes him feel special that way. Like they're the centre of his attention for that time. So it's really heartwarming."

CHAPTER NINETEEN

Playoffs and Curses

Given the team's playoff disappointments the past few years, it'd be easy to say the Leafs are cursed. It wasn't always so. They used to win. The last time was Canada's Centennial year, 1967, and Montreal was hosting Expo and wanted the Stanley Cup there to draw fans.

The Leafs had finished third at a time when four teams in the Original Six era made the playoffs. They had beaten the top-seeded Chicago Blackhawks and now had the favoured Montreal Canadiens on the ropes.

It was the evening of May 2, at Maple Leaf Gardens, Game 6. The underdog Maple Leafs had a 2–0 lead over the Montreal Canadiens going into the third period. Dick Duff had scored at 5:28 of the third period to cut the Leafs' lead in half. Late in the third, Habs Coach Toe Blake had pulled Gump Worsley for the extra attacker with less than a minute to go. Leaf defenceman Allan Stanley won the draw to the left of Terry Sawchuk and passed it to Red Kelly, who fed Bob Pulford, who fed Captain George Armstrong, who found the empty net to clinch the Stanley Cup. The eleventh as the Maple Leafs, the thirteenth in the NHL (including one as the Arenas, one as the St. Pats). The fourteenth for a top-level professional hockey team in Toronto (the Blueshirts won in 1914 in the defunct NHA).

On May 5, 1967, Toronto cheered its champions. It was a two-mile ticker-tape parade, a cavalcade of cars led by the 48th Highlanders. The parade route took the team from Maple Leaf Gardens, south on Church Street, west on Wellington, then north up Bay Street to Nathan Phillips Square. Children were sent home from school early so they could attend, and early in the day people stood at the best vantage points.

Armstrong hugged the Stanley Cup in a car with co-owner Harold Ballard. Dave Keon was feted as the Conn Smythe winner as the playoff MVP, the first Leaf so honoured. Mayor William Dennison greeted the team. "Such receptions have become a tradition," he told the crowd. "We are proud to honour this team."

The crowd size was about 2,500, smaller than the usual. Stanley Cup parades, in other words, had been a fairly common sight along Bay Street. If you missed this year's parade, there'd be another one next year. Or in a couple of years. Bobby Baun, in fact, didn't attend the 1967 parade, figuring there'd be another. That's just the way things worked for the Maple Leafs. But not anymore.

When Auston Matthews became a Maple Leaf in 2016, he joined hockey's most storied franchise. Not all the stories were good. Many of the stories told following 1967 focused on how the team was cursed in the playoffs. Larry Hillman, a six-time Stanley Cup winner, claimed to have put a hex on the Maple Leafs after he was fined $2,400 for a contract holdout following the 1967 Cup win.

Hillman was one of the unsung heroes of the Leafs 1967 Cup, having just turned thirty and played some of his best hockey. He had been earning about $15,000 a year and was hoping for a tidy raise to $20,000. Punch Imlach offered $19,000, then $19,500. Captain George Armstrong urged him to take it, but Hillman stood on principle.

Imlach fined him $100 a day for each day he failed to report (imagine what today's NHL Players' Association would say about that). Hillman eventually relented, but it cost him $2,400.

"I've left it on because they didn't pay me the $2,400 with interest," Hillman told the *Star*. "It would have been a lot cheaper to pay that than signing all those million-dollar players."

The Leafs became the first team in NHL history to win the Cup one year and miss the playoffs the next. Hillman would join the Montreal Canadiens to win his final Stanley Cup in 1969. The Leafs were swept in four games by the Boston Bruins that year, Boston only beginning a remarkable run of playoff dominance over Toronto that even Matthews would suffer through.

In retrospect, the Maple Leafs botched the 1967 expansion process, and the years that followed, selling players and their minor league affiliates, pinching the pipeline of young talent. They failed to invest in scouting, not understanding just how important the annual draft might become. No longer would they simply sponsor minor hockey teams to get access to their best players, essentially with the ability to claim playing rights for life. And cheapskate Harold Ballard took over as owner, letting players leave in the 1970s for the rival upstart World Hockey Association.

Thanks to the hard work of underappreciated GM Jim Gregory, the Leafs punched above their weight despite being hamstrung by Ballard. He scoured Europe, bringing in Swedes Börje Salming and Inge Hammarström. The Leafs had a very good team in the 1970s, with Darryl Sittler, Lanny McDonald, and Salming, and routinely made the playoffs. The high point of that era was an overtime goal by McDonald on April 29, 1978, to upset the budding powerhouse New York Islanders in the second round. That highlight goal is ingrained in the memory of every Leaf fan of the era, not the four-game sweep at the hands of Montreal that followed.

The Leafs had at least been Stanley Cup contenders in the

1970s, be it by the world of General Manager Jim Gregory, the "pyramid power" of Coach Red Kelly, or the visionary video-based coaching of Roger Neilson.

The 1980s Leafs really only had Rick Vaive's consecutive fifty-goal seasons to cheer for. A dead-last season in 1984–85 offered hope in the choice of future Captain Wendel Clark at first overall in 1985. They made the playoffs in six of ten seasons—hardly anything to celebrate with sixteen of twenty-one teams making the postseason. They won two rounds.

The death of Ballard in 1990 was the cause of macabre celebrations—maybe he was the curse—among Leaf Nation. The arrival of Doug Gilmour in 1992 and Mats Sundin in 1995, aided by top-tier coaches in Pat Burns and Pat Quinn, finally made the Leafs more competitive.

But curses? They continued.

The Leafs made it all the way to the Western Conference Final in 1993 and were up three games to two on the Los Angeles Kings with the Montreal Canadiens lying in wait to see who they'd play in the Stanley Cup Final. It was overtime and the Kings had a power play, with Glenn Anderson called for boarding with thirteen seconds to go in the third period.

Linesman Kevin Collins dropped the puck, and Gretzky shot it so quickly it hit Leafs defenceman Jamie Macoun and rebounded to the Great One, with Gilmour—bloodied—lying on the ice. Referee Kerry Fraser blew the whistle.

The league had a single-referee system back then. Fraser simply didn't see that Gretzky had not only high-sticked Gilmour but drew blood. Fraser thought it might have happened because of the follow-through on the initial shot, which is legal, rather than a battle for position. Neither of the linesmen, Collins nor Ron Finn, saw it either.

Under the rules of the day, Gretzky should have been penalized with a five-minute major and a game misconduct. But refs can't call what they don't see. There was no call.

To make matters worse, Gretzky scored the overtime winner to force Game 7 in Toronto. And he had his self-described greatest game ever in Game 7 to eliminate the Maple Leafs. Gretzky had a hat trick, including the winner, and an assist in a 5–4 decision over the Leafs.

Gilmour had had the greatest season—statistically speaking—by any Leaf. Gretzky praised him as the greatest player on the planet for that season. And he came up empty.

The Leafs went right back to the Western Conference Final in 1994. Doug Gilmour played with a broken foot from the opening series against Chicago. They fell in five games to Vancouver, a 2–3–2 format that saw the Leafs win the opener at Maple Leaf Gardens, then Vancouver take the next four, including all three at the Pacific Coliseum.

Of any of the Leaf legends of the post-1967 era, Auston Matthews most closely resembles Mats Sundin as a hockey player. Sundin was six feet, five inches, 233 pounds—two inches taller and fifteen pounds heavier than Matthews. Sundin was somewhat of a gentle giant. But he could do it all. He was a great skater, passer, and shooter.

And until Matthews came along, many believed that Sundin was the greatest player in Leafs history. His 420 goals and 987 points for the Leafs stand first in franchise history.

One of Auston's many nicknames is "Matts"—also spelt "Mats"—given to him by his Maple Leaf teammates who know all too well the kind of player Sundin was.

"I won't compare him to me," Sundin said in a 2017 interview with Rosie DiManno of the *Toronto Star*. "I will say it's fantastic watching him play, seeing a young man maturing, developing even from last year, and he's hardly even started his career yet. I have him right up there with Connor McDavid. The Leafs have waited so long to have a young franchise player to build around. He's that player." Matthews was just twenty when Sundin praised him.

"Just think of the average twenty-year-old, where they are in their lives," said Sundin. "I look at myself. At the beginning, there's all kinds of barriers that you're not used to, facing the media and being the face of an organization. Toronto is probably the toughest market to face that kind of challenge."

Sundin never got to the Stanley Cup either, his near-misses becoming frustratingly common. He arrived in 1994 in a multiplayer trade that involved Captain Wendel Clark joining the Quebec Nordiques. With Sundin, the Leafs made it to the conference finals twice. The Leafs moved to the Eastern Conference in 1999, possessing a postseason mastery of the Ottawa Senators. And with Sundin installed as captain, they made it to the Eastern Conference Final in 1999, bowing out to Dominik Hašek and the Buffalo Sabres in five games.

But it's the 2002 Eastern Conference loss to the Carolina Hurricanes that probably hurt the most. The two top seeds—Boston and Philadelphia—fell in the first round. But so did Sundin. He'd had his best season as a Leaf, with forty-one goals, including nine game-winners. But he broke his left wrist in the first round against the Islanders, missed all seven games against the Senators, and missed the start of the conference final against Carolina. Sundin came back for Game 2 of the conference final, but the Leafs soon lost their coach, Pat Quinn, for a couple of games to a heart arrhythmia. More than just Sundin were injured during those playoffs, a list that became comically long.

Sundin's era as Leaf captain came to an inglorious end in 2007–08, when, inexplicably, he wasn't re-signed for the 2008–09 season. He played his final season as a Vancouver Canuck while the Maple Leafs organizationally spun their wheels.

Between 2006 and the arrival of Auston Matthews, the Maple Leafs made the playoffs precisely one time. That was 2013. And again, it was against the Boston Bruins. The Leafs should get some credit for that series, given they hadn't beaten Boston all season and took the top-seeded Bruins to overtime in Game 7. But it was how they lost Game 7 that sticks in the minds of their fans.

"It was 4–1" is a mantra you hear around town when things go horribly bad. Yes, the Leafs, captained by Dion Phaneuf, looked like they were going to pull off the upset of upsets, until it all came crashing down. Nathan Horton scored at 9:18 of the third period, Milan Lucic scored at 18:38, and Patrice Bergeron forced overtime at 19:09.

The Bruins simply overwhelmed the Maple Leafs, Bergeron scoring again at 6:05 of overtime, proof to many that an unexplainable cloud hangs over the Maple Leafs, whom people simply started to believe were not allowed to have good things.

Brendan Shanahan arrived as president. As the team's Centennial Season approached in 2016–17, not only did Shanahan put his heralded Shanaplan in place, but he knew he had to do—or at least try to do—two things: Not only did he get Keon back in the fold, but he had to end that Hillman Hex.

"Yes, it's still there," Hillman told the *Toronto Star* in its January 23, 2016, edition. "It seems to have worked."

When the drought hit fifty that spring, Shanahan very quietly went to his board of directors at MLSE to get approval to pay Hillman.

"Shanahan knows the history of us older players," Hillman told the *Star* in the April 7, 2019, edition. "He checked into it and said he would like to correct the wrong. I was pleased."

The hex was lifted in time for the 2016–17 season. Auston Matthews, Mitch Marner, and William Nylander were free to create their own legacies.

By the skin of their teeth, the Maple Leafs made the 2017 Stanley Cup playoffs. Starting a run of consecutive postseason appearances superseded the Leafs of Sundin's era, Gilmour's era, Sittler's era, or even Keon's era. Eight seasons in the playoffs consecutively—and counting—as of 2024.

Making the playoffs in the NHL used to be easy: Four of six teams made it, later sixteen of twenty-one teams made it. Now it's sixteen of thirty-two, and the Matthews-led team continues to set the pace, if not ultimately winning the grand prize.

And though hexes and curses were lifted, the Matthews-era Maple Leafs faced some bewildering developments in their own playoff journeys, none ending the way they wanted them to. Often it was injuries that were added to insults.

Things started off well enough, postseason-wise, in 2017. The Leafs were the new kids on the block as far as the playoffs went, and teams were wary of this group led by seven rookies, including Matthews.

Ultimately, they fell in six games to Alex Ovechkin and the Washington Capitals, though Matthews tried everything to try to force a Game 7. He scored the first goal of Game 6, at 7:45 of the third period, to put Toronto up 1–0. The Capitals tied. And Marcus Johansson won it in overtime. It was the fifth overtime of the series. All six games were decided by one goal.

They'd punched above their weight all season, and finally a veteran team put them down 359 days after those Ping-Pong balls bounced the Leafs' way.

"They're young but they're strong," Ovechkin said of the Leafs. "They have a very good future."

Fans had hoped for better in 2018 and 2019, both winnable series against the Boston Bruins. The Leafs had a 4–3 lead going into the third period of Game 7, but Boston scored four times in the third against an overwhelmed Frederik Andersen, and Jake Gardiner had himself a historically horrific minus-5 evening.

It was the first inkling of a rift between Matthews and his coach, Mike Babcock. Matthews has always yearned to be the difference maker, the game breaker. Babcock sat him for stretches in the third period of Game 7. Matthews twice seemed visibly upset at the decision during the game.

If there was truly a rift—Matthews recoiling at Babcock's democratization of playing time—neither ever said so publicly.

"Sometimes people snap [on the bench]," Babcock told the media in a postseason scrum. "So what? That's the game. I asked him flat out, 'Do we have any problem?' He was sitting right there. We don't seem to [have a problem]."

The 2019 series against Boston was a head-scratcher. Nazem Kadri deserves some of the blame. An overly rambunctious hit on Jake DeBrusk in Game 2 saw him expelled for the length of the series. Even so, the Leafs were up three games to two after five. They failed to put the Bruins away at home and had to trudge back to Boston, where Gardiner again showed off his ability to give away the puck and Babcock stuck to his rigid use of players. No one was overplayed.

If the narrative around the Leafs postseason was taking a stranger-than-life turn, the 2020 playoffs might have trumped them all.

That was the first year of the coronavirus pandemic, a season stalled in mid-March. The NHL was desperate to get the playoffs going in the summer but decided simply to end the season and rate the teams by points percentage since so many had played a different number of games. Toronto and Edmonton opened their doors to the NHL, which had decided twenty teams—ten from each conference—would be invited to the postseason.

The Leafs, by virtue of a .579 point percentage based on a 35–25–9 record, placed eighth in the final standings. They'd face ninth-place Columbus in what was called the "Qualifying Round."

That whole season had been a ramshackle one, played a little off-kilter. There were plenty of injuries. Babcock had been fired, replaced by Sheldon Keefe. And the Leafs, embarrassingly, lost to a Zamboni driver. Their own, it turns out. David Ayres, who was a jack-of-all-trades in working for the Ricoh Coliseum, home of the Marlies. But he was also a practice goalie, and on the night of February 20, 2020, the Leafs were trailing 4–1 when Carolina ran out of goalies. James Reimer got hurt in the first period, Petr Mrázek in the second.

The Hurricanes were forced to use Ayres, Marlies helmet and all, on hand that night as the emergency backup. John Tavares and Pierre Engvall made it look easy as the Leafs closed to 4–3 by the end of the second period. And then? Perplexing history was made. The Hurricanes scored twice in the third period. Ayres became the first-ever emergency backup goalie to win a game. He stopped eight of ten shots and logged 28:41 time on ice in the Hurricanes' 6–3 win at Toronto.

Had Toronto won that game, their points percentage would have been .586. Had Carolina lost, their percentage would have been .580. The Leafs would have finished seventh and faced the Florida Panthers, a young team like the Leafs who bowed out rather easily to the New York Islanders.

Instead, it was the Blue Jackets, who'd developed a history of being giant-killers.

There was one warm-up game at Scotiabank Arena, against the Montreal Canadiens. The Habs were the home team and used the Leaf dressing room that night.

No fans were allowed in the building. Only a handful of media. Things couldn't get much more off-kilter than that.

No surprise then that Columbus—who had taken down the mighty Tampa Bay Lightning in a four-game sweep in 2019—took down the Leafs, three games to two.

None of the early exits might have hurt as hard as the one that followed: a 2021 loss to the Montreal Canadiens.

It was a strange season from the get-go. A delayed start due to the coronavirus pandemic, and with different rules regarding travel in Canada and the United States, the NHL was forced into a one-season realignment. The seven Canadian teams would be in their own division: the North. Border crossings wouldn't be an issue, since borders wouldn't be crossed. The league laid out a baseball-like schedule: two- and three-game series to reduce travel costs. The Leafs dominated the division, finished first, and drew fourth-place Montreal in the first round. It was the first time since Sittler's era—1979—that the Leafs and Canadiens would face each other in the postseason.

It shouldn't have been close. But Captain John Tavares was concussed in the first period of Game 1 and didn't play again. Trade deadline acquisition Nick Foligno was never fully healthy. Zach Hyman was injured late in the season but gamely played through it. The Leafs had a three-games-to-one series lead. But they couldn't put away the Habs.

Montreal won Game 5 in Toronto. The Habs were bolstered by the presence of 2,500 fans for Game 6 at the Bell Centre. It was the first crowd inside a sporting event in Canada since the pandemic hit more than a year previous. Montreal rode that momentum to take Game 6. The Leafs were allowed 550 fans—frontline workers in health care—for Game 7 but alas, it was a familiar finish.

"We realize that we let an opportunity slip," Morgan Rielly said.

Montreal went on to the final, losing ultimately to Tampa.

The Leafs lost in the first round to Tampa in 2022 and 2023, finally breaking through to the second round. The 2022 Leafs were probably the healthiest in some time. But Florida was not to be denied in the second round, en route to the final.

But all those cursed injuries returned for a rematch against Boston in 2024. William Nylander missed the first three games. Matthews was an absolute monster in Game 2 with two goals, including the winner in a 3–2 decision.

"What I have been impressed about with him is how tenacious he has been on pucks and how tenacious he has been on the forecheck. He has been relentless with his forecheck," said Bruins Coach Jim Montgomery.

"On the first goal, he wins the battle and rings it off the crossbar. It ends up in our net, right? On the other play, he gets in behind us. We can't let him in behind us. That is the most dangerous man on the ice. You have to be tighter.

"He is the most dangerous man on the ice because he has earned it."

Alas—and maybe this is some sort of hex that's never been addressed—Matthews got sick in Game 3; got hurt, a head injury, in Game 4; missed Games 5 and 6; and came back gamely in Game 7, assisting on the first goal in what turned into a 2–1 overtime loss and another early elimination.

The end of the 2023–24 season was a big disappointment on many fronts for Auston Matthews, both personally and professionally. It wasn't just another early playoff exit, because with the Leafs, there will always be next year.

There wouldn't be a next year for his beloved Arizona Coyotes. It was with some sadness in his voice that Auston Matthews addressed the fact that the NHL was leaving Arizona. The team's assets—including the active contracts of players and coaches—were sold to business interests in Utah. The Coyotes were no longer, shocking news that popped up just as the 2023–24 season was winding down and the Stanley Cup playoffs were beginning.

"Selfishly, it's kind of sad, disappointing," Matthews said at a season-ending scrum. "And I understand the NHL's viewpoint on it. So definitely a sad day when it happened for Arizona hockey, but hopefully they'll be able to bring a team back there at some point and be able to figure out that situation."

The promises of Coyotes owner Meruelo seemed empty. Mullett Arena wasn't good enough. The Suns had turned their facility into basketball only, and the Coyotes most certainly were not welcome in Glendale.

Utah came in as the white knight.

Matthews is well aware of what his legacy is to Arizona hockey. He's known it all along.

"I'm just a normal kid, I guess," Matthews told *The Arizona Republic* in its June 15, 2016, edition. "You do what you can do, and you work hard and put your mind to something. I don't think it matters if you're from Arizona or Ontario. Anybody that plays in the NHL, you obviously put in countless hours of work and have the talent and motivation along with it. I don't think it matters where you're from."

His bigger legacy, which continues to grow, will be to Leaf Nation. If Dave Keon is the benchmark of the first hundred years, then Matthews has rightfully inherited the mantle.

They say the Stanley Cup is the hardest trophy to win. It may well be now, but it wasn't back when the illustrious part of Maple Leafs history was being written. With four of six teams making the playoffs, you were more likely to be in the postseason than not. And with the rules essentially designed so that Toronto and Montreal could build dynasties, it was more a surprise if one of the teams didn't make the final than did.

By the time Keon left the team in 1975, he was the franchise's all-time leading scorer (365 goals, 493 assists for 858 points in 1,062 games). By 2016, he had been surpassed by only Mats Sundin (425 goals, 567 assists, 987 points) and Darryl Sittler (389 goals, 527 assists, 916 points), and Börje Salming in assists (the franchise leader in that category at 620).

Keon's thirty-two goals, sixty-seven points in eighty-nine playoff games also led the team at the time of his departure, until surpassed by Wendel Clark (thirty-four goals), Doug Gilmour (seventy-seven points), and Sundin (seventy points).

Keon was also among the most decorated Maple Leafs. He won the Calder Memorial Trophy as rookie of the year in 1961 and the Lady Byng Memorial Trophy as the league's best defensive forward in 1962 and 1963. And he won the Conn Smythe Trophy in 1967—the last of his four Stanley Cup triumphs—as most valuable player in the playoffs.

Understandably, Keon firmly believes that winning the Stanley Cup separates the great from good players.

"What is the object of this exercise?" said Keon to me in 2024. "At the start of the year when you gather in training camp, the object of the exercise to win the Stanley Cup. If you have all of these players putting up great numbers and you've won one playoff series in eight years or nine years, and you haven't even played for the Stanley Cup, then you have to take a look in the mirror."

The good news for Leaf fans, and Matthews and his teammates, is there's always next year. Matthews owned or surpassed most franchise scoring records by the time he was twenty-six.

Steve Yzerman was thirty-two—fourteen years in the league—before he won his first Stanley Cup. Alex Ovechkin was thirty-three—also fourteen years in the NHL. There's plenty of hockey left for Matthews to add on to that legacy, to prove he's the greatest Maple Leaf of all time, the greatest American player of all time, and secure that elusive Stanley Cup.

CHAPTER TWENTY

Captain Auston

Auston Matthews has answered to plenty of nicknames in his life, Papi and Matts among them. But there's one that might be more appropriate for the latter half of his career: Tone, a play on the last three letters of his first name. Sometimes it's Big Tone. That's because on the ice, in the dressing room, and around the team, Matthews is the one who sets the tone. He had done so as a rookie. He did so wearing the A as an alternate captain as he established team scoring records. Starting in the 2024–25 season, he would set the tone as captain.

There was one big issue: John Tavares was already captain, and the team's history of captaincy changes have always been messy.

Dave Keon spent an awkward first season as captain while George Armstrong was still playing. Armstrong had retired in training camp but returned out of boredom. In the interim, Keon was handed the C. "I think the C is where it should be," Armstrong said after he returned in November 1969. "It should be worn by a player of Keon's calibre."

Keon's final year as captain was spent battling owner Harold Ballard. Ballard thought Keon should be fierier, like Flyers' Captain Bobby Clarke, and frequently called out his players as lazy "fat cats."

Ballard let Keon go to the WHA—Keon's acrimony with the team only at its beginning—with Armstrong handing Darryl Sittler the captain's C. Sittler started his captaincy by blasting Ballard, saying he had mishandled Keon.

Sittler ripped the C from his jersey in a dispute with GM Punch Imlach, after Sittler's best friend, Lanny McDonald, had been traded to the Colorado Rockies in December 1979.

Sittler eventually put the C back on but found himself mentally stressed enough to leave the team and was ultimately traded in 1982 to Philadelphia.

Rick Vaive took over from Sittler, setting single-season scoring records Matthews would break. But his time as captain came to a rocky end as well in 1986. Vaive had been out late—hockey culture was very different then—on a road trip to Minnesota. He was with ex-teammate John Anderson, who had been traded to Quebec. The Nords had just played the North Stars. The Leafs were up next. Hot-tempered Coach Don Maloney called a 7:15 a.m. practice the next day, but Vaive overslept and missed that practice. He lost the C and ultimately was traded to the Chicago Blackhawks in 1987.

Rob Ramage was coming off a Stanley Cup win as a Calgary Flame in 1989 when traded to Toronto and almost instantly named captain, the first to have the honour without ever having played a game for the team. His two-year captaincy ended when the Leafs lost him to Minnesota in the 1991 expansion and dispersal draft. That draft would help stock the new San Jose Sharks while restocking the Minnesota North Stars.

A high-water mark for the Maple Leafs was on the horizon when Wendel Clark took over as captain in 1991. Two trips to the Western Conference Final later—in 1993 and 1994—saw Clark shipped out of town in a massive deal for Mats Sundin.

Doug Gilmour took over from Clark as captain, but by then the team had aged out, the heights of 1993 and 1994 playoff runs not to be repeated.

Gilmour more or less asked to be traded in 1997, complaining of a "fishbowl existence" in Toronto.

Sundin's tenure as captain was closest in class to that of Armstrong's. Long. Reliable. No Stanley Cup, of course, but decent playoff success and a reasonable amount of roster stability. But even the end of his time in Toronto was tumultuous.

The Leafs had missed the playoffs in 2006 and 2007 and were trending that way again in 2008. Cliff Fletcher, who'd traded Clark for Sundin in 1994, was back as an interim GM between the reigns of John Ferguson Jr. and Brian Burke. Fletcher had tried to trade Sundin at the deadline, along with Darcy Tucker, Pavel Kubina, Bryan McCabe, and Tomáš Kaberle. All had no-trade deals. All wanted to stay, hoping to pull off a playoff miracle. It wasn't to be. The Leafs missed the playoffs again in 2008, the five derided as "the Muskoka Five," the inference being they'd rather be at a cottage than in the playoffs.

Sundin was thirty-seven by then and still producing at a point-a-game pace, but unsure of his future. He became engaged. He wanted to play and retire as a Leaf, one of the reasons he refused to waive his no-trade deal.

The season over, his future hung in the balance. The Leafs let the Canadiens have a word before July 1 free agency. Sundin balked at a deal with the Habs.

Fletcher didn't sign up the classy Swede. Sundin ultimately signed with Vancouver and fittingly scored the shoot-out winner in his return to the Air Canada Centre on February 21, 2009, as a Vancouver Canuck.

Sundin would prove to be a tough act to follow, so it took a couple of years. By then Brian Burke was running the show, and his choice was Dion Phaneuf. Burke had admonished the media about making too big a deal that the team had been without a captain since 2008, that it simply wasn't that important, then threw a big bash for the Phaneuf announcement at Real Sports, the bar across the street from the downtown rink that is also owned by Maple Leaf Sports & Entertainment. Former captains George Armstrong, Darryl Sittler, and Wendel Clark were in attendance.

Phaneuf's tenure was an awkward one, just one playoff appearance, a Game 7 meltdown for the ages in Boston against the Bruins. His trade to Ottawa on February 9, 2016, helped set the stage for the Leafs to plummet to the bottom of the standings to give them the best odds to draft Auston Matthews first overall.

The Leafs remained without a captain until Tavares was named captain in 2019.

As GM Kyle Dubas put it then: "He's everything we thought he would be, and there's nothing negative about him whatsoever."

By the summer of 2024, Matthews had blossomed in many ways. But a team without playoff success needed change. The contract situations of the team's most important players suggested trading any of them would be impossible. Matthews, Tavares, William Nylander, Mitch Marner, and Morgan Rielly all had no-movement clauses. Like Sundin a generation before them, none expressed an interest to try to win elsewhere. They wanted to do the job in Toronto.

GM Brad Treliving did what he could. Coach Sheldon Keefe was fired, replaced by Craig Berube. That was a tangible change.

An intangible: Make Matthews captain, let him spread his wings more, let him lead.

But to name Matthews with Tavares still on the team, the Leafs needed to find a way to make this work.

Tavares was a good role model, a hard worker, easy to talk to, always striving to be better—all admirable traits in a captain. But he was stoic, almost too reasonable.

Matthews was looser, prone to sharing barbs in scrums, not afraid to show his personality. Maybe, Treliving reasoned, that could make a difference come playoff time.

It would take some massaging to get Tavares to give up the C, and to do it in such a way that there would be no acrimony, no controversy.

After a series of back-and-forth conversations among Tavares, Treliving, Shanahan, and even Berube, Tavares saw which way the wind was blowing and got on board.

In late July, Tavares called Matthews. "I remember after he let me know, I told him I was shaking. I had chills," Matthews said. "Like I said, it's just such a big honour to represent the Maple Leafs, to put on that jersey every night. To be a captain is truly special. For him to call me and let me know that he wanted to pass on the captaincy to me was very emotional. I felt a lot of things. But it was truly an honour."

As he took centre stage on the dais at Real Sports, the past and future of Auston Matthews collided.

It was Wednesday, August 14, 2023. John Tavares was to his right. GM Brad Treliving was to his left. His parents, Brian and Ema, sat in front of him, in the front row.

He looked comfortable in a pin-striped suit, peg-legged trousers, a casual white T-shirt, and white high-tops. That's not how hockey players used to dress, certainly not ones who are about to be named captain. But Auston Matthews had already broken that mould.

Now the team was embarking on another ceremony, one that looked and felt right, one that could be the template for future captaincy transitions.

Tavares was front and centre, truly the hero of the day. The

Tavares family were beside Brian and Ema Matthews in the front row, John's sons wearing Matthews sweaters. Tavares's last act as captain was to pass the C to Matthews, doing so quite literally in the form of a gift box: Matthews's new 34 sweater emblazoned with a C on it.

"What I've seen is Auston's evolution," said Tavares. "Obviously, we're talking about one of the best players in the game of hockey. The growth though has been incredible. I've learned so much. It's amazing how he pushes the team. I think a lot of the time, without him realizing it, you can just tell by the way he inspires us with his talent, his work ethic, and just being so level-grounded, just being one of the guys every single day. What he's shown to the team, the game, the drive to win is remarkable. And now with having this honour and responsibility, it really gives him the chance to spread his wings and grow through all that, through different areas that will help elevate him even more in our team. It's been amazing to learn from him, to play alongside him, and to continue that going forward."

Matthews became the first American to be captain of the Maple Leafs, the twenty-sixth captain in the team's history.

"We're very proud," said Brian.

CHAPTER TWENTY-ONE

Becoming a Leader

The Maple Leafs were not the only team for which Matthews wore the C in the 2024–25 season. He was one of the first to be named to Team USA's group for the Four Nations Face-Off, an event that marked the NHL's return to best-on-best international play. A month before the event, he was named captain, an acknowledgement by USA Hockey of just how dominant a player he had become.

"Auston's a guy that just has a quiet confidence about him," Team USA Head Coach Mike Sullivan said. "He carries himself with such humility. I think the best way he leads in my observation has been how he carries himself on the ice, how he carries himself off the ice. He's not an overly vocal guy, but when he speaks, he commands a lot of respect. Everyone has an incredible amount of respect for what he's accomplished in the game. He's a terrific player. He's one of the elite players in the game, and he's a quiet leader."

The core of the team was made up of players Matthews knew well from the US National Team Development Program. They quickly reverted to their high-school selves in their interactions with each other, recounting their "back-in-the-day" stories.

Zach Werenski remembered back to the summer of 2016, after

Matthews had been drafted first overall. The two were goofing around on Jet Skis on Lake St. Clair.

"We were doing some turns that I was pretty familiar with because I grew up with them and he's like, 'How do you turn like that?' I say, 'You go pretty fast, and lean one way and turn the other way.' So he tries it and he goes flying off the Jet Ski. And I go flying over there. I'm like, he's just drafted first overall, like a month ago. I'm like, 'Dude, are you okay, what happened?' And he was in the water laughing. He was fine."

Dylan Larkin remembered Matthews getting a firsthand look at what Toronto was going to be like for him one night in September when they were teammates on the Under-23 Team North America at the 2016 World Cup of Hockey.

"The tournament was in Toronto and he had just been drafted," says Larkin. "It was his first time in the Air Canada Centre. I just remember on the first night there, we went out to dinner and we got chased down the street by fans. We tried to protect him, but he handled it really well. And I'm sure right then he learned what it was going to be like playing in and being a star player in Toronto."

Everything he'd accomplished with the Maple Leafs made him the perfect fit for the American captaincy, for a tournament with three hundred accredited media and the international spotlight on his team, the presumptive favourites. If anyone could handle the media duties, his teammates reasoned, it was the guy who was captain of the Maple Leafs.

"When you go to a Canadian city and turn on Sportsnet or TSN, it's all hockey, and they're talking about Auston and pretty much the Leafs the majority of the time," said Werenski. "When you go to Toronto and play, you get a feel for—I don't want to say pressure—but like the media and the fans and how much they really care about it. Hats off to them. They're a huge hockey market, a huge hockey city.

And it's definitely different than other organizations, other teams around the league. It's probably the number-one most-talked-about team. And it's a lot to deal with, especially for a kid his age to go in there and do what he did. It's pretty incredible."

Of course, his sixty-nine-goal season in 2023–24 was still resonating even if his injury-ravaged 2024–25 statistics paled somewhat by comparison.

"Obviously scoring sixty-nine goals like that exceeds anyone," says Dylan Larkin. "Geez, that's just amazing in our game to do that and with the goalies now and the defence and how people penalty-kill. I knew he was going to be special on being picked first overall in Toronto. He's just such a great guy. I can't say enough good things about him, and he's matured a lot and he's had to grow up really fast. And in that market, he's had to deal with a lot of things NHL players don't have to deal with. But he's handled it with grace and, you know, he's a great leader. I'm very impressed by his leadership. And he does have that aura about him."

The tournament didn't go the Americans' way. Matthews set up both American goals in the final against Canada and had his best game of the tournament. But Connor McDavid's overtime goal won it, 3–2, for Canada, with a rematch hoped for in the 2026 Winter Olympics.

Matthews was the best American player in the final against Canada. He had three scoring chances in overtime, and he just missed breaking up Mitch Marner's pass to McDavid on the winning goal.

I asked him if that was the kind of thing that would haunt him.

At first, he gave a sassy answer: "Sure, Kevin."

But he also said he'd be a better player going forward. "You learn a lot, too, being around other great players, great people. There's a lot that you can take away other than just the opportunity to represent your country, which is huge. But definitely there's a lot that you can learn."

Maple Leaf teammate Max Pacioretty watched the tournament from his home in Connecticut.

"He's always trying to play winning hockey," Pacioretty said of Matthews. "I was sitting on my couch and resting and watching him grind it out against the world's best players. I have a whole new appreciation of superstardom."

Statistically, it was a down season for Matthews. He took a hit late in training camp that led to his missing nine games in November. He met with medical experts in Germany. He didn't need surgery, but was sidelined again for six games in late December while Leaf Nation fretted about their captain.

When he returned from the Four Nations, he scored four goals in his first three games back to lead the Leafs to a five-game winning streak as the team headed down the stretch to the trade deadline and playoffs. There had been moments all year with the Maple Leafs where his leadership shone through, where he knew his voice now carried a bit more weight as he, politely, knew how to call out his teammates, fans, and even management when the time was right.

In early January, his injuries now behind him, he'd scored in four of the last six games, but the team was struggling in the midst of a three-game losing skid. They'd lost to Carolina, Vancouver, and Dallas by a collective score of 13–4. Fans were restless. They'd yet to establish themselves as a top-tier team.

"Our execution can be better," Matthews said after that January 14 loss to Dallas. "We're going through adversity right now. As much as you prefer not to go through that, it's necessary sometimes. These are the kind of moments where we're going to come together even more and stick with each other and work our way out of it. That's really all we can do. That's the mindset."

The call to be better worked. They'd go on to win twelve of the next fifteen. One of those three losses, however, came at the hands of the Columbus Blue Jackets. Fan favourite Ryan Reaves got into a fight, his first that season. The crowd was kind of dead afterward. Matthews noted it.

"Would have liked a little more energy from the crowd after that," Matthews said. "I thought it was a little quiet tonight, especially after two guys like that go at it. But it was a great moment for [Reaves]. Gave us some energy on the bench."

The Leafs, as an organization, are deathly afraid of offending their paying customers, even if they can be one of the least engaging fan bases within the building, seemingly unwilling or unable to really get into the game. The Leafs' media relations folks had nothing to worry about. In the days following his comment, the chatter on social media and talk radio backed Matthews. Yes, the crowd at Scotiabank Arena can be quiet at times. "He's our captain. We look up to him, we follow him in the battle and what he says, we're right there with him," said teammate Steven Lorentz.

As the trade deadline approached, Matthews noted their closest rivals, Florida and Tampa Bay, had beefed up with big moves. The Panthers added big right-handed defenceman Seth Jones on March 1, six days before the deadline, also adding winger Jesper Boqvist in a deal with Seattle. Tampa brought Yanni Gourde back into the fold on March 5, two days before the deadline. In a scrum in Vegas, Matthews sent a clear signal to the team's management that he was expecting GM Brad Treliving to add players at the March 7 trade deadline.

"You look at our division, in particular. It's obviously very tight, and we know management is gonna do the best they can. All we can do is just trust in them," Matthews said March 6. "I mean, of course, you'd love to see a boost, I think, with the way that we've played this year and the position that we're in right now."

Not every player will come out and say something like that. If the team didn't make a trade, it could be quite embarrassing all around, but especially for management. Matthews continued on the theme.

"We feel really confident, really good about our team and our group. But this time of year, obviously, you see teams adding, and you want to add as well," Matthews said. "So, I'm sure the management staff are doing a lot of thinking right now, doing a lot of homework and stuff like that. And we'll just leave it in their hands. I'm sure they'll do what's best for the team."

Indeed, the Leafs added defenceman Brandon Carlo from the Boston Bruins and centre Scott Laughton from the Philadelphia Flyers. They'd pass Florida (who'd added Brad Marchand on March 7) as a result, and pull away with in the division title. Part of the surge was a game by Matthews in Los Angeles. The Leafs had lost in a shoot-out to San Jose, and given that they'd been on the road for much of the month—Matthews even longer because of his Four Nations appearance—it would have been understandable to throw in the towel against Los Angeles, a team that's hard to beat in Crypto.com Arena.

The Kings were up 1–0 when Matthews scored shorthanded, and he later drew a penalty and scored the winner on the ensuing power play. After a low-event first forty minutes, after which the Kings led 1–0, he put his fingerprints all over the final frame, leading the Leafs to a 3–1 win to cap off a roller-coaster week.

"You're not going to find more of a complete player in the game [than] Auston," Leafs centre John Tavares said. "We all know what a tremendous offensive player and goal scorer he is, but he makes plays all over the ice. That's why he's the catalyst and leader in every facet of the game for us."

As the season came to a close, Matthews scored his four-hundredth career goal in a 4–0 win in Buffalo, the second-to-last game of the regular season. It was his 628th career game. He became the fastest Leaf to four hundred, and sixth-fastest to four hundred in NHL history, bumping Alex Ovechkin to seventh. That was notable, because only a couple of weeks prior, Ovechkin had supplanted Wayne Gretzky as the NHL's all-time leading goal scorer.

Despite an "off year," Matthews had the highest career goals-per-game rate among active players (0.64), and the fifth-highest goals-per-game rate in NHL history, behind only Mike Bossy (0.76), Mario Lemieux (0.75), Cy Denneny (0.75), and Babe Dye (0.75).

Matthews finished with ten goals and fifteen assists over the final twenty games to end the year with thirty-three goals and forty-five assists for seventy-eight points in sixty-seven games. He was the first Leaf and ninth player of all time to start his career with nine consecutive thirty-goal seasons.

But there was more to his game. His eighty-nine blocked shots—a defensive stat usually associated with third- and fourth-liners—led Leaf forwards and ranked fourth in the league among all forwards. He was excellent at takeaways and face-offs, other moves that give his team possession.

"A down year," chuckled GM Brad Treliving. "We talk about a down year because he didn't score sixty-nine goals. He's led our team. We've talked a little bit about a change and some tweaks in how we play. I think Auston has been front and centre of leading that way. He's an elite two-way, number-one centreman in the league. The evolution of Auston. Everything that gets talked about is goal scoring. And it should. He shoots it in the net as good as anybody. But what he does away from the puck sets the standard for everybody else. The way he checks. I know we can say, 'Okay, his goal scoring may be down.' I think his overall game is as good as I've ever seen it. Now, I've seen him for two years now. And he's been a top player ever since I got here and long before that. But just the way he sets the standard for how we have to check and play two hundred feet of the ice, he's set the standard for us."

With Matthews as captain, the Leafs won the Atlantic Division for the first time in their history. The franchise doesn't have a lot of division pennants to its credit: The COVID-shortened 2020–21 season in the all-Canadian North Division and the 1999 Northeast Division are the only post-1967 titles of any sort.

The team went into the 2025 postseason hoping for a different result, a deeper run than usual. They dispatched the Ottawa Senators in six games, Matthews scoring the first goal of the Game 6 clincher. Then it was on to the Florida Panthers. The Leafs won the first two, lost the next three. Facing elimination, Matthews scored the winner in Game 6 in Sunrise, Florida, on one of his signature deceptive shots, shifting the puck and his blade at the last second before firing.

It wasn't enough, though, as the Leafs bowed out in seven. Going seven games in the second round was their deepest run since making it to the Eastern Conference final in 2002, when Mats Sundin was captain. But that wasn't deep enough, of course.

The Leafs licked their wounds in the days following their elimination. Matthews was offered a chance to reveal his injury. He didn't. He doesn't like talking about injuries. It may be he still harbours some ill will toward the media going back to COVID, when some reporters revealed that he had contracted COVID. It may be that he simply doesn't want to offer a guide map to the opposition about his weak spot.

"It was tough physically," he said. "It was a very tough season. No need to get into the specifics. I got injured in training camp. Obviously wasn't feeling great throughout the first month or so. Took some time off, went to Germany, did all these things to try to feel better. There were stretches where I felt good. There were some stretches where I didn't feel very good."

He did reveal that Craig Berube, who finished his first season as head coach, "pushed" him to grow as captain with daily conversations, which caused him to take in new ideas, think of different approaches, make sure every player on the team felt valued.

"The person is even more important for me. Great character, great personality. I really enjoyed being around him," Berube said of Matthews. "I thought his leadership got better as we went along. I thought we worked well together from that standpoint. Towards the end of the season, he really took over that role. He's only going to grow as a leader now. I think understanding what it takes to be a leader and then the things you gotta do, not only on the ice but off the ice. There's a lot that goes into it. And I thought he did extremely well."

But the elimination in seven games at the hands of the defending Stanley Cup champions left a feeling of despondency hanging over the team, especially after losing Games 5 and 7 by identical 6–1 scores, at home no less. In some ways, it felt worse than losing to Montreal in the first round in 2021 or to Florida in the second round in 2023.

Changes were looming in ownership, with Rogers having engineered a deal to become majority owner of Maple Leaf Sports & Entertainment by buying out Bell's 37.5 percent share. Their handpicked chief executive, Keith Pelley, announced less than a week after the season was over that Brendan Shanahan would not be back as president.

The team was heading into a period of uncertainty, especially with Mitch Marner leaving as a free agent to go to the Vegas Golden Knights. Brad Treliving remained general manager, tasked with sorting out the team's immediate future and finding a way to go deeper than they have on this nine-year run of postseason appearances.

"We have to be able to find a way to push through at the most critical moments," said Treliving in his postseason media wrap-up. "We have a good team. There will be change. When you keep getting the same result, there's some DNA that needs to change."

The goal remains the same: to be the best. Matthews and the Maple Leafs will continue that journey together.

EPILOGUE

Maple Leaf Forever

After Auston's four-goal game, *USA Today* reached out to Brian Matthews to get a sense of the moment.

"He knew what was happening, but I don't think it had quite sunk in. He was still in the moment, trying to figure out what he had learned on his last shift. His brain was just starting to shut down. He was starting to reassess. The look on his face was like, 'Can you believe that?'"

Brian said Auston can be more effective than he was in his debut.

"There were things that he didn't like that he did or didn't do. He looks at every game in terms of 'How do I get better?'"

How does he get better?

That's a common theme among all those I interviewed. As much as they might have helped, as much as they might have coached him, or driven him to the rink, or introduced him to the right people, it was Auston who did the work and put in the time. They were his gifts, God-given or earned.

Hockey was his love, his passion, his obsession. From the time they actually played with each other, as the young stars of Team

North America, through their NHL careers, McDavid and Matthews were friends. McDavid would visit Matthews in the off-season and saw firsthand how Matthews trains.

"I'm really impressed how passionate he is for hockey, how much he puts into it," said McDavid. "I think a lot of people just assume that he's some God-given goal scorer, but he put a lot of work into it and is super passionate about the game."

They say where you end up usually depends on where you start.

It's easy to see that an elite hockey player would come from some snowbound country. Given all of what Matthews has achieved, his roots make the accomplishments to date all the more wondrous.

It would be incredibly difficult to predict a future like this one having been raised in the desert in the US Southwest.

"He's got a unique history, unique heritage that way, growing up in Scottsdale, of Mexican descent. A great story," McDavid told me in an interview. "It shows just how much the game has grown. And it's continuing to grow and spread out, and getting outside of Canada. And everyone knows what the game means in Canada. But the kind of player like Auston who comes from Scottsdale, think how many more have come from out of that area? Tage Thompson. Matt Knies. A few other guys. The game is growing. Auston and those other guys are proof of that."

For Matthews to become the greatest Maple Leaf of all time, the pieces of the puzzle had to land in a particular way, starting with the boy-meets-girl narrative of Brian and Ema, and the unique choices the family made that flew in the face of the usual path of hockey families in northern climes.

"They've done so much for me, a lot of sacrifices for me to get to this point," Matthews told Sportsnet in the 2020 documentary *I Am: Auston Matthews*. "They've been a huge part of this.

"There was one point in time where I wanted quit hockey, when

I was a lot younger, and my dad always told me, like, if I wanted today to play chess or do whatever, he would support me doing anything to help me be successful. And that's just the way it was. And I never ended up quitting hockey."

But there are no shortages of "sliding doors" moments, seemingly inconsequential at the time, but that altered the trajectory of Matthews's hockey life.

Consider that Sean Whyte might not have coached him at Ozzie Ice if the Kings had placed him with their farm team in Manchester instead of Phoenix. Or that Boris Dorozhenko might not have been his skating coach had the Iron Curtain not fallen. He wouldn't have gone to Mexico, where the Matthews family found him. He wouldn't have become friends with Robert Lopez, who invited his youth team to Arizona. Lopez might not have been there if not for a chance meeting with Pat Quinn.

Consider the Wayne Gretzky trade to the Kings on hockey's growth as a whole, and on Matthews's exposure to it in particular. The growth of the sport brought Claude Lemieux, Ron Filion, the Courtnall brothers, and a host of others into the growing hockey hotbed of the American Southwest.

Laurence Gilman was an executive with the Coyotes when Matthews was making headlines as the region's best player at a young age. Gilman wasn't sure how that would necessarily translate, because he didn't think the region's youth hockey teams were that good. By the time Gilman joined the Maple Leafs as assistant GM, he was a believer.

"He's the heartbeat of the team and the engine that drives it," said Gilman. "He is, without a doubt, such a unique player with the arsenal that he possesses. His release is among the top in the league. He's got tremendous puck skills. He's strong like an ox, and he is willing to take the puck into the very hard areas. He is a unique player. And the team is exceptionally lucky to have him."

The tanking Canadian dollar and the dire financial straits of Canadian teams changed the NHL's landscape, letting Auston's Uncle Billy bring him to a Phoenix Coyotes game.

Sure, if the Jets never left Winnipeg, or landed somewhere else, maybe Auston would have played baseball. Or golf. Or chess. Or something else.

"I can truly say I am blessed that I got to be a part of his journey," said Sean Whyte, the ex-NHLer who managed Ozzie Ice. "But I can also say that if it wasn't me, it wouldn't have mattered. He could be growing up in Australia and he was going to be in the NHL. The fact that the Jets moved here and he was exposed to hockey right in front of him and fell in love with it, that was the starting point. I'm just happy that I was able to help him progress, where he can move on to the next person to take him to the next level and so on."

That, of course, turned out to be number one overall to the Toronto Maple Leafs, a historic National Hockey League franchise that hit historic lows to make sure it got him. Even that almost didn't happen given the vagaries of the draft order determined by the drop of numbered Ping-Pong balls.

Even the date of his birth: September 17, 1997.

Little did anyone know back then, in San Ramon, California, that the date would have a major impact on his future. If he had been born two days earlier, he'd have been eligible for the 2015 NHL Draft, the one where Connor McDavid went first overall.

If not for the birth date, or the randomness that it was the fifteenth of September, and not the twentieth or thirtieth, Matthews might have gone first overall in 2015. Or second to McDavid. Or third to his friend and Team USA teammate, Jack Eichel. The Leafs chose fourth that season and took Mitch Marner. One thing: Had the cutoff date been later, Matthews wouldn't be a Leaf. He and

Marner wouldn't have been teammates for nine seasons, heading down the road together playing on the same line while rewriting the team's record books.

The Leafs had to do their bit, too. Tim Leiweke saw the going-nowhere mess the team had become and hired Brendan Shanahan, who was given the leeway to start it all over from scratch. That end of it—how the Leafs have been managed and coached during Matthews's time—wasn't their finest. But Matthews held up his end of the bargain. He made himself at home, made himself a part of the city. He absorbed what it meant to be a Maple Leaf. He thrives on it.

Mike Babcock used to call it his "drivetrain." Scouts called him singularly driven.

His former teammate, Tyler Bozak, marvelled at Matthews's commitment.

"The thing that impressed me the most was his work ethic," Bozak told me. "I think when you're already that good, I think it would be harder to try and get better. But he was always first one on the ice, last one off the ice, always working on his game, trying to get better. Always in the gym. I just find that impressive. When you're already told you're the best and have all these accolades and all this stuff is going well for you, I feel like it's harder to put in the extra work because you already feel so good about what you have. But he was always striving and working to get better."

That was what impressed his former coach, Sheldon Keefe. "Without a doubt, Auston truly wants to be great, and he wants help to do so. I think he's also grown tremendously as a leader, and he's ready to take on more. Obviously, he made me look good as a coach on a lot of nights. But I'll never forget my very first meeting with him and how engaged he was and how he worked to really evolve his game to be great on both sides of the puck."

And he's never let any of it go to his head.

"A lot of hockey guys are just regular guys. He is quite funny," said McDavid. "He loves hanging out with the guys. Every time I'm around him, it's always been a good time, whether you're talking hockey or anything else. He's just, just one of the guys and someone that's really fun to be around."

Wendel Clark, the only other player the Leafs chose at number one overall, has been a Matthews admirer from the beginning.

"He just wants to be a good player in his own right," said Clark. "He's not trying to be the best ever. All of us at the start, you just want to be as good as you can be. And who knows what that ceiling is, right? Because you don't. Every year you enter a new level. Midget to junior and so on. I think he's done an outstanding job.

"And I think we all knew he was gonna be a great player when in game one he had a four-goal game."

That, of course, set in motion the most nontraditional hockey journey to become the best player in the history of most storied franchise and its twenty-sixth captain.

"As a lot of people have stated, he came in obviously game one as a very talented young individual," said now former Leaf President Brendan Shanahan. "But just to see him as an eighteen-year-old, where he's evolved throughout the years, taking steps to grow, maturity on and off the ice, his game has matured. And it's the kind of thing you hope and expect when you draft a player of that talent. He's just going to continue to improve. The guy scored four goals in his first game. Then you see improvement coming on him from there, like I said, on the ice and off the ice. It's been good to see. I think he's ready and the time is right."

The Leaf captaincy is illustrious. Jack Adams had a division named after him as well as a coaching award (though more for his time in Detroit). Charlie Conacher had a cancer research wing named after him at Toronto General Hospital, as well as a league humanitarian award. George Armstrong used his clout to support Indigenous causes. Syl Apps served as a member of provincial Parliament. Dave Keon has a rink (Aréna Dave-Keon) named after him in Rouyn-Noranda, Quebec. Darryl Sittler raises money for the Special Olympics and cancer research. Doug Gilmour supports diabetes research. Wendel Clark is involved with Easter Seals. Mats Sundin helped fund a research fellowship on maternal health in a partnership with the University of Toronto and Stockholm's Karolinska Institutet.

With his work at Toronto's Hospital for Sick Children and his work ethic on the ice, Matthews fits the template.

"The intangible that was alluded to today is that he has the ability that people want to follow him. Not that John didn't have that, but Auston—we're now drafting players that had posters of Auston Matthews up on their wall when they were little kids," said Shanahan.

"So Auston has that ability. It's not something that he has worked on, it's just something he was born with. People want to follow him and bond with him. I think giving him this time and this runway up until this point of his career, not putting that kind of pressure on him as an eighteen-year-old and allowing him to watch some of the leaders that have been here in front of him, has helped get him to this point where he's evolved, where he's ready to do this."

As he donned that C for the first time, Matthews stated his goal: "To be a Leaf for life. To win here with my teammates."

Acknowledgements

A heartfelt thank-you to those who gave so graciously their time, chief among them Boris Dorozhenko, whose help cannot be quantified. Outside of his family, perhaps no one knows Auston Matthews better. No one else can explain how he does what he does on skates better than Boris.

The book also wouldn't have been possible without the help of Pat Mahan, a Matthews family friend and member of a tight-knit Arizona hockey community, and Sean Whyte, who watched Matthews grow as a player at Ozzie Ice.

Within that community, there were so many others: Ron Filion, Justin Rogers and his late father, Jim, Mike DeAngelis, Claude Lemieux, Hector Majul, and Dwayne Osadchuk.

USA Hockey was also generous with its time. Thank you especially to Don Granato, Charlie McAvoy, Zach Werenski, Noah Hanifin, Dylan Larkin, and Luke Opilka.

Thank you to the those involved with the Zurich Lions: Edgar Salis, Marc Crawford, Ryan Shannon, and Robert Nilsson.

To Stephanie Stavros and Matthew Sposito, thank you and good luck in your families' journeys through cystic fibrosis.

Those in and around the NHL were also quite helpful: Pat Brisson, Russ Courtnall, Geoff Courtnall, Danny Brière, Zach Hyman, James van Riemsdyk, Tyler Bozak, Lou Lamoriello, Sheldon Keefe,

Craig Anderson, Frederik Andersen, Mark Scheifele, Connor McDavid, Travis Dermott, Michael Bunting, Matthew Knies, Mark Hunter, Laurence Gilman, Lindsay Hofford, Wendel Clark, Rick Vaive, David Keon, Darryl Sittler, and Mats Sundin.

Thank you as well to my colleagues in storytelling whose work is frequently referenced: Gare Joyce, Lance Hornby, Mike Traikos, and Sarah McLellan, as well as my *Toronto Star* colleagues Dave Feschuk, Bruce Arthur, and Rosie DiManno.

I couldn't have researched any of this without a tip from *Toronto Star* librarian Astrid Lange, who turned me on to Newspapers.com. It's worth the subscription.

I'd like to thank my literary agent, Brian Wood, who knew one day I'd write a book; and my editor, Jim Gifford, who showed me how. Thanks as well to the team at Simon & Schuster for believing in a first-time author: Nicole Winstanley, Michael Guy-Haddock, Rita Silva, and Dan French. The book wouldn't read nearly as well without Chelsea Drysdale's keen eye.

Thank you, of course, to those closest to me: my daughters, Ellen and Shauna. They probably didn't hear from their father as much as they were used to in the year or so it took to write this.

Kisses to Fiona.

If I've left anyone out, if I've made a mistake, my apologies. Deadlines come and off we must go.

About the Author

Kevin McGran is a sports reporter covering the Toronto Maple Leafs and the National Hockey League for the *Toronto Star*. *Auston Matthews: A Life in Hockey* is his first book.